REEL WOMEN
Working in Film and Television

Julie James Bailey

AUSTRALIAN FILM TELEVISION AND RADIO SCHOOL

AFTRS

COVER IMAGES:
Top row l to r: Sara Bennett, Jan Kenny, ACS, Kany Cooper, Sue Kerr
Second row l to r: Lynne Cartwright, Mandy Smith
Third row l to r: Bronwyn Murphy, Carolyn Reid
Fourth row l to r: Gillian Armstrong, Glenys Gill, Jackie McKimmie,
Annabelle Sheehan
Bottom row l to r: Nerida Tyson-Chew, Sally Pryor

ISBN 1 876351 04 7
Printed in Australia by Southwood Press
Design: Liz Seymour

TABLE OF CONTENTS

ACKNOWLEDGMENTS

This book could not have been written without the help of many women, most importantly, all the women who agreed to be interviewed – not just those who agreed to have their stories presented as role models, but the many I interviewed in operations departments in television stations around Australia. These interviews were made possible by the station managing directors who supported my meetings with the women and their operations managers.

The idea for a book which would focus on women in film and television who work with technology was first suggested to me by Dale Spender about ten years ago. Had I tried to write it then I would not have found enough women working in these areas to speak to. Now there are, and so a big thank you must go to all those men who stuck their necks out, gave women a chance and supported the (ongoing) struggle for gender equity in this industry.

The research for the Women's History in Film and Research chapters was done by Glenda Carriere who answered my every query with incredible speed, efficiency and good humour. I am also grateful to Clare Burton, Elizabeth Hartnell, Leonie Morgan, Michael Flood, Rosslyn Reed and Jocelynne Scutt who responded to my call for research ideas on Ausfem Polnet. The travel was made possible by a small research grant from Griffith University.

At the Australian Film Television and Radio School (AFTRS), Jan Kenny, Sara Bennett, Annie Breslin, Linda Dement, Jan Preston, Anita Kemp, Karen Skelton, Annabelle Sheehan, George Whaley, Craig Collie, John Colette and Larry Eastwood assisted in providing information about the production processes. Sara Hourez, Manager Special Projects, provided me with ideas at the beginning. Catherine Griff, Research and Policy Adviser, and Juliette van Heyst provided the research on the younger women's perspective. Meredith Quinn and Rebecca Chiu steered the book through the publishing process.

At a personal level, Avrill Stark and my two daughters Pippa and Robin helped me understand the problems of the younger generation trying to make their way in this industry; and Robin Gurr and Sandra Lachlan gave me enormous support through the long gestation process.

INTRODUCTION

'So it's all just luck!' Robin Hughes (filmmaker, former head of Film Australia, former chair of the Australian Film Television and Radio School (AFTRS) Council, 1991-97) was standing at the podium of the main theatre at the AFTRS summing up a session given by ten top women in the film industry. 'Do you realise that every one of you has said that your success is "just luck". I wonder if ten men would have said that their brilliant careers were due to luck?'

It was 1992 at the first Women in Film and Television (WIFT) conference and we had just heard from celebrated producers and writers, a director, and a lawyer in the Tall Poppies session.[1]

This was the catalyst to proceed with this book. Women were excited by hearing successful women's stories, their problems, their fears, how they had got their breaks, and how they had been crumpled and put down and picked themselves up.

In other sessions Jenifer Hooks (then Director of Film Victoria and now Executive Director at Cinemedia) gave a hilarious analysis of the different types of men who work in film and television; Pru Goward (radio journalist and now First Assistant Secretary of the Office for the Status of Women) told us how she was so brutalised by her experiences in television that she chose to stick to radio where she was judged on content rather than appearance; and a commercial TV news journalist, who asked to remain nameless, explained an incident where she had gone to extraordinary lengths to get the first footage of the San Francisco earthquake only to be told by her producer in Sydney that he did not like the colour of the shirt she was wearing.

But there were no stories from successful women working on cameras, in sound or editing and no-one from the operations side of television. I decided to pursue their stories and give role models to young women who were interested in these areas.

I have selected fourteen 'tall poppies' from the film industry on the basis of their acknowledged position, the diversity of their backgrounds, career paths and working environments, five women in television management, and four drama directors in feature films and television. I included directors because directing is a job which requires a broad understanding of all aspects of the production process and, in spite of the major successes of some women, there are still proportionately very few women directors.

These stories are supported by the views of over sixty other women who have full-time jobs working on equipment or in senior management positions in twenty television stations in all mainland capital cities. They did not want to be named but generously recounted their experiences to help other women working in television. I also talked to television managing directors, human resources managers and operations managers to get their views on the issues raised by the women.

The more women I interviewed the more I was struck by the similarity of many of their stories to the experience of women working in quite different male dominated work areas such as building and construction, the army and management. I have therefore finished the book with a chapter outlining some of the research findings on the employment of women in these areas and some analysis about why certain male behaviour towards women occurs. I hope this will provide comfort for those who might at times feel despondent at progress in the film and television industry.

The purpose of this book is to tell women's stories so that all who work in this industry, or want to join it, can feel that they are not alone, understand what is involved in different jobs and learn how women have made their niche over the last 25 years using guts and tenacity.

FOOTNOTE

1 Selected papers from this conference were published in *Women in Film and Television*, 1993, WIFT, Sydney.

WOMEN'S HISTORY IN FILM

Australia has one of the earliest film histories but, as in so many areas, it is dominated by men. In the early silent days, film production came from live theatre and the only women were actors, scriptwriters and, sometimes, editors. Men operated the heavy cameras and often processed and edited their own short films. Of course, we do not know to what extent women have been written out of our film history. Linda Seger says that the first fiction film in the world [sic], *La Fee aux Choux* (*The Cabbage Fairy* [1896]) was directed by Alice Guy Blache but later credited to George Melies (Seger, 1996). (In Australia, of course, we claim that the first fictional film was *Ned Kelly* made in 1895 – another example of the powerful rewriting of history!)

Cutting and assistant editing were accepted as jobs for women and some women received credits as co-editor, such as Katherine Dawn (*For the Term of His Natural Life* [1927]), who had come from Hollywood with her husband Norman, who directed the picture. Lottie Lyell is supposed to have co-edited some of the films she starred in and Yvonne Previs, also an actor, 'arranged the content' (Speed, 1987) on some of her films, but the contribution they actually made is obscured. In Hollywood, Viola Lawrence, who began her career in 1915, was considered to be the first woman editor. Margaret Booth started as a neg cutter in 1920 and then, in 1937, became supervising editor of all MGM pictures in Europe and America and worked in that capacity for 32 years, overseeing 42 pictures a year. Alfred Hitchcock's editor was his wife Alma Reville (Seger, 1996).

In Australia, when sound arrived in the late 1920s, women were employed in the laboratories and as assistant editors and neg matchers. Phyllis O'Reilly was one of the early assistant editors, joining Cinesound in 1929 in the printing room. Later she was assistant editor to Bill Shepherd and Terry Banks on *The Squatters Daughter* (1933). Following the birth of her first child she edited Noel Monkton's two films, *The Power and the Glory* (1941) and the wartime short, *Alert* (1942). Mona Donaldson started in the print room at Cinesound and edited *Pearls and Savages* (1921) and *Adorable Outcast* (1928). She was a neg cutter for ten years and worked as a co-editor with Charles Chauvel in the 1940s. Margaret Cardin was an editor and started Cardin Film Services. She set up the ABC's news library in the 1950s and worked on *They're a Weird Mob* (1966). She was a neg cutter on most of the feature films in the 1970s. Marcia Anderson and Shirley Shirley were also editors in the late 1940s.

There appears to be only two women who worked in sound in the early years. Alma Brooks worked as a sound recordist with her partner Rupert Kathner in the early 1930s, soon after sound was introduced, and sometimes took the credit A Brooks. Gwen Oatley was also a sound recordist, who started in the 1940s at Supreme Sound.[1]

There were few women cinematographers. Marion Michelle had been a stills photographer in Hollywood and did the camera work for her partner Joris Ivens on *Indonesia Calling* (1946-7). Lilias Fraser wanted to be a cinematographer and studied photography in England. She came back to Australia in the 1950s with a Kodak Special 16mm camera, but no-one would employ her. She made her own film on Stradbroke Island for which she imported slow black and white stock. When it arrived, customs officers in Brisbane would not believe that a woman could want film for a camera. She had to get Kodak to stop them ripping open the unexposed film because they thought it must be pornographic material.

She had the film processed at Supreme Sound under the name L Fraser. When she finally came to Sydney and visited Supreme they said, 'We thought you were a man. The camerawork is so good we were going to offer you a job'. She showed the film to Stanley Hawes at the Commonwealth Film Unit who told her that she could not be employed as a cinematographer because 'How can a woman carry a 35mm Mitchell up Ayers Rock?'. She retorted 'It's the vision that counts, the men can carry the camera'. She was given a job in the library and eventually directed an educational film about Torrens Title because none of the men wanted to direct it. From there she directed other educational films and had many battles with the male cinematographers who did not like a woman telling them what to do.[2] In the 1980s her daughter Jane Castle had the advantage of training in cinematography at AFTRS, and Lilias, thirty years after her rejection by Stanley Hawes, had the pleasure of telling him that it was Jane's film he had just seen opening the Sydney Film Festival.

In Hollywood there were several women directors in the silent era but the only woman director in Hollywood between 1927 and 1943 was Dorothy Arzner (Seger, 1996).

In Australia between 1922 and 1933 sixteen feature films were either produced or directed by women (Speed, 1987). The directors were Kate Howard, Lottie Lyell, possibly Yvonne Pavis and Louise Lovely, and Paulette McDonagh, who sacked the male director on her first feature and directed another three. There were no feature films directed by women between Paulette McDonagh's *Two Minutes Silence*, shot in 1932, and Gillian Armstrong's *My Brilliant Career* in 1978. The Commonwealth Film Unit gave Joan Long and Catherine Duncan, who were both writers, opportunities to direct short films in the 1940s and '50s but there was no feature film industry in those days. Joan went on to write *Caddie* (1975) and *The Picture Showman* (1976) which she also produced, and then concentrated on producing other features.

When television started in Australia in the mid 1950s there were no jobs for women who wanted to direct or work on equipment, except for one or two editor's assistants.

The main centres of production from the 1950s to the 1970s were commercial television studios around the country, the ABC in each state, Crawfords in Melbourne and the Commonwealth Film Unit in Sydney. If you wanted to work in film and television you learnt on the job. Boys started in the mail room or shifting scenery and worked up into the sound department, editing or camera to eventually become directors. Girls were employed in the traditional female jobs of secretary, research, make-up or wardrobe which did not generally lead to other jobs.

Jan Kenny (p13) tells how the Commonwealth Film Unit still refused to allow women to become camera operators in 1970. She had to wait another six years until Russell Boyd took her on his crew. She was the first woman ever to have worked on a feature camera crew. Gillian Armstrong (p207) and Mandy Smith (p311) remember that the ABC would only employ them if they had typing speeds. Gillian went into editing and then a directing course at the AFTRS. She became the first woman since the 1930s to direct a big budget feature in Australia. Mandy had to work her way up through the traditional female jobs of continuity, wardrobe and the production office before she became the first woman allowed to direct at Crawfords in 1979.

There were no women employed on feature films or in television as cinematographers, sound recordists, boom operators or drama directors before the AFTRS started specialist courses in 1975.

The AFTRS and the Australian Film Commission (AFC) were crucial in changing attitudes about the employment of women. The renaissance of the Australian film industry in the early 1970s – led by the federally funded AFC, AFTRS and Australia Council – the AFTRS' first three-year intake in 1975 and its happy coincidence with International Women's Year, meant that women started to get equal opportunities with men in this renewed industry.

During the decade for women (1975-84) the AFTRS ran specialist courses for women in the industry to assist them out of their stereotyped jobs (Alexander, 1979), supported traineeships to persuade male managers that women could do traditional male jobs, (Wyndham, 1986; Stapleton, 1987), and ran education and information programs to ensure that there was an equal gender balance in the intake. More recently the AFTRS has published a leaflet explaining the importance of gender neutral language in the industry in order to stamp out the mindset that defines directors as 'he' and camera operators as 'cameramen'.[3]

The AFC reflected the government initiatives to provide equal employment opportunities and created the Women's Film Fund.[4]

Women have also been well represented on the staff of Commonwealth funding agencies – the AFC and the Australian Film Finance Corporation (FFC). At the time of writing, both the AFC and FFC had women chief executives.

The state funding bodies have also supported women and been sensitive to gender issues. Most of them also have women chief executives. The South Australian Film Corporation had a women's unit in the 1970s, where Gillian Armstrong directed her first film and Jan Kenny and Mandy Smith also worked. Gillian Armstrong is very certain the reason we have so many good women film directors is because the funding organisations had an arts-based philosophy and not one of big business.

The ABC was required to adopt the government's equal employment initiatives and over the years has had a number of affirmative action programs although, because of tenured employment, their impact was slow. SBS television began broadcasting in the early 1980s so missed the early affirmative action initiatives but it also comes under the same federal equal employment legislation.

Commercial television on the other hand has continued to be a male environment. At a 1997 industry breakfast for women,[5] the American feature producer Debra Hill (*Fisher King*) remarked on the number of women in the film industry in Australia compared to the few women in senior positions in television. She said that it was the reverse in the US where there are many women in senior executive positions in television. There, television managements have realised that the majority of the viewers and shoppers are women and, therefore, women should be making programming decisions.

Laura Ziskin, President of Fox 2000 Pictures (USA), added her support for this view at the AFC and television industry breakfast in November 1998. She said she was the first woman appointed to the senior management of Fox following a recognition by the company of the very large female proportion of its audience, and an understanding that women liked different films to men. She also said that she sometimes totally disagrees with the men about scripts that are being pitched and that her male colleagues take notice of her views. She believes that it is important to have women's perspectives on what is being made.

In Australia commercial television has enjoyed a cosy oligopoly (of three) and it is only with the competition of Pay TV and the introduction of enterprise bargaining in the 1990s that the commercial networks have started to look at their archaic 'boys club' employment practices. The AFTRS has also had an ambivalent attitude to training for television so that its women graduates have not made the same progress in television as they have in the film industry.[6]

FOOTNOTES

1 This information was supplied by Martha Ansara and Graham Shirley who have researched the pioneers of the Australian film industry.

2 Interview with Lilias Fraser 1997.

3 As early as 1980 Dale Spender wrote about inherent sexism in the English language and yet it is still a contentious issue (Spender, 1980). I have purposely used the feminine personal pronoun in this book and there are places where it will stand out because it is still uncommon to think of women in some roles.

4 Two articles on the history of the Women's Film Fund: Thornley, Jeni, 'Past, Present and Future: The Women's Film Fund', and Grieve, Anna, 'Big Mother/Little Sister: The Women's Film Fund', in Blonski, et al, 1987, *Don't Shoot Darling: Women's Independent Filmmaking*, Greenhouse Publications, Richmond, VIC.

5 International Women in Television: The Big Picture, November 1997, Sydney.

6 For additional research on women in film and television, and theories on the effects of gender in the workplace, see Research, p337.

A 'film' usually means a production which is shot on light sensitive film stock, although it is now also a generic word for moving picture productions whether shot on film stock or videotape.

This section concentrates on the production jobs associated with shooting a picture on film stock. It includes the editing process, although most films are now digitised into an electronic editing system's hard drive and then assembled on film.

Feature films are usually shot on film stock, as are some commercials, a small number of documentaries, short films, video clips and corporate productions. A feature production uses the largest crew – in other types of screen production the jobs and number of people employed depend on the budget and specific needs of the production. However, no two feature films are ever the same and therefore the jobs can vary considerably.

The key creative roles are the scriptwriter, the producer and the director. They have different jobs to do in developing the script to a point where the producer can get production funding.

In feature films the producer's role may be split among a number of different people. The producer is responsible for the film from original idea to finished product, but there may also be executive producers who are responsible to the investors and a line producer who is responsible for the day-to-day production. There can also be various associate and co-producers who have different roles.

Script ideas can be initiated by the writer, director or producer – or a combination of these. The director is either involved from the start or brought on early to work with the writer in the development of the script.

Once the money is found to produce the film it goes into pre-production. The director works with a casting consultant to select the actors and with the production office and the various production departments – especially design, cinematography, sound and editing – to discuss the script and the director's vision for it. An intensive process of collaboration begins – and continues until the production is completed.

The production office consists of:

▸ The production manager, who is responsible for ensuring that the production sticks to the budget. She is also responsible for negotiating contracts, hiring the crew and the daily progress report.

▸ The production coordinator, who works directly with the production manager organising the paperwork and looking after the day-to-day detail of ensuring that actors, equipment, facilities and transport are available when required.

▸ The production secretary, responsible for producing the daily paperwork which is the link between the cast and crew and the production office.

Other people who work with the production office in pre-production and then work with the crew during production:

▸ The first assistant director (1st AD), who plots the shooting schedule in pre-production and then works with the director and crew during production. She is responsible for ensuring that the production keeps on schedule. She also directs the extras. During the shoot she has one or two assistants, called 2nd AD and 3rd AD. The 1st AD is the producer's representative on the set.

▸ The location manager, who finds the locations and organises their availability. The location manager may well work with or become a unit manager looking after the facilities for the crew while on location.

▸ The continuity person, who in pre-production is responsible for timing the script, is the director's and the editor's eyes and ears during production, ensuring that shots match. Continuity also keeps full records of the shots.

The first day of principal photography is the beginning of a very intensive and expensive period when the production crew and actors are brought together and the film starts rolling through the camera.

The other departments involved in this process are:

▸ The camera department, whose head is the director of photography (DOP). She works with the director and designer in pre-production to find the locations, and works with her camera crew (camera operator, focus puller and clapper loader) and also with the key grip and the gaffer during the production.

▸ The grips department, whose head is the key grip. The key grip is responsible for positioning the camera and carrying out all tracking, dolly and crane shots as required by the director. The key grip works under instructions from the DOP and camera operator and usually comes with a fully equipped truck.

▸ The electrics department, whose head is the gaffer, provides the lights and sets them with the crew (best boy and electricians) under instructions from the DOP.

▸ The design department, whose head is the production designer. She is responsible for building and painting sets, dressing locations and organising the props and models. This department is employed very early in pre-production. The art director organises and administers the department and answers to the production designer.

▸ The wardrobe department, whose head is the costume designer. She is responsible for what the cast wears. She works with the director, the DOP and the production designer. For period or large cast productions, this can be a big department which starts work early in pre-production to make and organise all of the costumes.

▸ The make-up department, whose head is the make-up artist. She will have a number of assistants and hairdressers, their numbers depending on the size of the cast.

▸ The sound department, whose head is the sound recordist. She is responsible for recording the sound during the production both on location and in the studio. The boom operator positions the microphones, under the direction of the sound recordist.

As the production progresses the post production phase begins. Picture editors start work at the beginning of principal photography.

The editing department consists of:

▸ The picture editor, who is head of the department and works with the director in editing the film to the finished version. She liaises with the neg cutter and the laboratory over optical effects and the transfer back to film stock for screening. Increasingly, the editor also liaises with digital media artists in executing the special digital effects used in the production.

▸ The sound designer, who takes overall responsibility for the sound. She may be the sound editor who edits the soundtracks to the cut picture or these jobs may be delegated to the dialogue editor, the effects editor and the music editor. Sometimes the picture editor may do all or some of these jobs.

▸ The sound mixer, who works with the director, composer and editors. She mixes the various soundtracks to the finished picture.

There are other jobs such as music composers and those involved in digital effects who can also be involved in the post production process and need to be consulted in the pre-production phase. They tend to work on their own and consult with the director, the editors and the design department. Because of the expanding use of digital visual effects, it is becoming increasingly important for designers to understand 'digital language'.

The jobs in film production are a mix of creative, craft and trades. Women are well represented in the key creative roles of scriptwriter and producer and are increasingly making their mark as directors and editors; they are also well represented in the jobs in the production office, wardrobe and make-up; it is in the crew positions which use equipment that few women are found and therefore their stories are not heard.

This book concentrates on the jobs that use equipment in the production and post production phases and the job of director. The director is responsible for the vision, the interpretation and style of the storytelling and for the delivery of the finished production.

I hope these stories of successful women will inspire and encourage other women to tackle these jobs.

CINEMATOGRAPHY

Cinematography departments are still predominantly male areas but, increasingly, women are gaining access.

To be a cinematographer on a feature film is perceived as one of the 'glamorous' jobs. The director of photography (DOP) has a high profile on the crew and works closely with the director in a way that the other heads of departments do not.

FEATURE FILMS

Traditionally there are four basic positions on a camera crew for a feature film.

The DOP is in charge of the cinematography department and, with the director, determines the overall look of the film as well as the individual shots. She helps decide on the position of the camera and makes all the decisions about lighting, which are then communicated to the gaffer who, as head of the electrics team, implements the decisions.

The camera operator is a specific position on the crew. The DOP, however, sometimes chooses to operate the camera herself, even on major feature films. The camera may need to be positioned in a car, on a crane, on a dolly on tracks, or just on a tripod. The grip is responsible for the safe operation of everything that supports or moves the camera.

The focus puller takes full responsibility for decisions regarding focus, adjusting focus during the course of any shot by reading the calibrations on the lens. She is also totally responsible for the accuracy and maintenance of the camera equipment. Apart from keeping every shot in focus, the focus puller assembles the camera and all its accessories, sets the aperture according to the DOP's instructions and ensures that the DOP's choices, such as depth of field, are maintained. The focus puller is also required to 'check the gate' after each set-up, ie. ensure a clean image by keeping the lens free from dirt, hairs, or emulsion build-up.

The clapper loader loads the film into the magazines in readiness for handing to the focus puller for reloading and lacing up. The clapper loader is effectively an assistant to the focus puller. She labels the cans of exposed film and does the paperwork for the laboratories, noting which takes are to be printed and how much film is left in the magazine. The clapper loader is the general 'gopher' for the cinematography department and is responsible for making sure that the film gets to the laboratory and the rushes (or 'dailies') get back to be viewed the next day.

On a large feature there can be a second unit which usually comprises a second DOP, who follows the main unit DOP's instructions, a camera operator and a focus puller, who may also double as a clapper loader.

The camera crew works as a team. Because of the importance of knowing the work and capabilities of each person on the team, especially when the project is a major feature, a DOP will try to employ a camera operator she has worked with before. For the same reason, the operator will usually employ a focus puller and loader whose work she knows. Therefore it is only if someone is not available that a new person has a chance to join the team.

The grips department is also part of the cinematography department. It is responsible for the gear that is required to support or move the camera and for helping to get the camera and gear onto the site. The person in charge is called a key grip and will usually have a number of assistants. The key grip works closely with the camera operator and the focus puller. Key grips usually own their own truck and equipment and have generally spent a long apprenticeship as an assistant grip. Grips come from varying backgrounds, but are usually skilled carpenters or mechanics. A good dolly grip needs strength, sensitivity, a feel for drama and a 'sixth sense'. It is a specialised job and a really good grip is highly sought after.

DOCUMENTARIES, LOW BUDGET FILMS, COMMERCIALS AND CORPORATES

The size of the camera crew will depend on the gauge of the film and budget. 35mm cameras are much heavier than 16mm cameras so require at least two people, one to light the shot and operate the camera and the other to assist in the operation, look after the equipment and paperwork and set up the camera. 16mm cameras can be operated by one person, so on a small documentary shoot the DOP will set up the camera and the lights.

The size of crews on commercials will depend on the budget. Some big budget commercials can have a crew similar in size to that of a mini-feature.

OPPORTUNITIES FOR WOMEN

The basis of employment in the film industry is freelance. For newcomers, then, it is important to establish a reputation and network. In the early days of a film career, the opportunities are greatest in the documentary and low budget drama areas. The crew is often paid on 'deferrals' (payments are deferred until the film makes any money) and, with low budgets and smaller crews, there is far less pressure from investors or clients. More interestingly, there is an opportunity to experiment and try out people and ideas.

Many women choose to work in these areas because, although the hours are often longer and the work more demanding, it gives them the opportunity to work on their own projects with people they respect and like.

While twenty years ago it was extremely difficult for women to enter cinematography departments, the success of women who 'broke the barriers' and the existence of formal training has dramatically affected the opportunities and outlooks.

ROLE MODEL

Jan Kenny, ACS, is a legend for women cinematographers. She was the first. A number of women cinematographers have followed but there are still very few who have been DOP on a big budget feature.

Some came through the AFTRS – Erika Addis, Sally Bongers and Jane Castle, who are all working as DOPs in documentaries, commercials, features and television. In Melbourne, Mandy Walker blazed the trail for women, shooting commercials and features. She was followed by Kattina Bowell and Rosie Cass. There is now another younger generation – Kathryn Milliss, who was DOP on *Thank God He Met Lizzie*, and Carolyn Constantine, DOP on *Pent Up House*.

Jan Kenny began her film career in 1967 as a production assistant at the Commonwealth Film Unit (as Film Australia was then called). She was the first woman to work in the cinematography department of a feature film, as clapper loader on *Summer of Secrets* in 1975. She was also the first woman to receive accreditation by the Australian Cinematographers Society (ACS), an honour granted by your peers, who judge your work to be of a consistently high standard. It entitles you to use the letters 'ACS' after your name. Jan won the ACS Golden Award for her work as DOP on the feature film *Mary* in 1994. She is currently Head of Cinematography at the Australian Film Television and Radio School.

JAN KENNY ACS

Jan grew up in the south-west corner of Western Australia and the majority of her schooling was in Albany. She had no knowledge of film or theatre as a career and did not have a television set. She used to listen to plays on the radio and went to Hollywood films at the drive-in. She had her own half hour radio program once a week. She painted and was a member of the Albany Photographic Society and won some prizes for her photographs.

When she was 18 she was a sports mistress in a girls' college in Katanning.

interview

GETTING STARTED

How I got into film is a curious story. One night I was on the train chatting to a woman. I got off the train at Katanning and she continued on the train to Perth – end of story. Two or three weeks later, I was called to the telephone, a long distance call from Perth, and this voice said,

'Look, you may not remember me, but I met you on a train a few weeks ago, I'm so and so.'

'Yes', I said. I vaguely remembered chatting to someone on the train.

'I remember you were interested in film and theatre. There are these two gentlemen here from the Commonwealth Film Unit

[CFU]...' I said 'What's the Commonwealth Film Unit?' and she tried to explain.

'They're going back tomorrow, back to Sydney, and I've arranged an interview for you, tomorrow morning. Now this is what you must do', and she told me 'You catch this train... you get off here... you go to this address at this time... this is the excuse you can give to get off teaching tomorrow...'

I just followed her instructions.

I gave the excuse she told me to give, got the day off teaching, got the train she suggested which left Katanning at midnight and got to Perth at seven o'clock the next morning. I had to lie on the filthy floor which wasn't carpeted because I was too embarrassed to wake up the very large fat woman stretched across my compartment. I was 18. I arrived filthy, sweaty, tired and stiff.

I rang the number that was given to me and asked for Stanley Hawes or Dennis Brown and said I'd arrived, explained my condition and could I please have time to go and have a shower and change, and they said no, I'd have to go straight there because they had an aeroplane to catch. I think perhaps the fact that I'd braved this overnight trip impressed them more than anything else.

I had the interview with them in the morning and had the rest of the day to fill before my train went back to Katanning. I tracked the woman down and thanked her. I walked past the Playhouse Theatre so I thought I'd have a look. Being completely ignorant, naive and all those wonderful things, I marched past everybody straight into the auditorium and saw something happening on the stage, so I sat in the seats in the dark and watched a rehearsal. And finally the penny dropped. It's the middle of the day, these people must be at work! They do this for a living. At that moment I realised that that's what I had to do.

» **Ultimately you're working to put the director's vision up there, not your own. It is the director's film and you're responsible to them to get the job done as well as possible.**

There was an opportunity, there was an outlet, I could do it.

I tracked down the director of the theatre and phoned him. I said 'You don't know me, I'm from the country and I'm here and I want a job in your theatre'. There was a stunned silence I remember. He said something to the effect that he was on holiday, it was nothing to do with him but there was an ASM's job coming up in six weeks' time, but I should talk to the stage manager, thank you, goodbye. So I went and asked the woman in the box office what was an ASM and she said it was an assistant stage manager. I said 'Thank you, where can I find the stage manager?' I found the stage manager and said 'Edgar told me to talk to you about the ASM's job' – quite innocently. I walked out of there with a job lined up as an ASM and so began my theatre career. I caught the train back to Katanning, gave them my notice, and moved to the big bad city and started a whole new life.

When I got that job I wrote to Stanley and Dennis at the CFU and said I couldn't come to Sydney at the moment, I've got this job in the theatre and I think it will be good experience, and I'll let you know – one of those letters. I wouldn't dream of writing a letter like that today. I stayed there with the National Theatre Company for a year and I think from time to time during the year I dropped Stanley and Dennis a note to let them know how I was going, I'm sure they were extremely interested to know! It didn't occur to me they wouldn't be.

At the end of the year various people were leaving the theatre company and I thought, it's time to move now so I wrote to the CFU and said I think I'm ready to come to Sydney now – they wrote back and enclosed my air ticket and said I could start as a production assistant. I had to find out what a production assistant was, what the Commonwealth Film Unit really was, and think about living in Sydney.

So I didn't have to struggle to get in initially. Deep down I knew what I had to do, it wasn't following any particular plan, it was knowing that this was the next step, and it was instinct. I instinctively knew when it was time to move, and then I had a helluva lot to learn when I got to Sydney.

FIRST JOB

I think I started at the CFU in 1967 and I was a production assistant for three years, and those were the most important three years of my life. I think I was probably fifteen steps behind anyone else because I was rather ignorant in so many areas. But in those days the only training available was as production assistant at the CFU or you went to the ABC. There were no other courses or schools or funds or anything, and I was very lucky that I was in there.

It was during those three years that I realised the direction I wanted to take. When you first arrived you spent about six weeks in each department and I quickly realised that I had a passion for cinematography. There were 23 or 25 production assistants and only two or three of us were women. Every spare moment I'd be down in the camera department. I'd get magazines and spend hours in the dark room, teaching myself to load them. On location it was usually a crew of three, a director, a cinematographer and production assistant who filled many roles. Then once the film had been shot you became the assistant editor. The experience of being a production assistant was incredible. The best possible training.

I turned myself as often as possible into the camera assistant and when we were away on location I would try to keep all the camera gear in the room with me and I would take it on myself to maintain the gear and reload the magazines and I just learned as much as I could from all this.

On bigger jobs there were camera assistants employed and I started pushing to get a job as a camera assistant and that's where there was a very strong line of resistance.

Women simply didn't do that kind of work. It was definitely male territory only. Production assistants were being groomed to be directors or editors. I think I probably raised the issue two or three times but at that stage one just accepted it. It was a different era.

MOVING ON

I left to travel overseas, I took a year without pay but I stayed away for two or three years. I went back to theatre as stage manager at the Royal Court in London which was an extraordinary experience working with legends in theatre and film. When I came back, I'd decided to get straight back into film, but a week after I returned I found myself on tour with Barry Humphries, so I was back in theatre again.

I then became the project officer for the Film and Television Board of the Australia Council, managing the film production and script development funds for about two years. Then I was stage director touring *Jesus Christ Superstar*. After ten months I knew it was time for someone else to take over.

We happened to be in Adelaide, and I finished the Adelaide season, so I was thinking very hard about what I really wanted to do – theatre or film? I still really wanted to work with cameras and now things were different for women, society's attitudes towards women had changed considerably. That was about 1975. I thought, perhaps now is the time I'll set myself up as a freelance camera assistant, so that's what I decided to do.

During the six weeks' season of *Superstar* in Adelaide I got some little business cards made up that said I was a camera assistant. I tried to get an agent and couldn't because I didn't have a track record. I started writing and letting people know what I was doing now and phoning people I knew. I didn't know too many people, but I did know Penny Chapman. We had both been working as project officers in Sydney and we had started working on a film together which I shot and she directed. It was called *Sunday*, I don't think we ever finished it, but we used to borrow equipment on weekends and every Sunday we'd toddle off and shoot all this stuff.

Penny was directing a documentary at the South Australian Film Commission and they needed a camera assistant. It was one of those rare occasions where the cinematographer, who was Russell Boyd, didn't get a choice of assistant because he was brought in at the last minute and he arrived with me already in place. So I stumbled into my first camera assistant job in Adelaide, which by quite wonderful timing started the minute *Superstar* ended.

During the last couple of weeks of *Superstar*, I found out what equipment we were using on the film and I got hold of that equipment as often as I could and by the time the shoot came I was thoroughly familiar with it because I had spent hours changing magazines in the bag, so I was extremely fast and proficient.

There were no female camera assistants then – I understand I was the first one – so Russell was a bit unsure about this. The first morning he said, 'Do you know how to load a magazine?'

'Yes,' I said.

'Okay, let's see' – he was a bit nervous. I loaded a magazine very very fast, right in front of him. Then he said, with a wry grin, 'when did you learn to do that?'

I said 'yesterday' – big grin on his face.

We got on fine from then on. And that was the beginning of my career as a freelance camera assistant.

I gave myself twelve months. I thought if you can't get it together in a year at least you tried. And that was twenty-something years ago.

After that job I returned to Sydney with an official track record on one film with Russell Boyd. Russell gave me my next few jobs and he was responsible for my first feature.

I was apparently the first female to ever work in the camera department on a feature film, which was *Summer of Secrets*. I was clapper loader and I know for a fact that I only got that because of Russell. He was DOP and he had to really convince the operator and the focus puller to take me on board because they were dubious. But Russell was determined that I should have a chance and thanks to him I got that job.

There I did meet my first few problems because I got very little support from these guys. I'd never done the job before and in fact I'd never seen anyone be a clapper loader so I could only guess at what I was supposed to do. I was given absolutely no help or guidance or assistance or communication of any kind by the chaps on the team and any advice I got was from Russell.

So I just dug in and hung in there. It was physically a very hard job. The camera was a PVSR (an early Panavision), an extremely large camera which requires two people to carry it by the handles on either side and the magazines are large and very heavy. We were shooting across the lagoon and the far side of the beach at Wattamolla. It was a drive out there every day, down the cliff, across the lagoon and a long walk up the beach to the location. Trip after trip after trip, morning and night, we had to wrap in and wrap out because we couldn't leave anything there. It was incredibly hard physically. I could have used some guidance. Systems that I could have been shown, shortcuts I could have been told about. I had to learn myself.

Normally if you're the focus puller working with a loader, you help the loader all you can, and it's part of your obligation, to teach those who are coming up. A loader is a less experienced camera assistant than a focus puller. You expect that focus pullers on features are the best assistants around with the most experience, and you expect that they will pass on their knowledge to the loaders, which is what normally happens.

As it was, I gradually earned respect through sheer diligence and persistence and hard work. I was just clearly doing the best I could, learning from my mistakes, trying to be faster and quicker and more attentive and was basically self-taught on that film.

I did feel a bit isolated, but I was also incredibly determined, and I did have Russell. When I really came up against a wall and was not quite sure what I should do, I would have a quick word with Russ. I think he was conscious of the attitude but there wasn't a lot he could do. I just had to get on with it.

In those days we worked six-day weeks, and I'd spend all of Sunday in the back of the camera truck, re-organising trying to get the system better, finding a faster way to do something. I just worked at it seven days a week and well into the night, every night, after wrap. I got very little sleep for the first half of the shoot. I really did it hard.

But for my second feature as clapper loader, which was *Break of Day* [1976], again with Russell Boyd, I had my act together, I knew what I was doing so it was different. I had the experience of one job behind me, it wasn't as though I was coming in completely cold. John Seale was the operator on this next one, David Williamson was the focus puller. It was a superb team. By the end of the first week, which physically was an incredibly tough week, working on the beach down at Portsea in a howling gale with the sand flying at you sideways, the whole crew indicated their respect for the job I'd done that week.

David Williamson was quite wonderful and I worked with him several times. He taught me an enormous amount and I think he was impressed because I wasn't complaining about the boys' attitudes, I was just getting on with the job and trying to learn as much as I could. And I gradually earned their respect.

I got my first job as a focus puller through luck, through someone else's misfortune, which is often the way that it happens. I was working on *Dawn* [1977] as clapper loader, and dear David Williamson was the focus puller and he had what was very nearly a tragic accident. He ended up with a bad gash on his leg and was taken off to hospital, in the middle of one day. John Seale was the operator, Russell was DOP again, and they had to quickly decide whether to get in a new focus puller or get me to focus pull and get a clapper loader for the day until they found out what was happening with David. I had done quite a few pictures by then and John Seale and Russell both decided to give me a go as focus puller and get in a new loader. It's the way it often happens – someone gives you a chance.

I pulled it off that afternoon. David wasn't returning to work because of the injury and I stayed on and did the majority of the picture as focus puller, and I was a focus puller from then on.

The move to operating was very gradual and over a couple of years. I got to the point were I was starting to shoot a little. If you're shooting in the studio on something that is straightforward and you're a fairly experienced focus puller then the operator will say come on you do this one. That's how you get your first experience. If you've got to cover something on two cameras you might get the focus puller to operate the second camera. DOPs were doing that for me. You just build up your time. I think you have to have a few years of being a really well worked and good focus puller and camera assistant. The more years you can put in as a camera assistant the better for your career down the track. The more cinematographers you can work for, then the more you are going to learn, you learn different ways of doing the same thing quite often.

What I used to do was walk onto a new set and I'd just quietly think how I would light it, then I would listen to conversations between the DOP and the director, hovering and watching and then thinking, 'gee I wouldn't have done that, I wonder why they are doing that', then you start seeing why they did that. Then later, when it's an appropriate time, if there is something you didn't understand, you ask. 'Why did you do this, this and this. Why wouldn't you have done it this way?' That's where you learn.

I don't think there is any shortcut and I think that's a very appropriate way to do it.

I was letting it be known I wanted to shoot and operate but I kept my name on the books as an assistant. I think the transition came when I was doing a certain amount of shooting on documentaries, short dramas, things like that, and still a certain amount of assisting. I remember at some point I thought I've got to make a decision now to drop assisting and stick with shooting. I chose the beginning of a new year for the new start. I actually picked a date and I notified my booking service to take me off the assistants list and put me down as an operator.

These days it's much easier than back then, because now there are all sorts of funding bodies to help you along your way. There are schools and courses and things going on everywhere. There is no excuse not to be able to learn any more. I think the bottom line is you have to judge when the time is right and then stick by your decision. It's not going to happen immediately, it could take a year or two years or more and you need to be prepared to hang in there for the time that you've set yourself. No one is going to hand it to you, no one owes it to you. It is up to you to learn what you can.

ISSUES FOR WOMEN

Today of course one is much more aware of sexist attitudes and so on. They are openly discussed issues that everyone is aware of. But when I started I chose to just plug on and not complain, never ever complain, just learn what I could.

Early on when every set I walked on I was still a novelty, I do recall the grip on one picture calling out 'All hands come and help to get the crane out of the back of the truck'. That of course usually includes everyone in the camera department. I went over to help. There are at least six blokes there ready to haul this thing out, it's not heavy. I remember the grip standing at the back of the truck and in front of everyone, loudly declaring he wasn't moving any piece of equipment with a woman lifting.

My heart sank, I thought, 'here we go'. I thought just joke your way out of it, so with every eye on me, I said 'Ah come on, don't be so pompous, this is part of the job, come on guys', and he said 'No', and he was rather heavy about it. 'No, I'm not moving, women do not lift this equipment.' I said 'Okay mate, I'll go to tea, I'll see you later', trying to keep it light, so I went away and they got on with the job.

After wrap, I went up to him and said 'I want to have a talk with you.' He said 'Oh, what have I done now?' I said 'Right, number one, don't you ever speak to me like that again in front of the crew' I really got stuck into him. I said 'I've been really pissed off with you all day. I offered to help and instead I get ridiculed in front of the crew'. I went through what he'd actually done, and I said 'Put yourself in my position, how would you feel if...' and I went through it again. He said 'Gee, I'm sorry, I never looked at it like that'.

So I walked away and half an hour later I was finishing wrapping and he wandered over and said 'You know I really am sorry' and gave me a hug and I said 'That's okay' and from then on, no problem. He was terrific and we worked together very well. I don't know what I'd have done if I hadn't been able to resolve it because, especially if you're away, you're not only working with everyone you're living with everybody. If I had yelled abuse at him, which I have seen on other people's film sets, it doesn't do anything for anybody. It gets you nowhere, and it's not constructive and it's not acceptable behaviour on a film set.

I had to keep reminding myself I was breaking new ground. But when I look around now, it's another world completely, it's another political environment. But since I was first a loader on Jim

Sharman's film, or since 1967 when I was at CFU – the changes I've seen are enormous.

I probably view it a little differently from someone who is just coming up because I can see the differences. It is still very much a boys' club, there is no doubt about that. Even today it's a boys' club of which one could perhaps be considered an associate member if one wanted to be a member. I occasionally look at it like a golf club. Golf clubs are still very male oriented. Women who belong to a golf club are known as associates, they are not known as members. And in a way that could be compared to the film industry.

Today you look at the crew lists for booking services and there are a lot of women camera assistants. It is simply considered part of the system. A camera assistant, you don't think female or male, you think camera assistant – good or bad. That's where it's at today – a far cry from my early years.

I can now choose who *I* want to work with and they are the people who are the best at their job. But I make sure they are people who will not only get on with me but get on with each other. I actually think that's a very important part of crewing. In my crews, there is often a mixture of men and women.

I do feel some responsibility for women coming up. But I don't consciously choose women because they're women nor do I think I should. I think professionally first and if it's a dead heat between a male and a female it may go to the person who is going to fit in with the crew better, and has a good attitude, particularly if you're away. I think that it is irresponsible to the job, to the producers, to the production company, to the director, if people on the team aren't the best possible choice for that job. Ultimately you're working to put the director's vision up there, not your own. It is the director's film and you're responsible to them to get the job done as well as possible. There are now several female assistants who will in good time become cinematographers. You can't hurry that process and I don't think you should. I think we should be encouraging people to get in as much ground work as possible because in the future that's where it is going to tell.

DOMESTIC ARRANGEMENTS

As far as I'm concerned I'm on call 24 hours a day. There are times when you have phone calls early in the morning and are told to be at Tamworth or somewhere, by six o'clock tonight, and you're up there for two months. You often have to move very fast with no notice. My advice is stay as organised as you can at all times.

I can get a call and I can say 'No, I can't do it', but unless you've advised your booking service that you are not available for certain periods of time, you've decided you need a break, then you're on call.

ADVICE

A cinematographer is an odd mixture of talents, unlike a lot of other jobs where people are either technical or creative. A cinematographer has got to be a good balance of technical and creative. Not a lot of people have that, they tend to be really leaning one way or the other.

I suggest that a woman starting out should become an assistant for as long as she possibly can.

These are the things that I would be looking for in a camera assistant.

Technical and creative

A camera assistant has to be on top of the job technically, to know the equipment inside out better than anyone else, before you take it out on the road. If something happens to the equipment it is the assistant who is responsible for it. Knowledge of basic maintenance is vital.

Fit and strong

You need to be fit and strong, you need to be able to fit in with the rest of the crew.

Reliable and honest

You need to be reliable, you need to be honest, someone of high integrity. For instance, you don't want somebody who has dropped a lens or your light meter and not told you because they think they will be in trouble. They have to tell you because this could affect the job, it could affect the results of the work you are doing.

Self disciplined

You need to be a self disciplined person, you need to be someone who can be supportive of the people you are working for and with.

Respectful

Before you get on a film set you need to understand how the hierarchy of the film set works. Understand that it is the 1st AD who runs the set, know who you talk to about different things, know who you don't approach at certain times. Respect the fact that most of those people have probably got more experience than you and learn from it, respect it, treasure it, treasure everything you can learn from it. When you're just starting out you should listen to other people and watch and ask questions.

Sensitive and intelligent

You need to be somebody who is sensitive, somebody who is aware of when it is appropriate to keep quiet. How to behave appropriately, how to be sensitive to the situation you're in. We're often shooting in people's homes, people's workplaces and in public and one needs to show respect for other people's property.

Initiative and foresight

You need someone with initiative who doesn't have to be told every single thing. Someone who is intelligent, someone who can think on her feet. Someone who has a deal of creativity. Someone who has an ability to anticipate what equipment might be needed and keep it handy. Thinking ahead.

Thorough and organised

Someone who is thorough and organised, which a lot of people are not. Somebody who *wants* to keep the equipment clean and maintained, someone who enjoys it. I don't want to walk into a truck or look at a camera and find that it's filthy. The gear should always be kept clean and organised.

You have to learn to love the equipment. Someone who is happy to work out of hours to keep that gear looked after and not make demands on the production office. When we were working six days a week in the old days, on Sunday we'd get into the back of that truck and go through all the gear and clean everything, so on Monday morning everything had had a particularly good clean and we knew it was in good running order after a long and heavy week. You do that sort of thing in your own time because you care about the job.

Punctual

Somebody who turns up ahead of time. If the crew call is 7am I expect the gear to be ready to start working at 7am, not for the assistant to be pulling up in the car at 7am. Someone who really has their act together who is really organised, ready to roll at crew call and is happy to do it. *Wants* to do it. Somebody who cares enough to be mortified if they're five minutes late on the set. The first thing you do if you're late on a film set is you go to the head of your department, you tell the DOP and apologise and you tell the 1st AD that you're now here and apologise. I've seen assistants constantly arrive just a bit late and it doesn't seem to occur to them that there is something wrong with that. I find that inexcusable.

Concentrated

A very important one is the ability to concentrate. Quite often, especially on feature crews, there are long periods of time where you just have to sit and wait, it can be as boring as hell but a camera assistant has to be able to concentrate during that time and still be ready to jump into action and anticipate needs. Stand by your cinematographer or focus puller, or whoever it is, all the time and stay aware of what is going on.

As an assistant think that every day you go to work is an opportunity to learn.

Awareness of sexist issues

A female assistant should be aware of sexist issues but not be preoccupied by them. But you deal with any problems at the appropriate time and in a constructive way. There is no place for aggression on a film set. No-one wants to work with someone with a long face, drooping around all day. You keep your private problems off the set. If someone is giving you flack, consider if it is possible that you might have deserved it. Don't always presume that it's because it's a male that you're in the right and they're in the wrong. Maybe there was some truth in what was said but if you truly believe they were out of line, address the problem *after* work.

I would hate to think that women coming up now are looking at sexist issues ahead of professional issues. There is a point of view that you can't separate them. I personally tend to separate them.

Therein lies the problem for women – trying to find the balance. Because first and foremost you are a professional, your first awareness should be of the job as a professional. Somewhere at the back of your mind you have an awareness of someone who might be dealing with you in an unfair way because you are a woman but you deal with that when appropriate. But if that's your first and foremost thought on the set you are in the wrong place. Your job is to do the job you are paid to do, not be worrying about the way one of the guys spoke to you.

My advice would be to never confront anyone on the set, and resolve it as soon as possible when the working day is over. Having said all that, I must say that these issues rarely enter my head when I'm at work.

The greatest thing is to see the finished product on screen and experience that feeling of pride and satisfaction at your part in it.

SOUND RECORDING

FEATURE FILMS

The sound department on a feature film usually consists of a sound recordist and a boom operator (also called a boom swinger) and there may be a second boom operator or an assistant to help the boom operator if it is a complicated sound production. The head of the department is the sound recordist who is usually employed by the producer, the production manager or the director and in turn employs the boom operator and assistant. The sound recordist usually has to supply her own equipment for a shoot.

The sound department works closely with the DOP, the gaffer, the first assistant director (1st AD) and the actors in order to work out where the camera, lights and actors are going to be so that the boom operator can place the microphone (usually at the end of a pole or boom), in a position to get the dialogue without casting a shadow on the set.

The recordist will be very conscious of any unwanted sound on the set and particularly on location when it is much harder to control extraneous sounds such as planes and traffic. The sound recordist will often stop a shoot if the sound is unacceptable.

The recordist will also want to record atmosphere from the location which will require complete silence on the set at the end of a take.

Most sound recordists start by recording either on documentaries or short films and then move into recording features. Some come through boom operating.

DOCUMENTARIES

Sound recording on documentaries is quite different from feature films or drama productions because the shooting is less predictable and there is often no opportunity to re-record the sound if it is not acceptable.

There is usually one sound person on these shoots who is the recordist and looks after the placement of the microphone. If the budget is very tight the sound recordist is sometimes dispensed with and either the director records the sound or the microphone on the camera is used and the camera operator monitors the sound.

LOW BUDGET FILMS, COMMERCIALS AND CORPORATES

There is usually a sound recordist and a boom operator on these types of shoots. However, if it is a small crew a boom operator may be dispensed with.

ROLE MODELS

I have selected two sound recordists, Bronwyn Murphy and Gretchen Thornburn, who represent careers in Sydney and Melbourne which have been built in two different decades, and a boom operator Sue Kerr, one of the first woman operators.

Bronwyn Murphy was one of the first women sound recordists. She graduated from AFTRS in 1984 and is based in Sydney. She has made a substantial name for herself in documentaries and low budget features. She has been nominated six times in the AFI awards for best achievement in sound, most recently in 1997 for *The Well* and 1995 for *Vacant Possession*. In 1990 she won the award for best achievement in sound in a non-feature for *Land Bilong Islander*. Most recently she has worked on the features *Radiance*, *Dog Watch* and *A Wreck A Tangle*.

Gretchen Thornburn is based in Melbourne. She has been

working in sound since 1977 but has only been a full-time freelance sound recordist since 1994. For eight years she worked in the Melbourne office of AFTRS. She has recorded sound on documentaries, commercials, short films, low budget features and television series, most recently *Driven Crazy* and *High Flyers*. She got her break into big budget features on the Jackie Chan film *First Strike – Police Story IV* which was shot in Queensland, the Ukraine and Moscow, and went on to work with an international crew on Jimmy Chan's *Who Am I*, shot in South Africa and Holland. She has three AFI nominations for best achievement in sound, non-feature category, most recently in 1995 for *The Needy and the Greedy*.

Sue Kerr is one of the few women feature film boom operators. She graduated from AFTRS in 1983 and has been working as a boom operator ever since. Her recent credits include the television series *Murder Call, Fallen Angels, GP, Rescue IV* and *V* and her feature credits include *Looking for Alibrandi, The Sum of Us, Sweetie, Travelling North, Les Patterson Saves the World, The Right Hand Man*, and *For Love Alone*.

BRONWYN MURPHY

Bronwyn grew up in a working class family in Bourke with a younger brother. She went to the local high school where they did not encourage girls to have careers. 'There was a general expectation that you would get married.' She left school at fifteen and tried several things including nursing.

She got her first job in the industry in Brisbane at the University of Queensland's audio visual centre. She had answered an advertisement for a laboratory cadet and had studied camera operation, editing and electrical engineering for the BC OPS (Broadcasting Certificate: Operations) at TAFE.

There were no women in the department and the head of television wanted her to make him cups of tea. 'I did it for a very short while but I resented it. I was surrounded by male colleagues so I very, very gradually produced a climate where everyone shared. I made my point and it phased out.'

She got interested in sound through a couple of freelance sound guys in Brisbane who she assisted in her spare time. 'That was also an introduction to the lifestyle. Freelance filmmaking offers you a very different way of working – the long days and time off, which I enjoy. Also a film crew is a bit like a family.'

She also made a weekly radio program for the Bourke High School radio station with a group of people who came from Bourke. One of those programs was the basis of her application to AFTRS, where she began to study sound in 1980.

interview

Film school was a great apprenticeship. I did everything in sound but I liked the autonomy of sound recording. I enjoy mixing but there's something really frustrating about trying to achieve something that somebody else wants. You always feel that you never quite get it.

When second year came and you had the option to direct I chose not to. Instead I got to record or boom so many films and it gave me a really broad range of experience of directors and crew. In third year I mixed all the films I recorded.

▸▸**On documentaries sound is really important because you are half of it, the sound is often the content, but on feature films it's all ultimately replaceable.**

One of the reasons girls didn't go into sound in the studio was that it is very gadgety and there is a lot of one-upmanship with jargon, gadgets, toys. Also computers were beginning to come into that area as well.

However, it's something I've come back to a little bit because recently I've done a few sound edits and I've found that very satisfying. I edited the sound for *Land Bilong Islander* [1989]. I felt much closer to the film and I had a lot more job satisfaction because you are constructing it the way you think it should sound using your raw material and then it is up to a mixer to balance it.

Most of my work is on film. I prefer film because I'm not physically connected to the camera whereas video is, although there are systems now where you can have a radio link to connect you to the camera which means that you are free.

FIRST JOB

I left film school in '83 and my first job was with Mike Edols who was directing and shooting the documentary *The Child of the*

Bounty, which was a re-enactment. Wayne Taylor, who was in my year at film school, was his assistant. I got the job because it was a 10BA film and the money didn't come through so Bob Hayes, who was supposed to be recording it, pulled out and Michael offered the job to me.

Michael was a tutor for a while at the film school and he talked about his way of making documentaries, which was the fly on the wall, cinéma vérité approach. The cinematographer is the director and you move with the people who you are filming and treat them with respect and don't impose your stuff on them. It gives the sound recordist a lot of interest in the picture. Michael said that I had to be really unobtrusive and wanted me to work with a little SN Nagra which I wasn't happy with because it is very hard to use. It is also rigged through the camera and you can't hear anything until the camera is running.

When I graduated from film school I decided that I was going to be a freelance sound recordist. You can start as a boom operator and move up but I didn't. I was very lucky because there were a lot of women making films and a lot of films wanting to be made about women and it was a time when they were starting to realise that it was nice to have a bit more of a balanced crew. I was in the right place at the right time and very quickly got a reputation as a woman sound recordist for documentaries who could travel, which I did a lot of, and I was easy going enough to take in most situations. So there were male camera people and me.

GETTING INTO FEATURES

I didn't actually make a conscious decision to move into features. I was just offered one. I'd done a few short dramas and Dean Gowen, a sound editor, called from Melbourne. He likes to get sound recordists who are new when he works on low budget films and my name came up for a film called *Ghosts of the Civil Dead* [1987]. I had an interview with Dean, not really an interview, but I met with him, and he thought I could do it.

There aren't too many women sound recordists on features. Pat Fiske has done *On Guard* [1984]. All the features I've done have been low budget ones. The first timers. I was offered *The Small Man* [1995] which is John Hillcoat's second film. He was director of *Ghosts of the Civil Dead* and he tries to keep the same heads of departments, or the same crew. I was going to do that but I pulled out.

One of the major problems for me in feature films is the different channels of communication and also I find it very difficult to get used to the notion of being less important. I don't like having to live with something that is less than good.

On documentaries sound is really important because you are half of it, the sound is often the content, but on feature films it's all ultimately replaceable. People will say they haven't got the budget to post sync but somehow or another those small budget films always manage to find some money for post if they have to.

In America we are called 'sound catchers', people who catch whatever sound is there and then they post sync everything. It's happening here. Some sound recordists fight for their role and do it really well. People like Ben Osmo, who has a huge reputation as a sound recordist and he forces the issue to get things for sound.

Assertiveness is actually to do with experience and following one film with another. My problem is that I do one feature and then another in say three years so I seldom get a run at a few where I can learn something and move on and put it into practice.

I did a couple of films in a row – *Vacant Possession* [1993] and then Geoff Bennett's *Turning April* [1995]. That was good because on *Vacant Possession* I found myself feeling badly done by. At the end of that film I thought a lot about the mistakes that I had made and about the way I worked on it and then I had *Turning April* just a few months after that. I took a lot of those lessons with me and I felt a lot more comfortable.

Recording documentary and feature films is so different. I like the balance, it feels very good to move from one to the other, backwards and forwards.

HIGHLIGHTS

Meeting some of the people I've worked with. My favourite films nearly always come out of the experience of shooting them. It's about the people on the crew, the people you are filming. When you are doing drama, the actors can bring a lot to a set, they make your job harder or they can make it easier. Most Australian actors are fantastic.

Nights Belong to the Novelist [1986] – a long time ago now – was an interesting process, working with Erika [Addis, cinematographer] and Christina Wilcox [director], who hadn't made a lot of films. There were some difficulties working with Elizabeth [Jolly] who is very eccentric. We all loved her but she was difficult at times, as eccentric people are. I think it is a nice film. I think it gives you a good feel for both her and her work. I expect I am also very affected by the experiences that we had and the funny moments in the film. She is a lovely woman.

Land Bilong Islander [1989] I think is a really important film. That won an AFI Award for sound and that was the first film that I had worked on as a sound editor as well as recording it.

I talked to Trevor Graham, the director, about wanting to do sound editing and out of the blue he said 'Why don't you do it on this film'. So I did. Ken Sallows was the picture editor and he was happy so I had to do a lot of quick research. I only had three weeks, it was very hairy because they didn't give me enough time. It was on 16mm, finishing on sprockets not on tape and I had not done anything since film school. So that is a pretty proud film for me work wise.

CHALLENGES

The job has got so many facets. The working relationships can be fantastic. Feeling excited about the potential film. You always go with high hopes for the film.

Travel has been really important for me in documentaries. More in the past than now because I've done so much and the attraction of travelling with masses of gear and getting it on and off aeroplanes, into taxis, into hotels, into lifts, all that stuff begins to pall. If you work on one of those films where you go to a new city every two or three days it's a nightmare but it's also exciting, it is something everyone should do.

Being a role model is good too. When we went into schools in Arnhem Land the girls were completely enthralled by me. It was very unusual to see a woman walking round with a Nagra and microphone working with the crew. We would often be in a classroom situation and they would be watching me. I could just feel it. It was great. I didn't have to say anything it was great just being the role model. None of them may ever do anything like that but at least it won't be such an unusual thing to think about doing.

In Japan I was a little bit strange, too. No-one said anything but you can feel people's attitudes being challenged. In Asian countries they often think I am a man because I'm slim and tall and look a bit androgynous in an Asian society. The kids will ask if I'm a man because they are not quite sure when I am wearing all that gear.

ISSUES FOR WOMEN

There are all those gender specific things rather than sexist things. There are things in me that stop me. An example is having to be very assertive, fighting for what you want, rather than being cooperative and expecting something in return. I don't know how much of that is gender based and how much of that is background.

In feature films you need to be assertive, you can never expect that things will happen just because you are all working together and making a film. The problem is that sound is going to look bad unless you have certain things like quiet locations, a certain amount of equipment, access to actors, all that sort of stuff and you cannot take any of those things for granted. It's getting harder and harder for sound to negotiate because of the use of post production sound.

It is interesting because Kim [Batterham, cinematographer and Bronwyn's partner] has had more drama experience than me and he comes home occasionally such as when he was working on *Sun on the Stubble*, and says 'The sound recordist is fantastic you don't even know they're there'. And I say 'What! I don't like to be not there'. I think, that's not how I want to work, I like to be there, I want to be acknowledged. It's great if the director says 'How did that sound? A bit quiet? Do you want some more?' or something. I like a crew to think about sound and I'd like a bit more fun with the DOP rather than be seen and not heard.

But in documentaries sometimes you want to be anonymous. You develop a body language that sort of avoids people being comfortable about coming up to talk to you. The last thing you want when you are recording an atmosphere in the middle of Hong Kong is someone to come up and ask you what you are doing.

If the cinematographer is a woman it probably does make a difference. Although I did work with Erika on Susan Dermody's film [*Breathing Under Water* 1991] and that was hard but that was more about the situation. I was a one-woman sound crew and had to record what was unlimited atmosphere because they didn't have much dialogue. I did it on my own which is not great. When you are working on features it is nice to have two people to work as a team.

Crying

On *Return Home* [1989] with Ray Argall I was doing sound and Mandy [Walker, cinematographer] was shooting and there were separate days when we were both in tears. It was a very awkward location, a service station between two bus routes, and we were doing lots of dialogue on the tarmac at the service station and I wanted to go again and I wasn't allowed to and I insisted and I still wasn't allowed to. Basically I had to compromise and I thought it was unfair. I burst into tears.

I've done it one other time on *Harry Dare* [1994] and that was a situation where I was completely stitched up by the shot. The shots kept changing. You'd have a set-up, you'd be ready to go and they'd move the camera which meant that you couldn't put in the microphone, so then you had to run around putting radio microphones on and the pressure is on to do it quickly because we're running out of time. I was put in a position where they changed the parameters on me after we'd done what we believed was the right thing and I was stuck with something that is going to sound bad because I haven't got time to do more things. I thought it was unfair.

I do know of an occasion when a guy who was a production manager burst into tears because of pressure and I think that that is fantastic.

Dealing with men

I can only think of one example where I had difficulty and it is something I would never do again, it was a great learning curve. A 1st AD would just not hear me. I would give him forewarning like 'At the end of the scene before we break for lunch we need an atmosphere'. He'd nod or make some joke or whatever. I'd be ready to go into the atmosphere mode at the end, when the gate cleared on the last set up before lunch, and he'd call lunch. And that happened time and time again. Somehow everything I said just went straight past him. My reaction was to get silent and take it all home with me and be less assertive. I just retreated and thought I will never work with you again.

Afterwards I thought about being assertive and what I should have done, I should have stood my ground, I should have been louder, and not asked but said 'Now we will do it', all that stuff.

About eight months later I was offered a shoot with the same AD so I thought 'Alright I'm going to put it into practice' and it was fine. As soon as I started being the strong me, instead of the weak child who is being grounded, he was fine and he treated me like a person.

Occasionally grips and gaffers slip into that sexist stuff and then you just treat them like children. I usually say something, it wouldn't be anything hard, a sort of jokey thing with humour, occasionally I just walk away. As you get older you start to get the problem of them saying you're behaving like that about the sexist stuff because it's sour grapes.

Usually there are other women on the crew somewhere so you often get a kind of a group reaction if there is some sexist comments, something like the group hiss.

On the whole I get to work with people who are not male machos and they are chosen for that reason. But *Ghosts of the Civil Dead* was interesting. It was set in a male prison. There were very few women on the film and I was the only woman head of department. The dressing on the cell walls and the props were of course pornographic literature. It had been decorated by the art department and some of it was gross. What started to happen was the men were taking on the atmosphere that had been created for the film. It was coming out not directly but little comments and attitudes. It was actually comments about good bodies and things like that. It was very strange, all the women noticed it, the 2nd AD, the focus puller, wardrobe, make-up, the production manager but we didn't actually do anything about it. Usually you go 'give me a break' in a casual way but this was different.

DOMESTIC ARRANGEMENTS

At a personal level my relationship with Kim has meant a bit of a pause. We have been quite aware of what the film business can do with relationships, we've kind of decided not to work at the same time on something huge and we are still sorting out what that means, because there are two careers. We are at the same sort of level but Kim I suspect is going to break soon. Now I think I'm supporting him and I have to be very careful that I don't let my career disappear. For example when he was working on a miniseries he was six weeks in London and then in Melbourne. That meant that I would work on whatever came up in Sydney but I would not take an eight-week job because we then could not have weekends together.

THE FUTURE

On features the future is scary because of the expectation of what you are supposed to supply in your sound kit. Money is getting tighter and tighter and producers don't like hiring equipment because it costs a fortune but you can only do as good a job as the equipment you have. You are expected to have radio microphones, monitoring systems for directors, DOPs, continuity and whoever else, so that they can watch a monitor and listen. You have got to have a lot of up-front money to buy lots of what the new technology offers.

You can get into a situation where it would just be expected, but unspoken, that you have all this equipment and then on the shoot they ask for something and you haven't got it. Initially I was too inexperienced to know this but now I just put it up front. So when I did *Turning April* [1995] at my interview I said that if we want this and this then we will have to hire them because I don't have them.

The capital outlay for that would be at least $60,000. Sometimes recordists have two or three recorders, a stereo Nagra, stereo microphones. One good radio microphone costs $7,000-$8,000 and you are usually expected to have at least two. You get the equipment gradually, you buy second-hand things. I borrowed $10,000 to buy my first sound kit and for that I got a really old Nagra that did me well, 416 and 816 microphones, a boom pole, a pair of headphones.

Most sound recordists are not very comfortable sorting out what should be charged for equipment costs. The notion that a sound recordist comes with the basic kit which includes two radio mics I don't think is fair, if a shoot uses radio mics then they should be charged for them.

In documentaries the problem is different. Now the ABC is encouraging the documentary directors to get their little DVC cameras and go out and start shooting their films. So we are going to get a series of documentaries with a lot of wide shots with no dialogue, which is dead boring. You have got to hear what is going on. I think it is really scary. I know of two films that have been shot that way but the sound editors and mixers are hating it.

ADVICE

The important thing is to get the training so that you have the knowledge. You also have to be passionate about sound. You have to think about the way things sound and why, and create moods. There was a time earlier where some women moved into the film industry because it was a male area and not necessarily because they were passionate about it.

I'd advise starting as a boom operator first, or getting a job as an observer or an assistant to the sound recordist. Your place in the crew is a really hard thing to negotiate especially if you go in as a sound recordist and haven't boom operated. A boom operator at least gets to observe the sound crew at work and they get to see different sound methods and styles. Ben Osmo is really big on training people, he wants to get new young people to do cables and second boom. Ben's idea is that we should be using people who are keen and not necessarily from film school but I think that film school graduates could do that. I didn't and I suffered for that.

I'd say, after film school, work on anything that you can. I didn't say no to anything in the beginning and I don't think you can afford to. It's also how people know that you're keen. I did a Christian television series. I considered myself an atheist at the time and lots of people thought that I shouldn't do it. I didn't need to be a Christian to do the job and it was a fantastic experience because I went overseas. It was my first experience with a radio mic, and so from a career point of view I learnt how to work with a particular piece of equipment.

Also it is a good thing to contact other sound people. Women come to me. Leonie [Dickinson] talked to me about recording sound in Vietnam, we had a long conversation and I told her what I thought she should take if there should be a breakdown. Gretchen [Thornburn] talked to me about some problems. They are mostly practical advice things about going into particular situations.

It is not until later on in my career in feature films that the problems with people came up. If there was any aspect of training that I lacked it was that. The film school didn't provide any training in dealing with larger groups of people and the hierarchy of communication. That would be a very valuable thing for women.

GRETCHEN THORNBURN

Gretchen Thornburn has been a freelance sound recordist only since 1994. She has worked on all sorts of productions in Melbourne and got her break into big budget features on the Jackie Chan films.

Gretchen went to PLC in Melbourne. Her father was an industrial chemist and a racing car driver. 'I was brought up in the pits at Sandown. I have two elder brothers and there's not a gender bias in our family'. She always liked films. 'I use to sneak into the film festival before I was eighteen but working in films was a dream that I never thought would ever come true.' She planned to be a potter but realised she wasn't going to get anywhere and her parents insisted she did a receptionist course.

In 1973 she was a receptionist in a printing company and saw an advertisement in the paper for a receptionist's job at Film House, which she got. For two years she answered the phones and was used as a production assistant on commercials. 'It was cheaper to use me as a production assistant on a receptionist's pay, and get a freelance receptionist in to cover for me. That was my first experience of non equal pay'. She finally took them to the Department of Labour and Industry and won.

She left and got her next job with a video company called Infotel. Gretchen was a receptionist, Girl Friday type person and they let her work the video camera to make animated storyboards. 'I knew my way around a film set and it was great because the advertising agencies at that stage didn't have set ideas so you were at the very start of the creative process.' She stayed there for two years and had her first experience of sound recording for one of the partners who did voice-overs.

She then got married in 1977 and moved to Geelong where her husband worked in the family business. 'I had no thought of a career, I left Melbourne and all the things I love. Looking back it is just bizarre.'

Deakin University was just starting in Geelong and Gretchen got a job in the media department screening films. 'The off campus courses were starting and they had a studio but no-one knew anything so I thought I am going to have to do something here. The still photographer was interested in the camera and he was better than I so I slotted myself into the audio because no-one else was interested in doing it and it fascinated me. I wasn't phased by the technical side. My mother said 'I've always hated cooking but if you can read you can cook' and I always say if you can read you can be technical. I got hold of the manual, the microphones and the machine and worked out how to use them. No-one knew what I was doing, I was one step ahead of them all the time.'

She topped and tailed the British Open University courses and produced audio programs for distant learning students on a bench model Tanberg and one microphone, and seven years later she ended up with an eight-track studio and the Open University bought her programs.

In 1984, after seven years, her marriage broke up and she went overseas and returned home in 1986. She realised that working in feature films was what she wanted to do because that would pay her to travel. She knocked on doors for seven months and then saw a job in the paper for a receptionist at the AFTRS. 'I thought that's the best place to make contacts; I had been out of Melbourne for nine years and I needed to work somewhere where I could build up contacts.' She was told that she was overqualified for a receptionist but got a job as a project officer and stayed at AFTRS from 1987 to 1994. During that time she made many contacts and started recording again. In 1989 Solrun Hoaas asked her to record for *Green Tea and Cherry Ripe*. In the seven years she was at AFTRS she took leave without pay and worked on three films a year. 'They were happy for me to do that because I was keeping up with the industry but I was in a very privileged position because I could actually choose the projects, I didn't have to make a living out of it.'

Just before she left AFTRS, digital technology came in and she applied to the Australian Film Commission for a technical grant to learn about DAT (digital audio tape). She got a job on a short film *The Sewing Room* (1993) which was recorded on DAT and released on 35mm Dolby SR. She borrowed gear and played with it, setting herself exercises, and set up a liaison with Craig Carter, a post production person. He became a mentor and he agreed to post produce *The Sewing Room*. 'I loved the technology. I grabbed it with two hands and that is something that helped me.'

In 1994, aged 40, Gretchen became a freelance sound recordist, joining only one or two other women in Melbourne. In her first two years she got into the major commercial companies, made some documentaries and decided to get into drama, worked on a couple of low budget dramas and then in 1995 got the job of sound recordist on the Jackie Chan film *First Strike: Police Story IV* through Craig Carter who suggested her when Gary Wilkins didn't want to go to Queensland.

interview

HIGHLIGHTS

The Jackie Chan films because they broke the stereotype completely. This huge macho over-the-top action film recorded by a woman. I just loved doing it, they are such a hoot. I'd only recorded one stunt before I did the Jackie Chan film now you name it I've done it. Seventeen cars, blowing up houses, it appeals to my sense of adventure.

I signed a ten-week contract and 22 weeks later it finishes on the deck of a submarine in Russia. I had no idea that was going to happen. As I stepped off a nuclear sub in the Black Sea onto a police boat with a Fostex round my neck I thought 'Jesus what am

I doing?'. All these guys trying to carry the Fostex and I said 'I've carried a handbag all my life boys. Go away – I'm better at it than you are'.

I've travelled with many docos overseas but to go with a huge crew, sit in a room with the whole top brass Russian Navy and Air Force, asking for two helicopters, a submarine, a police boat and a missile base... I was the only woman apart from the producer. Everything was 'niet, niet, niet' and finally Jackie came in in all his glory and their faces lit up, the hats came off, the Polaroids came out, signed photos and we had the lot.

▸▸ I have other ways of working with the technical thing. I actually use the way I think as a woman. In other words, I think of sound in colour rather than in technical numbers. I will actually ask a director what colour their script is.

Jackie introducing me as head of a department – he's good, he says 'This is my sound man' and I keep saying 'Yes, I've had a sex change'. People laugh. There is no word in Chinese for sound woman. There were seven camera teams and me, I was the only woman head of department and I employed about five recordists which meant I could compare their work. That was good because as a sound recordist you are usually out there on your own and you rarely ever get a chance to compare your work with others.

Other highlights are achieving my dreams. Selling audio programs to the Open University, looking after Peter Greenaway at AFTRS. I had seen *The Draughtsman's Contract* at the film festival years ago and heard Peter Greenaway and thought 'I am going to meet you one day' and ten years later I welcomed him to Melbourne. Taking Sacha Vierny, the French cinematographer to lunch with Fred Schepisi when I was at the AFTRS. They talked about how Fred shot *Six Degrees of Separation*. I just wished I could have shared it with twenty other people.

Three AFI nominations, *As The Mirror Burns* [1990] which was the first doco I'd done overseas, *The Sewing Room* [1993] and *The Needy and the Greedy* [1995]. I haven't actually won one yet but being nominated is good.

AMBITION

I am more interested in drama, I love documentaries for the content, it is an incredible privilege to be invited into people's lives and they are a huge challenge technically. But you just can't get the quality of sound whereas in drama you have more control and I like the creative element. I am also fascinated by the acting process.

I still want to do that great feature. The Jackie Chan films were huge but only 30 percent of what I record is used. I'd like to do a big budget film where my input is up there on the screen and it's a film I'm incredibly proud of because I've had some journey through the creative process.

By the time I'm 50 I am not going to want particularly to lug that gear around, particularly travelling. I'd like to get into post production sound but I don't think I could be a sound designer. I'd love to edit the stuff I record. I never approach a job without talking to the post production people. I liaise with them.

ISSUES FOR WOMEN

At Deakin I had a battle. I was always employed as the assistant audio producer. There wasn't an audio producer. Peter, who was on camera, was the video producer but I was always the 'assistant'. I fought it, I've always fought these things. It's been one long battle in my life. Fortunately I had Fay Marles' daughter in a radio play I recorded and she said I should ring her mother who was head of the Equal Opportunity Board and also on the Council of the University. She took it to the Council and said 'I don't want this case to appear on my desk because if it does you are going to lose'. So I finally became the audio producer for the last two years I was there. Then of course they promoted the video guy so he continued to earn more than I did.

One of the main problems is being recognised as a head of a department and being listened to and taken seriously on set. Of course we have to be twice as good and we are just not recognised for that. I know that I am as good as any of those boys but I am just not recognised as such. People will not listen to you or they will be constantly reminding you that you are a woman. I was looking at some C stands with somebody one day, and the guys were joking 'Yeah C stands, men's work' and I said 'Yeah that's why they are so simple' and walked off. And they said 'Oh alright'.

On the Jackie Chan films I had Paul Jones as a boom operator. He's very good. He is 6'4" [193cm] tall and intimidates the hell out of the Chinese. He is a lovely guy and it is not an issue that I am a woman but people constantly talk to him rather than me about sound problems, because he's a man. He'll listen and finally he'll say 'Well you'd better ask the boss'.

Other problems are talking to other sound recordists and trying to get information from them because there is a male thing of boasting and learning. Guys tell each other how much they know and that way they glean information whereas I would walk in and say 'how does this work' and they think I'm an idiot. I get that constantly.

In the technical world I find I walk into service places to talk about gear and I am not taken seriously. Trying to get things fixed, trying to buy a couple of transistors or something. They don't believe you can know what they are. They don't believe you can use tools. If I go to shows like the Audio Engineering Society show I'll walk in and ask about a DAT machine, they brush me off. It happens all the time. If you're a woman you do not exist. I have a standard joke, I say 'Too much Ponds vanishing cream this morning. I've vanished'. That makes people sit up a bit. I know it's sarcastic and it gets people's backs up but at least it makes the point.

I have other ways of working with the technical thing. I actually use the way I think as a woman. In other words, I think of sound in colour rather than in technical numbers. I will actually ask a director what colour their script is. 'Do you see your basic production as being in yellow or blue or green or red, or is it warm or cool', and from that I know exactly what microphones they want and the style of sound they want, whether it is really crisp and cold or warm. It is really interesting because it's a common language and I say the choice of microphone will give you an extra element of sound for your film. Directors aren't usually technical and a lot of them have said no-one has ever asked them that before.

I had a camera operator tell me that I didn't know what I was doing when I complained that he was running off a whole lot of film without me. It was on a low budget documentary which desperately needed every sound effect that could possibly be got. It was the most vicious attack and he wouldn't have done it if I was a man. I just reeled. I chose to get on with the film, took responsibility as women do, and let it go because it was a small crew. But in hindsight I should have resolved it either there, or within a day or so, and I didn't. It was such a personal attack it completely unnerved me. I couldn't resolve it and it still festers.

On the first Jackie Chan film the DOP hated me. He was a particularly nasty man – 90 percent of it was in Cantonese but you can tell from the body language. I just said 'Look I don't understand what you're saying, I'm here to do a job'.

When I have had a problem I tend to get around it with humour. With firsts [1st ADs] I go in with a positive attitude, that we are all a team and we are going to make this together. The first thing I will do is ask the AD to walk through the location. I will ask them specifically for a script. It's about knowing what their job is, too. I found that being precise about knowing what they should give me and instantly asking for it always works. Walking through will also tell me a lot about how much they know about sound because everyone says, 'Look I care about sound' and no-one gives a shit about sound and very few people do know about it. Some DOPs do and light for sound so that I can get a microphone in. When they do, it all works. It is such a dream.

I use some of the management psychology that I learnt at AFTRS. I stake out my territory very quickly on set. I walk straight in with my hand out and say 'Hi' and introduce myself. I always have a trolley which denotes my office space. I often put a tarp down which defines my space and means they have to ask if they are going to put lights there. I try to look neat and tidy but androgynous.

I also find having the latest equipment helps. I usually take the lot, I have all the bells and whistles. I have very professional sound sheets with the name of my company on the top.

One of the hardest things is being employed for your skills and not because they want a woman on the set. The first commercial I did was for Huggies, because they thought it would be good to have a woman on set. I was the only person on set who didn't have kids and all the guys knew far more about it than me.

The younger generation are not sexist and these are the people who are coming up in the industry. When I was running courses at AFTRS being a woman was not an issue with anybody under the age of 30. They just want someone who records sound well and has some input. It's not an issue for a lot of people I work with and they're the ones that you go back and continue working with.

It will take three generations to get rid of the sexist attitudes. It has to be talked about, people have to be reminded of it all the time. I have had no support. *Encore* [the industry magazine] hasn't mentioned my name once.* They came down on the set and it is pretty unusual to see a woman behind a sound trolley – I don't know whether they thought I was just sitting on the seat, which is quite often what happens. *Variety* were really interested and they did a little piece.

When we had an all female crew instantly they thought we were students. The guy that I hire gear from pulls out a microphone and says 'you know you have got these switches here' and I said 'I am a sound recordist not a secretary, I can pick up a microphone. Alright. Thank you' and walked out the door.

The other thing is that people think women are cheaper, and I hate to say this but it's often women producers. You'll always find that women are the first people asked to work for less money by women producers which I think is a very insidious untalked about thing. And yet the smaller the budget, the greater the responsibility.

Charging is a problem and I do often find myself not charging enough or feeling guilty about charging. It is a real bind. There is an assumption out there that people employ me because they think I'm cheap, I still do women's issue films, I've done nearly every women's health video in Melbourne. I didn't have my own gear until a couple of years ago and then I was able to start buying it gradually. I hire it from a sound recordist who has a hiring business and he's able to buy the newest and the best.

Sexual harassment

At the university there were many occasions. The worst was a couple of academics. I talked to a few people about it and then it started getting back 'Gretchen is being uncooperative'. I was uncooperative because I wouldn't have a sexual relationship with them. Saying I was uncooperative professionally is the classic old line, it undermines me and defends their position in case it gets out. The one thing you could not call me is uncooperative and the head of the department rang me and said 'I don't believe that for a minute, what is going on?'. So I told him what had happened and words were said and that was that.

Sexist comments

I walked on the set as a boom swinger once and someone turned round and said 'Oh look, a boom swinger with tits' and I said 'Oh look, a camera operator with a dick, surprise, surprise' and he just laughed and said 'Oh alright, alright' and I said 'Okay, I'll just walk outside and walk in again and we'll start again shall we?' I walked outside and walked in with my hand out and said 'My name's Gretchen, how are you today' joking all the way.

I really don't let people get away with that sort of stuff. I'm quick on the repartee, it's always been a survival technique. I don't let the moment pass. I'll call them boy or lovey if they call me girly, and slowly they get the message. You have to identify what the problem is, and once you've identified that you can cope with it.

I had a classic female put down on just a really simple corporate for a council, it was nothing big. I walked in as a mixer and there was the television cowboy on camera in the cuban heels, the moleskins and the gold chain and pink polo shirt, and he said 'Oh that's an expensive mixer' I said 'Yeah' and got on with my job, looked at the shadows, put the microphone in and he turned round and he said 'Ladies and gentlemen this is a very clever little sound recordist. She knows where the lights are, she really knows what she is doing' and he thought he was being complimentary. He continued to say things like that in this incredulous voice. I said nothing for a while, I waited, which is what I do, and noticed that he had taped off the camera to try and make it look like 35mm. I said 'Oh, what is the last 35mm thing you shot?' and he said 'I do television'. And then he said 'What was the last one you did' and I said 'Jackie Chan'. Then he said 'What did you do on it' and I said 'I was the sound recordist' and he said 'Oh, I heard Gary Wilkins did it' and I said 'Gary did second unit for me'.

Working on the Jackie Chan films has been terrific, suddenly people stand up and go 'Whoa,' because it is such a recognised multi-million dollar feature and we don't do many of them here.

Compromises

The whole art of filmmaking is one big compromise. My whole day is one of compromises. Particularly in the sound department, every location in the world is under a flight path or on a main highway. Being a woman you are a good problem solver – we are very good at thinking sideways and making those kinds of compromises.

Being 45 and still not there – I know I've only been freelance for $4^1/_2$ years but I should, with my experience, be further than I am. My personal life is often very difficult, you just become severely independent. I don't think I'd survive if I was in a long-term relationship. I would find it difficult. It is very hard you know you are very intimidating as a woman in these positions. I made a decision not to have children. It's taken me years to get my own space. Every time I thought I'd got a deposit together I didn't work for three months, I barely hung in there, but I chose this life.

Portrayal of women

As a sound recordist there is not much you can do. I need the money, I'm not in a position where I can knock back work. You put your values in your back pocket and turn up and grin and bear it.

I work out what is worth fighting for. Sometimes you're not going to change the way these people think so what's the point.

I end up on some extraordinary difficult docos because I am a woman and they need that sensitivity but there is actually no debriefing. I did a thing called *Guns and Roses* [1990] with Carole Sklan on domestic violence and for two weeks I heard the most horrific stories, really difficult stuff. A director makes a film and resolves it and comes out with a product but as a technician I've got to listen, that is my job. The camera puts a lens in front of her, but I can't just switch off and look at the pictures and frame it and reframe it. The sound is directly into your head. At the end of that film I was shattered. There was no debriefing.

Working with an all-women crew

It is different. It's usually a small crew and I enjoy it. We have lots of jokes and we laugh. All the heads of departments on *Life* [1995] were women, but on set it was an all-male cast. It is set in a prison and I heard that one of the male actors complained that because of all the women on the crew there were no jokes. We were in stitches about all sorts of things, but they weren't sexist jokes.

If I can I will use women boom operators but there are not many in town and there is an issue as to whether, as a woman, I am harder on them. I think it does happen. I certainly know that it has happened to me where women have been harder on me than they would be on a man and I suddenly find myself doing it. So I have to be careful.

Feeling vulnerable

Not having done something before – although that is an interesting double-edged sword because it is also what drives me. I feel very vulnerable when I am in a situation where I am being undermined, not being listened to, when I don't have any sense of authority.

If I am attacked on something that is professional but it is put in a personal way. Being asked very technical questions by people, that is the classic put down. My answer is 'Oh God, another radio parts catalogue question, go and read the catalogue'. I'll say that I am an intuitive sound recordist and I will usually try and work out why they are asking, whether it is to big note or whether it is genuine and I say 'Oh you're trying to reduce this to the lowest common denominator again, oh God I forgot you are a boy. If you insist'. You can get away with it with some people, you can't with others.

Criticism

I usually crawl into a heap. I take it on board but I don't deal with it well. I've had it all my life. Sometimes it hurts, sometimes it doesn't, it depends on whether you're vulnerable at the time. It depends on the type of criticism, if it's from someone who is constantly undermining you. Sometimes it's awful, sometimes it doesn't affect me.

Crying

Sometimes the guys just get at me. I've gone home in tears a number of times. When I was an attachment on a job with a very top sound recordist I don't think he understood that I was already a sound recordist and he kept putting me down, he treated me like absolute dirt. I had a complete attack of the klutzes. I tripped over, I pulled a boom pole over, I hit the light fitting, you name it I did it because he destroyed my self confidence. I came home every night in tears, luckily I was in a household where people would build me up again.

Once I cried and my male boom operator said 'Don't show them' and I thought 'I don't care, I'm that upset, then I don't care'. It was out of frustration with the electric department, they were very, very difficult television boys and television boys are the worst. Most film people are okay, they are getting used to us. It was a gaffer who started off by parking the generator in the middle of the front door. It was obviously noisy for me and I said 'Guys could we move this after lunch, do you mind' and they said 'Yes we do mind, it's staying there.' Luckily, I thought, it's also in shot. So I just went to the director and said do you know that that generator is in shot. He said 'What? Boys move it'. You have to think laterally to cover your base. Then they lit it in an absolutely impossible way for sound. They were really victimising me. They'd come up and put a ballast right next to me and I said 'Move it' and they said 'No, we were there first'. I said 'No you were not' and pulled it out of the wall and all the lights went. It just got me. They were there to get me and they just went niggle niggle niggle. Then I discovered a mistake I'd made under all this pressure and it was the last straw so I thought 'Oh bugger it' and cried. I tend not to but if it's too much I will. When you do cry you think it's unprofessional, and then you think 'Oh bugger it, I'm reduced to this, I can't think of anything else, I am a woman, so what'.

I don't consciously put on a performance but sometimes the headphones come off and the hands go in the air. It was a first [AD] who said when your hands go in the air we know she's off, that this is a big one.

STRENGTH TO COPE

Film is my vocation and once I recognised that I let it drive me. I have a network of friends who I talk to in the film industry. The rest of my friends are not in the film industry and that is also what keeps me going. I'm also very worldly and I travel. I have an attitude to film... we are not finding a cure for cancer, we're only making a film. I think that also helps me out of a lot of things because every now and again when it gets too hard I think 'we're only making a film here, let's get this back into perspective'.

I have great confidence in my intuition. I am a very perceptive, very intuitive person and I've learnt to trust that. That gives me the confidence. Years ago I went trekking in Nepal and got very, very sick but I survived and that was such a liberating experience. Whenever I am in a really tight situation I know it can't be as hard as that, and I survived. I have always had the strength since then. I know I can do it.

ADVICE

The thing I absolutely believe in is that you must have a dream. Have a five-year plan and a ten-year plan. I think you need both because, if you have that dream when opportunities present themselves you recognise them and that dream is what keeps you going. It's what allows you to recognise opportunities when they appear.

As far as technology is concerned, if you can read you can be technical. Don't be intimidated by it, it's alright to not know. Dealing with the guys you've got to believe that you are better than they are. My motto is 'don't let your skirt get in the way'. It's arrogance really, and that's what keeps me going, but you have to be good. You have to be absolutely sure.

I would highly recommend going to film school, VCA or AFTRS – it's really up to you where you want to live. If you go to AFTRS in Sydney you will end up there because you set up your creative team, your creative networks. Getting qualifications helps enormously with your self confidence, it helps you to measure up to other people. Sometimes I wish I had gone to a school, other times I am happy I didn't.

You won't get anything that helps you deal with the male culture in the industry. When I worked at AFTRS no-one ever talked about it, or about receiving negative feedback. It's as if it doesn't exist. I had to battle with my male colleagues, it was always 'he' this and 'he' that, every director was 'he' and every producer was 'he'. It was a constant battle. It wasn't until the gender neutral leaflet came out that I had the authority to pull them up.

It's getting better, the attitude to language, and the type of films they screen. It's the fact that women's films are not celebrated and a lot of women don't celebrate them either. They are a bit scared. It helped me a lot when I admitted that I was a woman and I wasn't trying to be a man and deal in those terms. Mandy Walker [cinematographer] is wonderful, she celebrates the fact that she is a woman. She used to wear overalls to work, now she wears gorgeous sexy clothes, she looks into the lens with the lippy and puts it back on. Her camera assistant has a little lippy holder on the dolly. She's a real role model. I love working with her.

If you want to go into sound, first I'd ask why, what is it about sound that interests you, second I would suggest you do a little test to see whether you are aurally or visually orientated. Get involved in a technical position just to know how to use the tools and speak that language. Buy a recorder walkman. Go and see twenty films and try and remember the soundtrack. Walk out at the end of the film analysing whether you heard the film or whether you saw it, how much you remember of the soundtrack and what that soundtrack actually did to you.

The reason I love sound is because it is a window instantly to an emotion. I always use that description of an egg frying – when you add the sound you can smell it, the smell is a real memory trigger and you can remember when you last had bacon and eggs. Sound has such a dimension to it, but it's rarely talked about.

---

* Subsequent to this interview, *Encore* did publish a piece about Gretchen.

SUE KERR

Sue comes from Mirboo North, a small country town in south Gippsland. She has two brothers either side of her. Her mother wanted her to be a teacher and then she was expected to settle down and have a family. 'I don't think they regard the film industry as a career at all. It is outside their experience. I know they are very proud of me, but they don't tell me.'

She went to Rusden College where she started to do philosophy and sociology and quite by chance picked up a media studies elective. 'I didn't know anything about it, the most expensive piece of technological equipment I had ever owned was a cassette player. I mostly did graphics and photography, very little film or television, but studied radio.'

Sue took a year off between her third and fourth year because she wasn't sure that she wanted to be a teacher. She had been doing a lot of still photography and people started asking her to light their independent films. One day she lit a low budget film and the sound recordist didn't turn up so she was asked to record it. 'I was really bored with camera by then. I was bored with being obscured, but when I put on a pair of headphones it was like the world opened out.'

In her last year at college a lecturer suggested that she should go to the film school [AFTRS]. 'He said that there were three types of people in the world. There were the creative people, there were the technical people and there were the people who were luckily between the two. He said that if I stayed in Melbourne I would just specialise and that wouldn't be enough for me. I needed to be pushed and I needed to be challenged and that the film school was the only institution where that was possible.'

'He helped me fill out the application form and when I got an interview he said 'We will have to tone you down a bit' which meant that we had to cover up the fact that I was out and gay and not 'feminine' which was the word he used. It was his idea of making my future secure which was very nice of him'. So she grew her hair and got a perm and was flown up to Sydney for the tests and interviews and she got in.

'They let me in, then they tried to discipline me. I had the worst times of my life and the best. The film school prepared me for anything I could take within the industry. Before I went to the film school I actually thought film could change things, that it was possible to change the world. At film school I learnt that it wasn't and you actually had to work out who was changing the world'.

AFTRS gave her the opportunity of recording and boom operating on a large number of films and television programs and recording a wide range of musical instruments and an orchestra. After her first year she realised that she was not going to be a sound recordist and that she would concentrate on boom operating.

Her first job when she left AFTRS was boom operating on a health educational film for another film school graduate, Annie Cocksedge (pp108-117), who was recording. She then did a whole lot of recording for documentaries and not much boom operating.

She wanted to go back to Melbourne and attempted to in her first year. She did a couple of films with a sound recordist she had worked with but he was reluctant to take her on because he had someone he had been regularly working with. 'I was doing a lot of documentaries at that time and everybody I seemed to know was in Sydney and suddenly I didn't know many people in Melbourne. 'One of the problems with the film school is that they take you to one state and you build up your networks there and to actually go back to your home state is quite difficult'.

Her first feature was *On Guard* (1984) swinging for Pat Fiske who was recording. She did some other short films with Pat and with Leo Sullivan who was a film school graduate sound recordist.

Then she worked with Syd Butterworth on *For Love Alone* (1985). Noel Quinn, who was his swinger, knew Sue through teaching her at AFTRS and he wanted to go back to teaching and wanted Syd to take Sue to replace him.

Sue worked solely with Syd for five years and did several features including *Travelling North* (1986), *Kokoda Crescent* (1988), and a range of miniseries – *Harp in the South* (1986), *Poor Man's Orange* (1987) and *Skytracker* (1989). Syd then wanted to do more commercials, which Sue was not interested in, and because she had only worked with Syd for a while she found it difficult to get work without him. She started house painting. She then swung for Leo Sullivan on *Sweetie* (1988) and Phil Keros and when she started working with Peter Grace at the ABC her career took off again. She worked on *Police Rescue 2, 3* and *4* (1991-94), with Leo Sullivan on the feature *The Sum of Us* (1993), *Joh's Jury* (1993), the movie *Police Rescue* (1994), some stints on *GP*, *Heartland* (1994), *Bordertown* (1995), *Fallen Angels* (1996) and worked again with Phil Keros on *Murder Call* (1997).

interview

HIGHLIGHTS

[*Police*] *Rescue* was a major highlight. *Rescue* was the hardest thing I have ever done in my life because of the physical difficulty of swinging on those locations. One of the problems was that we didn't have very good radio mics so that unless there was a boom on it you didn't get good sound.

Basically I had to hang off ropes, I had to hang off cliffs, crawl into wrecked cars, wherever the actors were I went. It was a case of getting the microphone anywhere you could and if that meant moving the microphone between people's legs then back over their head then I did it. It was physically very very demanding. The trouble with series television is that you are shooting so much so quickly you need two boom operators. I used to run from the time

I got there to the time I got home. I'd be running from set up to set up, from cliff top to cliff top. It was just frantic. It was completely under-equipped in the sound department. It was stupid of me to continue doing it but at another level I am pretty proud of my work. I think there is some brilliant boom swinging on that gig, some extraordinary physical boom swings.

I think my career is a bit of a highlight. I am very good at what I do and I have always given my best to productions and most of my productions are well over 90 percent sync. In series television most of the ADR [automatic dialogue replacement] is extra dialogue to explain the stories, not because of sound problems.

>> **I just love watching actors work... There is nothing more exciting than watching some performances unfold... I'm in a prime position because I see things that don't get captured by the cameras, it could be an off screen performance that I could be swinging for.**

Being aware that you are good at something, that is probably a highlight. David Williamson told me how good I was. He was the camera operator on a film called *Going Sane* [1985]. He is one of the most respected camera operators in this country. After week one he walked up to me and he said 'How many features have you done?' I think that might have been my second. I said 'Oh not many. Am I not communicating clearly or something' thinking this was a big lecture and he said 'You're one of the best boom swingers I've ever worked with. You always tell me what you are doing. If you've got a problem you come and talk to me'. I regard that praise as very high.

He is a very good camera operator to work with because he knows the problems. To him the frameline is not sacrosanct, he will float it a little so that he can help you out. I'd say to him 'At this point in the walk along the verandah I've got a problem because I've got to come under the beam. Can you slightly adjust the shot' and he will do that. He will have a look. He's an old fashioned camera operator and would rather see where the boom is than not see it and he'd rather know exactly where you were. A lot of new camera operators haven't got that concept at all. There is nothing worse than working with an inexperienced camera operator because they make you look bad. They keep getting you in frame because they never hold their head room. And they get nervous if the boom comes anywhere near the frame line.

I did some beautiful work on a Di Drew picture *The Right Hand Man* [1985] and I had a really good time on that show. That was my third feature. Peter James was the DOP. He set up some lighting situations he thought that I wouldn't be able to get round and I solved them all progressively. He wasn't setting them up as a trap, he wasn't setting me up to fail, he just thought it would make it far too difficult for me to swing. He was just astounded at what I did to get around things. I was helped a lot by Syd's gear because it was really solid and you could throw the microphones and poles around a bit. If you have to get round things you do it really quickly. If someone's got gear you can't move quickly that just makes your job harder.

Syd said that I was really good but my attitude could use a bit of improvement because I was a bit too argy bargy. I was a bit too keen when I was young. I left the film school and everything was fabulous. I just wanted to be in there and I wanted to help the grips. I wanted to help the electricians and I wanted to help continuity, which I learnt you should never do. You should speak to them quietly and privately.

I've enjoyed a lot of the kids shows I've done. I've got a big commitment to kids television.

Other highlights are excellent performances. *Bordertown* was pretty good. Cate Blanchett, what a delight. She is just eye opening, amazing. Mitchell Buchanan who played the halfwit in *Bordertown* was delightful. *Fallen Angels,* Gary McDonald was very good, and Celia Burke. I've never seen anybody that good, she just took my breath away. She was playing a complex character, a woman who drank all the time and yet had to appear to be in control. She played that to perfection. A lot of the other crew had a problem with her because her technical awareness was not good and in television it has to be. But they never explained to her what the problem was. They use to say 'No, no, no, she leans out of frame' I'd say ' Just tell her what you want and she'll do it. She's an actor she's not looking at you guys and where you're pointing your bloody thing. Tell her if she leans that way she'll lean out of frame and she'll lean the other way'. That's a major problem with technicians, they think actors are robots.

I love watching actors work. I think they are remarkable, magical. There is nothing more exciting than watching some performances unfold, and I have seen some excellent performances. I am in a prime position because I see things that don't get captured by cameras, it could be an off screen performance that I could also be swinging for. I've seen just some remarkable things. I've been really privileged.

You just watch an actor and they will transform what is tripe on the page to something that is real and alive. That is what is really good about the film industry, watching a performance emerge which is like watching a butterfly come out of its cocoon. I've learnt so much from watching.

GP was my first experience of working with another boom swinger and I love that. Although it has its moments because I tend to regard myself as being the better boom swinger and never let the other boom swinger do anything. One boom swinger is not necessarily a senior and that creates problems. Generally seniority is created by the sound recordist's choice. For instance, Phil [Keros] got *Murder Call* and rang me and said 'I want you'. We were getting a second boom swinger and we were arguing about who the boom swinger should be. We ended up with a guy who became a mixer and he's not as overall concerned as I am. I'm a really finicky boom swinger. I don't like to hear heels. I do a lot of set quietening stuff and he doesn't do a lot of that yet. He is really good to work with and he doesn't mind me being bossy.

At the ABC I worked a lot with Todd Kirkness who's their only boom swinger on the payroll, and he is brilliant. We work really well together because he's a bit taller and he'd work on the long pole and I'd work on the shorter pole. We could actually work side by side in a very cramped space and swing the whole thing together. He's got a very similar boom swinging attitude. He is always hunting for the best sound all the time. Not all boom swingers are like that. The boom swingers from a television tradition generally don't hunt so that when you've got two people talking they just put a boom in the middle and just slightly favour whoever is talking. Whereas I'd be hunting, moving the mic backwards and forwards all the way through, there were times when I would choose to be in the centre for the spilt but for the rest of the time I'd be hunting.

BOOM SWINGING AND SOUND RECORDING

When you look through a camera you're putting a frame around the world so you're selecting specifically what you will see. Sound is not like that, sound gives you back the world, it makes it real. Camera gives a flat image on a screen and it wouldn't breath, it wouldn't live, it wouldn't tell you anything unless you could hear the sound. The sound tells you where you are, how big everything is around it and what is happening.

Possibly my whole life was built up to becoming a boom swinger. When I was at school I learnt to read in blocks. I don't read word by word and that's really useful for dialogue. I've got a photographic memory for dialogue. I was a middle distance runner when I was at school and that gave me an incredibly big strong upper body for a female. I played state league basketball for five years which gave me a whole sense of where my balance and gravity is.

Boom swinging, physically moving a pole, is a whole body action. You can't just flip your little wrists around, you move your legs, you move your arms, you move your eyes. I am a freak. It is completely natural for me to have my hands in the air and to move a pole for the period of time that is required.

I don't have parallax error which sets up a situation where your eyes would lie to you and calculate that the microphone was in a place where it isn't. I never had a fear of lights or camera because

I operated them and worked them for three years. I knew what lens was going to be on. None of that technical stuff was an issue for me. I am always learning about new lights and what they will do and what they won't do.

I enjoy learning about new film stocks. They are getting so sensitive that shadows you can barely see with the naked eye show up. Before, you used to hide boom shadows all over the set, you just had to know where to hide them. You can't do that anymore with modern film stocks because they will get picked out.

Boom swinging is a philosophy for me, it is what I do really well in my life, it suits me down to the ground. Filmmaking is like a pyramid, there are people that start off at the base. There are always things that have to happen before the next bit. But as you progressively move forward into shooting, those numbers of people get whittled down until you come to a take and the only people that are working on the take, who are physically involved in the performance, are the camera operator, the focus puller, the boom swinger, sometimes the grip if the camera is moving, and that's it. There is nobody else. You are all working to capture the actors performance. The sound recordist, the director, the DOP, are all standing there focused and watching but the only people who are really working are those four people, sometimes even less. That's what I like.

Getting the performance is what we are there for. Filmmaking is a whole lot of palaver to capture a performance in its absolute crystal best. That's our job and any technician who doesn't recognise that, who thinks that their job is more important than the performance, is a wanker.

The technology has changed. All Syd and I used to have on the set was a Nagra, a chair, a small microphone case and an Esky. Syd never used a mixer, he just used his normal Nagra. Now a sound recordist on drama wouldn't dream of not having a mixer. You come onto our set and we've got a high trolley filled with gear. We've got anything up to twelve microphones to choose from.

Boom swingers need to be responsible for what they are using, the cable and the microphones and all the equipment. Now I actually supply all my own boom poles – I have about seven – and I wouldn't want to use other people's boom poles. I think it is much more important that I actually control my piece of technology. I often carry mike mounts, particularly to commercials where I don't actually know whose gear I am going to be using. But you have to be careful not to offend the sound recordist.

I make sure that every piece of equipment is there at the end of the day. I order stock on TV series – on a feature I wouldn't be doing that. I make sure that there are enough DATs, that we've got enough batteries operating. I learnt to do that on *Rescue* because we didn't have time to scratch ourselves on that show. We had to think at least two weeks ahead. When I was shooting in the studio I would spend part of my lunchtime up in the production office making sure that we had enough stock to get through the next block before I came back into the studio.

Temperamentally I am a perfectionist about what I do. You can't be a perfectionist and be a sound recordist because you will go crazy. You can never get a perfect sound, there are too many compromises and frustrations.

Boom swinging is all care but no responsibility. If a plane goes over and you have completed your end of the bargain, which is a perfect boom swing, everybody is on mic, everybody is in perspective and balanced, and you didn't come in frame, what can you do?

The sound recordist sits there and listens to amplified noise in her ear drums all day and most of it is crap. It's very rare that you get a quiet rehearsal on series television because they are setting up lights and somebody is usually talking all the way through it. So the sound recordist listens to crap all day. They are never on set, they are in a vacuum, and they don't know why someone has gone off mic. Their only involvement is what is fed down the line to them and I can't cope with that. It is not me. I was lucky that I realised that really early without having to buy the equipment.

Sound recordists in this country are expected to carry far too much gear and it's getting worse. They don't get paid anywhere the amount they should for the amount of gear that they are expected to have. I think their wage is probably the most unrealistic wage on a film crew now. They have much more personal outgoings than any other crew member and yet no one is prepared to pay for the amount of gear that they have.

What you want from a sound recordist is loyalty. Someone who will back you in a dispute, if there's a boom shadow or a problem that has to be resolved. On drama, sometimes, you really have to exert yourself just to do your job and that is when it just gets all a bit too hard. When you say 'I can't do any more' then it's time for the sound recordist to come in and try and add their weight. Some camera people believe that sound should never be seen or never heard. I don't agree with that. I think that we are all trying to make the picture together and we all negotiate. But some sound recordists won't back you in that situation. They'll just sit back and you cop it.

I did like documentary sound recording. It is the only sound recording that I would even contemplate doing. It's exciting, it's vital, and one of the really good things about documentary is that it is a very small crew so that it is a much more intimate experience. But it is not something I have a burning passion for and I still have a burning passion for drama. It is the reason I am still in the industry. The only thing that keeps me there is that I love boom swinging. The day I stop liking boom swinging is the day I walk because it is not an industry for the faint hearted to be involved in.

Except for boom swinging, sound is such a vastly technical area. If you want to be a sound recordist you have to understand how the equipment works. Cameras are basically very simple, sound recording is not. I am not very good technically with the equipment, the stats, the figures and the signal-to-noise ratios. It does not interest me. I need to know what a microphone polar pattern looks like. I need to understand what that piece of equipment is used for, how to plug it up, how to unplug it, how to change the configurations, but I don't care about the internal guts of it.

Until recently a lot of people fixed their Nagras themselves. Now with DATs you can't and maybe the push button technology will attract more women to it. But I think it is perceived as being not very attractive.

ISSUES FOR WOMEN

When I first started I had major problems because I was a girl doing a boy's job and there was a great deal of resentment about that. Sheer bloody minded rudeness and no help. People just wouldn't help you and it was a constant problem. I had a particular grip who decided that any time I was near the dolly he would hit me with it. The camera operator was incredibly embarrassed because he kept losing his track halfway through rehearsals. The grip would see me cross the track and he would come up and hit me. Tedious.

There are sound recordists who won't use me because I am a woman and there are some sound recordists who won't use me because I'm known to be gay. There are some sound recordists who won't use me because I am outspoken. Those problems are ever present in the film industry.

The most unpleasant thing I have had to put up with is strange versions of sexual harassment from some of the guys. The implication is that I should sleep with them. I don't know if it is to do with me just being a woman or whether it is to do with my sexuality as well. There is an implication that if I sleep with them it would solve everything. Not that I've got any problems to be solved but they obviously do. So that's probably more to do with my sexuality.

The biggest problem I have faced, and still do, is to get credibility – that I am good at my job. In the film industry they say that you are only as good as your last job but that actually is not true, it depends what sex you are.

The other thing that has also changed is that the production manager used to be the representative of the crew to the producer, they used to be the intermediary. They don't do that now because they have all got producer credits. So you go to deal with these people and they're not looking at what would be best for the production, they are looking at their producer credit.

I used to have a commitment to low budget filmmaking and every year I would try and do a low budget film. I would fit it in. I'd take the pay cut and I'd do it. I've stopped doing it because they treat you like a dog. What they don't recognise is that you are actually doing them a favour. They cannot afford to pay you for your ability so they should treat you better. But instead the reverse happens.

I am not a hard headed negotiator. Usually if I want to do a picture I'll do it. I am not in the business to make a heap of money but it does irritate me that I've been swinging for seventeen years, I'm one of the best, and they will not pay me for my abilities and, quite frankly, my experience is worth more money. It's very hard to prove why you don't get a job. In another industry you could say unfair dismissal or whatever but here they just don't employ you ever again and you don't know why. Nobody ever comes up to you and says you can't work with him because he hates your guts. You only hear about it further down the track.

I was almost unemployable for eight months. Syd was the only person who told me 'You've got to stop being involved with the union'. I hadn't done anything that was bad. I'd understand if I'd led a big revolution.

Mostly I get on pretty well with the guys. You have to play the guys' game so that's what I learnt. I grew up with men. They don't particularly bother me. It was much harder for me to get the respect of the women because they had a problem with me doing a boy's job too. Make-up, hair, wardrobe, they are tough. If they have been in the film industry any length of time they have just about seen and done everything and they were always my toughest critics.

But the industry has changed so much, even since I came into it. Quite often there used to be just three women on set and the rest would be all men. That just does not happen any more, even on the most male testosterone set. There are women everywhere now.

There are women on camera but most of them have stopped at focus puller level. They don't get the breaks. What seems to happen to a lot of these girls is that they just seem to get to a certain point and that's where they get held up, unless they get adopted by one of the guys they just don't get any further. Maybe that's what happens to the guys, too. Maybe the women need to be more outgoing.

I can't explain why Erika Addis is not a top feature cinematographer. Her work is brilliant. She is incredibly capable and she doesn't get the work. She should be one of the top feature film cinematographers. She can't even get a commercial gig.

It will change again in the next ten years providing the industry survives the upheavals. I think what will eventually happen is that they won't be able to keep the girls out because they are too good. There are women DOPs in Melbourne who are breaking through.

Sound will be an area where there is always a problem for women because sound recordists have an incredibly long working life. Bronwyn [Murphy, see p29] is the only person who I've worked with who could do it. She has got the ability.

Ambition

I have an ambition to be a boom swinger and to probably have a slightly easier time than I have had in the last five years on *Rescue*. I just want to do quality Australian drama. I don't care whether it is television or feature film. I want to make films that mean something to me. I've never been interested in American pictures. I don't want to work on something where my work is meaningless. What's the point of going along and recording good quality guide tracks.

If conditions go downhill I'm not prepared to stay in it for very long at all. I work more hours than anyone I know, except for residents in a hospital, and they are only going to do it for a very short period of time. I've been doing it for seventeen years. Between Monday and Friday I can't see anybody and I can't do anything because I'm exhausted. I go to work for ten hours every day, I come home and I go into grunt mode. I can't see people socially. There are two days that I have for the rest of my life.

Working with women

One of the great things about working with Bronwyn is that there is no bullshit. You just do your job. The difference between working with Bronwyn and other sound recordists, and I am not including Phil [Keros] in this, is the tension that exists between the sexes. There is the 'Well I have to be boss now'. It just doesn't happen with Bronwyn, we could actually concentrate on making the other departments work for us instead of having to constantly explain the reason we were doing things.

I personally react differently if there is a female director. I am much more circumspect with men. I'm very direct with them, I say 'This is going to be a problem here and here. Is that an issue for you?' If it was a woman I would probably speak differently to her. I think I'm very protective of female directors because I don't get to see many of them and they are usually having a hard time anyway and I'll defend them. The crew will criticise the men and I'll let them but with women I will defend them.

One of the great losses to the Australian film industry is [director] Di Drew. She is incredibly talented. I believe Di Drew has actually been robbed of her career. She probably believes that too. Maybe it's because of her gender and because she never actually learnt to play the producers' game. Di Drew is one of the few people I have worked with who you could actually go up to and say 'Here is a problem, here is a problem, here is a problem', and she'll go 'We'll do this here, we'll do that here and we'll do this here'. One of her technical problems is that she tends to be a bit of a romantic and gets sucked into a performance and tends to not cut it. All she needs is a really good creative producer.

Jane Campion is brilliant with producers. I did all of Jane's pictures at film school except for *Passionless Moments*, and I did *Sweetie* [1988]. She is out there, she understands, she can breath celluloid that girl and she has a unique vision too. Jane is able to produce a shot out of nowhere. She is just extraordinary.

Feeling vulnerable

I think lack of personal respect. It makes me angry as well but what makes me really vulnerable is when I believe that I am not actually being listened to, whatever I am saying is being devalued. Some film crews are like that, if you're not in the right gang then you're not allowed to say anything. You have to be completely silent. It happens in the ABC and on feature films where there are the chosen few who have the director's ear. You have to work out that sort of thing for yourself.

Crying

The first feature film I ever did, *For Love Alone* [1985], I cried most of the way through because I had a particularly difficult time. I was a bit clumsy about crew hierarchy and people decide to have scapegoats on film sets and I was the scapegoat on that film and that was really hard. I used to go and hide behind sets and have a little cry, I didn't know Syd very well so I didn't know how he would react to it. What I should have done was tell him what was going on but I didn't. It was my little journey. I didn't actually tell him till a year later and maybe it would have been better if I had told him at the time.

I cried a lot on *Rescue* just because sometimes it was so hard and I couldn't work out a way to make the set work. Normally I can find my space in the set and work around it. I just couldn't seem to make any headway on that set at all. There was a lot of antagonism to me because I was an outsider and they figured it should have gone to an ABC person so there was not much help or sympathy coming to me at all. The other times I've cried is when I've been so tired.

It used to worry me. It's not something that I actually endeavour to do in public on a set or anything. I would hide it. I tend not to show it. I used to smoke which was the way I contained my emotions so whenever it was getting too much for me I would walk off and light up a cigarette.

Anger is as difficult as crying for a person in my position in a film crew because you're not supposed to show it. Anger is not acceptable unless you're in particular positions. Then you are allowed to be angry. Unfortunately I am not very good at hiding it.

We are all so polite and terribly middle class that we don't actually openly fight on a film crew. It would be a more genuine exchange if you just turned around and said 'Fuck you' and belted somebody. But there is sniping and undermining and all sorts of things are said about your work behind your back by various people, sometimes in post production, and you find about this later down the line. You don't actually hear about it at the time.

Film crews can be the worst type of dysfunctional family. It's not uncommon to be in a situation which is basically domestic violence but it is in the workplace. You get that because there can be a particularly strong personality high enough in the hierarchy, for whatever reason, who is allowed to express their full fury at everybody, and everybody will tippy toe around them. People who normally wouldn't stand for any bullshit from anybody kowtow to them and get out of their way. Everybody turns when they arrive at the breakfast table to check out the sort of mood they're in. That's where the first [AD] becomes important but if the first isn't strong enough to stand up to that stuff then everybody's life is miserable. If it is the first who is like that, then it is a real disaster.

STYLE

I am a bit in your face really. I am very there. People know I'm there. I think my style is pretty verbal. I like to enjoy myself at work. I like to be interactive with people and I like to negotiate with people and if people are pissing me off I generally let them know. I've learnt that I have to be a bit of a diplomat at times because the argy bargy style doesn't work very effectively.

ADVICE

I would advise anyone to go to the film school because I think the sound workshop was extraordinary training. You could start work in community radio, that is not actually a bad background provided you maintain an interest in learning technical stuff, how to cut sound together. I learnt an enormous amount, even before I became involved in recording for film, from doing radio work.

The other thing you can do is become involved in lower budget films and offer to record effects for people. You can go to a mixing studio. They are great places to learn. Editing suites are great places to go, too. I went to an editing suite when I was at Rusden. They put me on a three-week attachment and they were cutting *The Chant of Jimmy Blacksmith* [1977] and that was fantastic just to see how the picture was constructed and actually working out how you relate the sound to that. I had no idea of the layering. It never occurred to me there were so many elements in the soundtrack. Anything to do with post production is really useful. So is anything to do with music.

It's just getting used to handling equipment and not being worried about it. When it breaks down just sort it out. If you can't sort it out find out what actually happened to the equipment when you take it back to whoever you borrowed it from.

Record anything that moves. If you've got home video equipment with external microphones, run different soundtracks. One of the best things you can learn about sound is to watch television with the sound off because you then realise exactly what you are missing. See if you can have any involvement with the image with no sound. As soon as you remove the sound you remove all emotional involvement and as soon as you realise how important sound is then you can actually see ways that sound can be useful.

What I used to do was come home and re-swing the entire day and work out whether I had made all the right choices. If I'd had a bad interaction with somebody at work where there was a compromise forced upon me, I'd work out if there was another way I could have done that better. When I went to see the first feature which I swung, which was *For Love Alone,* it was at the State Theatre. Big gala occasion, I had never been to anything like this before. I was so excited. I sat in the theatre and boomswung the entire film. I was covered in sweat. I came out, I went through every bloody set-up we did for every close-up. I boomswung all over again. I've learnt to contain that.

For women to come into the film industry they don't necessarily have to be completely certain of their job ability but they need to be confident that they can do it. If they're not confident then they have to find a way of learning that they can do it. You can't afford to show weakness on a film crew. As soon as you show weakness on the film crew they'll slaughter you in very subtle ways.

You can't let yourself be trampled over. I can't really think of any guidelines you just have to have a degree of self respect. If you don't have that you have to find self esteem before you become involved in the film industry. You have got to be able to believe in yourself, what you can do, what you can cope with. If you can't do that you can't survive in the film industry.

All film jobs are confidence jobs. You have to know that you're okay at what you do. You have to know, within parameters, that 'Yes I'm making the right decisions' because you could make another decision which might be equally as valid. I could choose to go here with a microphone, I could choose to go there, I could choose to be underneath, I could choose to be over the top, and you weigh it up in the pros and cons of what you are doing at that particular time.

You just have to work out what is your point, what is your line, where you say 'No, that's enough, I'm not wearing this any more' and you take responsibility for it. That's probably been my biggest lesson in the film industry, when to fight and when not to. What to fight for and what not to.

SOUND EDITING

Sound editors start as assistants and because sound specialisation is relatively new (since the introduction of Dolby sound), most sound editors have started as assistant picture editors and learnt to edit sound when picture editing documentaries.

Sound editors are now training in sound only and not necessarily looking at it as a stepping stone to picture editing as it often was in the days of celluloid.

Today feature film soundtracks have expanded so that there are many sound editors and they work with computers rather than physically handling magnetic soundtracks on editing machines.

There is the dialogue editor, whose job it is to cut the dialogue track. If they have been responsible for post sync recording they are called ADR editor (automatic dialogue replacement). This means that they have had to arrange to re-record the dialogue in a recording studio after the picture has been shot. This involves identifying with the director those sequences that need re-recording; organising the actors, the director and the recording studio with the production office; and monitoring the recording to ensure continuity with the location sound.

There are sound effects and atmosphere (atmos) editors who work with foley artists to recreate sound effects and specialist atmospheres and cut them into tracks to match the picture.

In Australia there are rarely specific music editors who work with the composer and organise the music recording as is done in the United States. The sound editor or sound designer will lay up the tracks.

The person who takes overall responsibility for the sound is a sound designer, who usually comes from effects editing and often works as one of the editors. She and all the sound editors work closely with the picture editor.

There are many women assistant editors and they are moving into ADR editing and dialogue editing. Some are effects and atmos editors but this is still seen as a male preserve responsible for guns and car doors whereas an ADR editor is more people-oriented, organising the actors.

ROLE MODEL

One or two women are beginning to get major feature film credits as sound editors, particularly on films directed by women.

I have selected Annabelle Sheehan. She is a successful sound editor who trained at the University of Technology, Sydney in the late 1970s. She started out wanting to be a picture editor but with the development of Dolby stereo and more complicated soundtracks she realised that there were more sound editing jobs available so she decided to specialise in sound editing. She also developed a parallel teaching career in screen studies and has navigated both careers around having two children. She has found that teaching has been a useful career for those periods when childcare hours are difficult to combine with production hours.

Annabelle has seventeen feature film credits including *The Piano, Lorenzo's Oil, Fearless, The Portrait of a Lady* and *Dead Calm.* She has won an AFI best achievement in sound award for *The Piano* as well as the US Motion Picture Sound Editors Guild award for *The Piano* and *Dead Calm.* She is currently head of teaching at the AFTRS.

ANNABELLE SHEEHAN

Annabelle, with three sisters and a brother, is the youngest of five children. She went to PLC (Presbyterian Ladies College) and then the Australian International Independent School and credits that school with raising her consciousness about representation in the media.

Her mother was an infants teacher and a very staunch unionist. She was the first woman president of the Hornsby Association of the NSW Teachers Federation. 'She was a big influence on me because she was very strong about women's issues and politics in general. We went to our first women's march together.' Her father was a doctor but died when she was young. Annabelle's sisters are a barrister, a scientist and a music teacher and her brother teaches drama.

She and her sisters watched a lot of television as children and in her HSC year in 1977 she became interested in the communications degree at the University of Technology, Sydney (then called the NSW Institute of Technology). At UTS she focused on film studies, film production subjects and radio where she enjoyed sound editing. While at UTS Annabelle worked as a production assistant on commercials, for the Jaffa Picture Company.

After finishing her degree at UTS she didn't go on to apply to AFTRS. 'In the late '70s we thought that they just didn't make anything political and therefore you couldn't possibly go there. I really regret that now.'

'We had visions that we were going to be radical filmmakers but in fact I didn't have the confidence to see myself as a producer or a director. It's different to the students at AFTRS where by their very selection they gain confidence. At UTS there was a very big emphasis on politics and breaking down hierarchies. They were rightly concerned with developing *what* you want to say but less able to deliver practical support because their funding and their gear wasn't that fantastic. However I credit that degree with providing a strong ongoing basis from which to analyse film and industry structures that I still draw from now.'

When Annabelle left UTS the idealism of working as a filmmaker quickly gave way to the reality of the industry apprenticeship system. Through her sister, Annabelle got a job as an edge-numberer on *Stir* (1979). Someone saw her there and suggested her as second assistant on *Hoodwink* (1980). She was then asked to stay on as a sound assistant. Sound designer Andrew Stewart went on to work on *Winter of Our Dreams* (1981) and took her with him. Having done two features as a sound assistant she really wanted to picture edit and refused a couple of sound assistant jobs and got a job on *Mad Max 2* (1981) as a picture assistant.

> **»Men... are not afraid to go for things if they don't actually know it. Women don't like to do something they can't do well.**

At the time of *Mad Max 2* the number of films in production was increasing due to the boom of the 10BA tax incentive. She went from one film to the next with ease. After *Mad Max 2* she was asked to be picture assistant on *Kitty and the Bagman* (1981) followed by *Brothers* (1982). During this time she was also doing radio work on 2SER, presenting a breakfast show one morning a week with a group of people from her years at UTS.

To try to move on from being an assistant to being an editor she went to Film Australia as a picture assistant because she thought that there she could move to picture editor a bit faster on lower budget projects. 'I actually didn't get a chance. It was a very busy time at Film Australia and there was a whole bunch of assistants waiting as well. At that time it was more likely that male assistants were given a chance to edit, and the survey of women working in the industry which the Australian Film Commission (AFC) did then, supports that. This has changed and in the nineties women are moving through to editing positions more easily.'

She did get to sound edit *Out Of Sight Out Of Mind* (1982), which she had picture assisted on, and through her Film Australia connections she was offered sound editor on *For Love or Money* (1983). 'Maureen Walsh was head of editing and she was often rung up by low budget producers and asked if there was an assistant who would like to get a leap up. She was very supportive of women and wanted women assistants to get to edit.'

'When I took on *For Love or Money* there were enormous gaps in my understanding of the soundtrack but at least I had seen a number of tracks through to the mix stage. I knew what you were supposed to do and could do it but when I look back now I think "My God, how did I manage it". I had an enjoyable time inventing ways of getting sound effects.'

She assisted on some other films but also wanted to direct so she went to New Caledonia and researched a documentary about independence which she put up to the AFC but it was knocked back. 'I think it has taken me another twenty years to work out how I could put in another proposal. I had not learnt that part of being a filmmaker is to know how to understand refusals. I was very confused about my career at this stage. I had no idea really how it all worked, I felt producers were very high up important people who I could never be. There were women producers but I didn't identify with them. I didn't know how they got there and I just thought they were like "parents". I was in my early twenties, I should have been more brave but I just thought that that couldn't be me. There were a lot of men in the industry and women were mostly assistants at that stage. So I was starting to wonder how I was ever going to picture edit.'

She worked on the American version of *Mad Max 2* as an associate to an American editor. She then went on to be picture assistant on *Annie's Coming Out* (1983). 'I accepted that job because it would include assembly editing but I didn't get a credit for it. I could not work out how you could get recognition for what you had done.'

After travelling overseas in 1984 she returned to take up an editor's position with the Women's Film Unit which was to be run out of Film Australia with women directors and writers to give women a chance. Jane Campion was one of the directors straight out of film school and Annabelle edited her film *After Hours* (1984). 'Jane said to me you should hold out and not do any more sound work, you should just wait until picture editing jobs come up, but I couldn't do that because I had to earn money.'

With that in mind and because she liked to work with Kennedy Miller she took up a job as an assistant sound editor on *Mad Max – Beyond Thunderdome* (1984). 'I had this feeling that in sound you could become an editor more quickly than in picture because sound crews were expanding to respond to Dolby stereo. Tracks were becoming more complex and there were job opportunities. Instead of one or two sound editors there were now three or four. A lot of my friends who were at UTS, Andrew Plain and Adrienne Parr for example, had shifted from being picture assistants to sound. We liked sound. We could have more control.' During this time Annabelle was also doing reviews for the Sunday program *Razor's Edge* on 2SER and some reviews for the *Sydney Morning Herald*.

Mad Max – Beyond Thunderdome was Annabelle's first Dolby stereo experience. She was doing a lot of the scheduling and planning for the ADR (automatic dialogue replacement) editor, Tim Jordan, and they needed an extra editor so she started doing the ADR herself to keep things going. 'Basically I put my hand up and said – look I am happy to keep the wage I've got as an assistant but I just want a sound editing credit.' and so she was promoted to dialogue editor on that film.

In 1985 after making the move to ADR editor she went to the US for two years for a mixture of personal and career reasons. She was accepted into the Masters program in Cinema Studies at New York University (NYU). 'I was feeling that maybe I could develop my career in film further by doing film studies for a while – enriching the way I thought and talked about film, not necessarily getting out of sound but thinking about it again. I was also interested in lecturing in screen studies, I had done a few talks by that stage and a bit of film criticism and I was interested in returning to that part of myself.'

'I often say that I have a dual career, film reviews and analysis and the industry work. I was very passionate about film and just saw film constantly and was totally surprised if all the crew didn't go to five films a week.'

Annabelle completed an MA in Cinema Studies at NYU and started a doctorate. While there she tutored in the film production department and developed a liking for teaching. She also researched and completed interviews for a major radio documentary on the radio work of Orson Welles. 'This experience of research confirmed for me my ongoing interest in cultural studies and academic work.'

The first job she got when she came back to Australia was as a sound editor on Ian Munro's film *Custody* (1987). She was then rung by Kennedy Miller and asked if she would like to be an assistant sound editor on *Dead Calm* (1987) which was the position she had originally been employed in on *Mad Max – Beyond Thunderdome*. She said that she wouldn't be an assistant but she would accept the role of ADR editor that she had achieved by the end of *Mad Max – Beyond Thunderdome* and they agreed. 'At that time I was living at home and I had the confidence to say "I don't want the job if it is assisting". This was a big breakthrough for me.'

In 1988 her son was born and she taught in the editing department at AFTRS and screen studies at TAFE. In that time she completed a diploma in education and started writing more on film education issues and on the effects of digital technology on post production work practices.

In 1991 she was offered *Lorenzo's Oil* (1991). They wanted someone to do ADR on the boy's fits and coughs and they needed someone during the fine cut phase to work out whether it was going to work or not. Lee Smith, who was the sound designer on *Lorenzo's Oil*, then took her onto *The Piano* (1992) where she got a credit as a supervising ADR editor. She then decided to leave TAFE permanently and was dialogue editor on *Fearless* (1992) and ADR editor on *Rapa Nui* (1993). She was also doing reviews for *Filmnews*.

When she was pregnant with her second child in 1994 she did a study of career paths for the AFC and, after her daughter was born, she lectured one day a week in screen studies at UTS. When her daughter was one year old her husband took over as the main carer so that Annabelle could work as curriculum manager at AFTRS supervising the rewrite of the curriculum. She had a longstanding engagement as ADR supervisor on *The Portrait of a Lady* (1996) for Jane Campion. She is now head of teaching at AFTRS.

interview

HIGHLIGHTS

The films that have stayed with me are *Mad Max 2* because it was really exciting to be part of the Kennedy Miller team as an assistant. There were four editors and George Miller was running between all four of them. It was a bit of a revelation about scope and size. The Kennedy Miller people were very positive about what I could do, so any film I have done with them has always stretched me a bit.

Mad Max – Beyond Thunderdome had Bruce Lampshed as sound designer. I was very conscious of him being a talented person who was doing interesting things, coordinating a team and devising ideas. He was in charge of specific special sounds and I found that interesting. The challenge of the film is what makes it special because inevitably it extends your skills and knowledge.

Dead Calm was a real development for me and Phil Noyce was really stimulating to work with. The ADR was a good puzzle to solve, a whole lot of breath editing which was fantastic. It was the first film I did with Lee Smith as sound designer, I was the ADR editor and within the first week I was having lots of planning discussions with the editor and the director about how to organise all the post sync dialogue for the key actors because they were leaving the country and we needed to do a week of dialogue recording with each of them. It was a great experience.

Talking about the meaning in the film was what attracted me to being a picture editor and it's more one-to-one, editor and director. Picture editing is still a thing that I would like to do. With ADR there is also a great deal of communication and analysis. There's planning, there's talking to whoever is the post production coordinator, the producer, the director, the designer, and then sometimes agents. Then you have to ensure the facility is appropriate to record in and work with the operator and recordist. I also love watching how directors work with actors. You're virtually in another production phase. There are a lot of people to interact with and that's why I find it enjoyable.

Both *Lorenzo's Oil* and *The Piano* were highlights. The directors experimented a lot on the ADR stage trying to find how to get the performance back, trying to find how to do good breathing scenes or struggle noises. In both cases it was finding out how good and precise ADR could be, how real it could be and how it could make a person have more presence in a scene.

George Miller was very interested in ways to get actors to do the coughing scenes and reproduce performance. It was equally fascinating to work with Jane Campion because she works in a slightly different way to other directors.

We also had to travel. We went to Los Angeles and New York for *Lorenzo's Oil* and to New Zealand and Los Angeles for *The Piano*. We looked at other studios, how they work, and we saw the similarities between the way we work and the way Americans work.

The ADR editor goes with the director, you're there to say whether it is going to sync or not and whether it will match. You are there also to inform the director and actor of exactly why a particular line might need to be re-recorded. There is a lot of technology to get across every time you go into a new studio – you work with new people, and you have to tell them what you want and what the director wants.

The Piano gave me a credit as a supervising ADR editor because the work involved a higher degree of supervision. When there is an international component, and you go to two or three other countries and manage sound from different studios, you have to really manage a lot of people to keep some continuity in the way each studio records it. Time constraints also mean that another dialogue editor needs to work with you to edit the material recorded overseas.

Rapa Nui was fantastic in some ways but not in others. It was an interesting experience to work with Americans but it was a bad film. It was depressing. When you work on a film that you actually don't like it is depressing to put the reels up every day. I've been very lucky that almost every film I've done I've really liked but *Rapa Nui* was just a politically bad film, badly acted with a poor script and that feels bad. From that experience I now know that I don't want to work on films I don't like.

Portrait of a Lady was a fantastic challenge because that again was a big puzzle. There was a good director to work with [Jane Campion] and a good sound crew. When a film has so much detail in theme and style it provides a lot of opportunities to be creative in sound.

AMBITION

It's hard for me to say what I want to do because I've got a two year old and a seven year old. It's not only always trying to balance film culture and film education, which I really love, but there's the whole other part which is parenting and I am trying to balance all three.

I have been really lucky. I've been able to go overseas and come back and find work, have children, come back and find work. But I think that in terms of the career choices I've made, my sense of what I could do has been a little bit stunted by not quite recognising what sort of career I could have had in film. However I don't think anyone really knew in the 1970s. You probably had to be more confident than I was.

While I think about whether I should venture into directing or not, there is another part of me which enjoys solving a big puzzle that involves screen culture. In fact I very much enjoyed being part of decision-making and planning for film education in my curriculum work at AFTRS and I think that in doing that I combined the two strands of my career so far.

CHANGING TECHNOLOGY

We've changed to digital workstations and the whole transition in sound has actually gone well. At first a lot of people thought that they were never going to be able to achieve the same results they were used to on 35mm and yet almost everyone I know can now operate one or two of the new digital audio stations and appreciates the different version of editing flexibility that these systems provide.

I had to learn digital editing for *Fearless*. The company – Soundfirm – which was mixing the sound and which also developed a digital audio workstation called Edi Tracker, arranged for a two day teaching session for the two dialogue editors – both women. We didn't find it all that difficult in editing terms. I think the hardest thing is coming to grips with troubleshooting technical breakdowns. Most editors who came out of the eighties, both men and women, don't necessarily know about patching or audio engineering because you just don't have to know it when you are simply sound editing. The workstations tend to mean you must have more contact with that aspect of sound.

ROLE MODELS

Jane Campion is a role model for many women. I like the way she works with people, and she works with a sound mixing crew in an interesting way. She has to work quite hard at the mixture of playful versus assertive. She has to do the blokey bit along with all the rest of us. But I think she has a good mix of it and she gets performance.

I like the way sound designer and editor Lee Smith works. I think he is a great role model. He makes people who are working with him in his team feel good. He is calm all the time and doesn't blame, and he cares about people's lifestyles and if they are working long hours.

Sara Bennett is a good person to consider in terms of balance between film production and education in her career. I think she has done a fantastic job in the editing department at the AFTRS and she has done a lot for women editors. If you really look at why women editors are getting somewhere in Australia you would have to say a lot of them have come through the AFTRS.

ISSUES FOR WOMEN

The problems that I have had working out who I am in the industry may not be specific to women. I am sure there are men who have exactly the same trouble. But I am aware both anecdotally and via studies that women are much less likely to apply for positions that they don't absolutely feel confident about.

I have had a very good run for a woman in sound and in fact there are a number of women who also have – Karin Whittington, Helen Brown, Livia Rusic, Annie Breslin. However women are much more likely to become dialogue editors and much less likely to become sound designers or supervising sound editors.

Initially, when I first got work in post production sound there was a culture of it being men's business, and very secret men's business it was, the mixing and the pressing of the buttons and patching leads. There is that entrenched masculine culture in the mixing room where to get on you've got to be a bit clubby about it. You also have to know when to stop – if you get too clubby you can see them think 'Hold on, you're meant to be a girl, stop it'. You are treading a fine line which is about how to make friendships in the room. I really like the many different men involved in sound, they're fantastic people but the culture is probably hard for women and there would be a lot of women really put off by it.

Because I've had people be kind to me I feel churlish to say that there are problems. But in fact I have to admit that there is a lot of information which can be passed on between men that women have found it hard to break into. I suspect that men find it easier to pass on knowledge to each other. I've been lucky enough to work with some men who are open and I feel alright saying 'Look I don't know how to do this' and they'll tell me if they know how to do it, or they'll admit that they don't know either. But the culture is about not passing information on unless you're part of a club. Of course it's not a conscious decision on the part of all men to avoid telling women, it's just the way they have learnt to relate to people.

I also believe that there is a sense in which men look after each other a bit better than they look after women colleagues. They might save a male colleague from a mistake because they don't want another man to mess up in front of other people, whereas they are quite happy for women to make mistakes... they might not save you, and that is very scary. It's the public embarrassment of making a mistake that can make you sick with fear sometimes. So, as a woman, if you know there is no safety net then that would make you fearful of doing it again. I do believe that men are saved from their mistakes a lot in sound and so there are more women casualties.

I have been in a room where a mixer has said to we three female editors 'Women don't track car effects as well as men do because they don't know about cars'. The two other women, who had done effects editing, as well as dialogue editing, were obviously outraged. I found it offensive and just amazing that someone could say that quite happily in front of three women. But there is a sense in which effects *are* 'car things'. They are big and noisy and that is considered boys work. A bit like the song about boys liking puppies and all things smelly and girls, well girls do dialogue. There are female effects editors but not many. One of the reasons I don't do sound effects is because I am deeply uninterested in car doors and horses and I am more interested in humans.

Sound mixing

There are practically no women mixers these days. Annie Coxsedge used to be a mixer at the ABC but she has left the industry [see p108]. On *Portrait of a Lady* there was a woman who did some ADR recording at Spectrum, which is how you could start if you want to be a mixer.

In gaining early confidence to mix I think men would find it easier to say to a mixer 'Can I just hop on the desk for a minute and fiddle with this' man-to-man. If there was a female mixer, women might feel a bit more confident about doing that too. Also I suppose I would find it easier to judge the mood of a woman at a desk and then to ask her why she chose a particular equalisation and what do those three buttons do, etc etc. I am less likely to ask that of a male mixer.

I certainly know more men than women who like to read the sound technology magazines. I really can't bear to read them and I actually don't even like thinking about patching and audio engineering in detail. I prefer considering which sounds will work with the story and not how to make sure they'll translate in the 'DS4'. This lack of interest in deep technology issues is most likely cultural for women and goes back a long way. I hope there are now young women ready to contradict me and say they love reading sound magazines.

Dealing with difficult men

I have probably most often chosen the path of least resistance which would have to involve compromises on my part. I accept that, especially if they are in charge.

There are times when I do think I have a relationship with some men which is sort of 'gamey', it's not sexy, but it is a sexist relationship. I probably use lots of submissive body language without knowing it. I probably do jokey friendly talk if I sense I might be seen as threatening. I see it as part of how we play our roles and if I like the man as a friend then I am prepared to let that be unless it affects my work. I basically see that we are all stuck in this culture and I am not going to make a point of getting this particular guy for it.

However there are times when a man is difficult in a way that affects my work. In one case I worked on two different films with an American ADR recordist who was particularly difficult but by the second film I think I had learnt a way of dealing with him. My first session with him was on *Lorenzo's Oil* and he was patronising and irritating and saying negative things about choices I was making. He made comments I'm sure he would never have made if

I was a man. Initially I ignored him. He was a real griper and he didn't like the fact that we were going to DAT tape instead of reel-to-reel and would say 'Well I don't know why you are doing that' and I'd be thinking, 'Why is he talking about this to me, I just want to get on with the job'. Gradually he irritated and upset me in such a way that I felt I might lose concentration and so I said, 'You might like to ring the sound designer because he is the one who has made this decision'. So I chose to deal with it by telling him that it was actually a man who had made the decision. He accepted that.

We went back there for *Portrait* and I responded to any of his comments with something along the lines of 'I am the client, this is inappropriate. I've made my decisions for specific reasons'.

It didn't stop him. He griped all the time. He was even complaining about the way Jane Campion directed. The man was unstoppable, he was just a negative patronising sort of man. Occasionally I joked about it. A couple of times I would try out my little assertiveness statements: 'I find this inappropriate'. It made me feel better and sometimes it did work. In fact, our US post production supervisor complained to the studio management because she had been on the receiving end as well and they were surprised as no one had spoken up before. In fact we knew of some other female ADR editors who had not liked it but they had just never gone back to that recording studio.

Another example of where I've tried to actively improve a work relationship with a male colleague was when I had a male editor working to me who was 'white anting' me because essentially he was finding it hard to accept that he was not my supervisor. I decided that I couldn't let it go on as it would irritate me and I'd be distracted in my work. This person was obviously unhappy and felt threatened by me. So I very consciously set up a meeting with him and tried to get him to say why he was feeling unhappy. I had to sit him down at various times when I could see him building up into a state and talk with him saying, 'I understand how you feel that I should be doing something different. Can you tell me about that'. He'd tell me and I'd explain what I was doing and I think it worked well. That's an example when I felt quite good. He was quite easy to deal with ultimately because he was not really an aggressive man. With an aggressive man I don't know quite what I would do but I would probably try the same thing.

The climate is changing but I still think there is some malevolence towards women in technical sound positions. If a woman seems to know, and uses the same strategies and makes the same statements the men do, I think men feel put off by it and she will be disliked by them. Some men don't like women to do what they do.

Sexist remarks and sexual harassment

I was told that the job I got on *Hoodwink* was because a guy said to the editor 'There's a girl doing edge-numbering over at Film Production Services, she's got big tits and you'll probably like her.' The editor was luckily not at all interested in this particular selection criteria but he did tell me later that that's how I was recommended for the job.

From time to time I've had people come up behind me in the editing room and with their body language indicate that they think that that is the place to have an affair! I think I've just felt embarrassed because they have usually been senior to me and I didn't quite know what to do. I've basically ignored it and walked away. I haven't said 'Stop doing that' or similar. I think I have felt afraid of making a scene. I was not well equipped with strategies to deal with it. I regret not pointing out to them how inappropriate they were.

When I was quite young a producer insisted on sitting right next to the Steenbeck so I had to constantly push past him to lace up the film and I knew he was doing it on purpose to kind of humiliate me. I just ignored it, despite three years of feminism at university.

You have to be able to find the words. It is probably less prevalent now with the publicity and media attention to the whole sexual harassment issue. But I am sure some people don't realise that they are doing things that could be considered sexual harassment so they would be shocked for someone to turn and say 'This is inappropriate'. I guess I didn't want to shock them or be considered difficult. It's sad that even with a sense of feminism a woman knows she will not easily find work if she complains.

However I do think there is some point in not always speaking out instantly, just moving away instantly. I would probably advise women to move away from the immediate danger or humiliation, just absent themselves geographically so they can gather their thoughts. You do need a bit of air between yourself and the event to work out what you want to say. If I turn on a person at the time I would feel so emotionally caught and distressed that I wouldn't think clearly and I like to have more control over the situation.

Child-rearing

While I was pregnant and after I had Angus I knew I couldn't work on sound because the hours are too impossible to be compatible with childcare arrangements so I taught at AFTRS and TAFE and did a Dip Ed.

A year later I was beginning to think I should work again and Kennedy Miller offered me dialogue editor on *Bangkok Hilton* [1989]. My husband took his holidays, and Kennedy Miller were very supportive – they let Neil bring Angus in so I could feed him at work, and then when Neil's holiday leave was over and he returned to work they let me work odd hours, from 6pm when Neil got home until 2am, and I would just bill them for my specific hours. This was quite workable if you were given a set number of reels to prepare for a mix.

I have almost always done ADR. On *Flirting* they offered me sound designer after a number of people had turned it down for one reason or another. I accepted it but after two weeks I said that I wouldn't be able to do it because I was still breastfeeding Angus and I found it too hard. If he got a temperature or was sick, even though I had a very supportive husband, I just found it too hard to cope. So I said I'd stay on and do dialogues. It wasn't a very hard decision with children. I suppose I can hardly gripe about how a post sync dialogue editor would never get asked to be a sound designer because I have been asked once!

When Claudia was born I was teaching one day a week at UTS and it was pretty hard. I used to have someone mind her in the room next to the lecture room and I'd feed her even while I was lecturing.

Students were very understanding about it, as they had been when I had Angus. In fact, women students were particularly interested to discuss how to balance career and family. The fact that my partner is able to support me by taking time off and through his ongoing commitment to sharing the responsibility has meant that I can almost balance both with some compromises in each case.

Claudia went to childcare five days a week, I would have preferred she didn't because I missed her a lot. I'd also rather they didn't go to after school every day because I'd like more time for homework, soccer and trumpet and all the things that we also do. And it is a real drama running out of the house at 8am and not getting back again till 7pm. It's just so difficult, I don't know how we all keep doing it.

Ultimately if you want to work on feature films you need a partner to give up their work. The hours are so long and with both working you'd have to pay someone to live your life for you.

Feeling vulnerable

I feel vulnerable when I haven't prepared well or I make a mistake in public. I don't like to show that I've been lazy, or that I don't know the answer to something that I could have looked up and found in advance, or that I haven't thought ahead.

A lot of research shows that women don't go for jobs because they don't believe they are qualified, while men will do it at the drop of a hat. They are not afraid to go for things if they don't actually know it. Women don't like to do something they can't do well.

Crying

I've cried at work mainly when I'm sick and therefore floundering. It is to do with frustration, of feeling that I am not going fast enough. I don't feel embarrassed about it really. I do feel that I have exposed a weakness but if I can relate it to illness I don't feel at all worried about it. However I wouldn't say that I cry much at work.

Coping with criticism

I consciously want to be good at that because I believe it is important. Jane [Campion] is a good role model. I learnt a lot from her about how to interact with people. She has a particularly good, gentle approach if she's not happy with what someone is doing. I also think she is able to give them an opportunity to tell her they're not happy with what she's doing. I think that skill is worth learning.

If there has been a mistake – mine or someone else's – I try to say 'Okay, what can I do to fix it'. If it was me I would just say that I am very sorry I made a mistake but I would want to explain how it came about, especially if there were extenuating circumstances. I wouldn't want to feel that I'd been blamed for something that actually wasn't my fault. In the heat of the moment I'm sure I've blamed someone else if it really was their fault but I try to keep that to a minimum as it's a bad habit in the film industry.

PERSONAL STYLE

I do try to be organised in my cutting room, to produce information and put things up on walls and have things organised and communicate well with the people so that they know what I am doing. I don't like to think that anyone spent an hour or so being held up in their work because I haven't informed them.

Over the years I've noticed I've had times when I was too overwrought and intense on perfection. Hurrying and worrying! I've consciously tried to be calm and to want to make people feel happy and jokey and playful in their work. I am a natural 'want to get things done fast' type of person and I probably oscillate between being intensely anxious and attempting to project a calm purposeful image!

LESSONS

I think you have to be aware of sexism and the culture that has produced it. You have to be aware of your rights and be strong and assertive, not aggressive. Then at times you have to lose and accept the mistakes of the men and the women around you because otherwise you get too distracted.

There is a kind of a balance of acceptance which means that I am just going to ignore problems for a while so that I can get my job done but also an awareness that it shouldn't be like this. If you can't keep the balance you get walked all over or you get intensely anxious and frustrated and leave the business yourself. In fact you also might get forced out because you're not getting on with people.

I know that at times I err on the side of being too relaxed then I think, given my background at UTS and interest in feminism, I should be more concerned for women and for improving how we relate. Basically I think you need to give positive responses to men who treat you well. When men treat you badly perhaps you continue to model for them how you think humane people should interact – but sometimes you have to put your foot down.

ADVICE

I think there are all sorts of issues for people wanting to enter the industry at the moment. It is always a hard job working freelance, never being certain of work. For women it is about preparing yourself so you can't be made to feel a lack of confidence. Making notes and lists and feeling well prepared so that people can see you feel strong. It is about confidence and about getting rid of negative thoughts in your mind as you work.

In a more direct sense it's about knowing that mixing desks, sound engineering and editing are all absolutely attainable skills. Also, harder skills you need are communicating with people – discussing and analysing. Culturally women are considered to excel at these things so make the most of that!

Part of being prepared for a sound career, or any media career, is having a course behind you. I think if you are new and raw and an apprentice you are probably much more vulnerable to the old culture that divides women from certain skills. If you have done a course you can judge that older perspective against something that you have learnt in a potentially more friendly environment like an education institution. And of course you have the confidence of having skills learnt before you arrive on the job. However, film and television education is relatively new so the general issues of learning are still being explored. The gender issues associated with learning highly technical areas such as sound have not really been drawn out and that's the next challenge.

SOUND COMPOSING

Composers are another group of film professionals who have found computers becoming essential for their work. Composers use computers as a tool to give an impression to the director of the music they have composed, before they go into a recording session with instruments, as a 'mock-up' full orchestra, or as an instrument to create electronic music which will be on the final soundtrack.

In past years a composer needed only a video recorder to watch the final cut of the film which had time code on it, a piano to compose and paper to write the score – a small number of composers still work like this. They would then either orchestrate the score and copy the parts for the instruments themselves, or employ others to orchestrate and copy.

Today composers can compose using the computer and it will print out their orchestrations. Most composers therefore have invested large sums in electronic recording facilities in their home studios.

A composer will usually read the script before production and discuss the amount and type of music and the length of the recording sessions with the director. She may even start composing rough sketches but cannot start work in earnest until the final cut has been locked off by the editor. Sometimes pre-recorded music for playback is required for the shoot.

Music is the emotional life of the film and is usually used to underscore dialogue and reinforce the dramaturgy of specific scenes at particular moments. The composer will sit with the director 'spotting' the film points, ie, noting where music is required, and discuss with the director the style and type of music she wants. She will then measure the exact time that the music is required according to the time code burnt into the VHS copy of the film and compose music to fit the cues.

Depending on the amount of time she has, she will discuss the music with the picture editor and the sound designer, if there is one, or the sound editor. There may well be collaboration regarding the sound effects, the placement of the music, and the type of music under the dialogue. In Australia – unlike in the US – there is very seldom a music editor so that the composer also takes on that coordinating role which involves organising recording and scoring sessions, and booking musicians.

If the composer also likes to conduct, she will then conduct the instruments or orchestra to the projected film. The music cues will be recorded in the order that is most economic in the use of the musicians. To help the musicians play with precision, a click track is generated by a digital metronome and fed into the conductor's headphones and sometimes also fed to the players.

The sound mixer will record the music, which will be laid by the sound editor on a separate soundtrack, and mixed with the dialogue and effects tracks against the picture at the final sound mix. The composer may attend the final mix of sound to picture with the sound editors and the director and producer. She will help to solve problems when all the tracks are heard together with the picture.

If the music is electronic then the composer will record the music track in her home studio and there will be no need for a music recording session with instruments. Of course, there may also be a combination of electronic and instrumental music, which will be recorded on separate tracks and laid against the picture by the sound editor.

The budget allocated for the composer will determine the amount and type of music to be used. If the film is late in production or the editing has overrun then there can be enormous pressure on the composer to work against difficult deadlines to meet recording sessions with booked musicians. It is not uncommon for composers to be composing and recording one reel while the editor is finalising the next.

Film composers are often trained musicians who have acquired the additional skill of composing within the strict limits of film. Although there is a growing number of women composers there are very few women film composers. This is partly because of the male culture of sound recording but also because there is very little training in Australia for film composers. This is an important consideration because the availability of training in other aspects of film production has given women access to areas traditionally seen as male preserves. In 1999, the first full-time course for film composers began at the AFTRS.

ROLE MODEL

I have chosen Nerida Tyson-Chew, who is only in her early 30s. Her career is in stark contrast to anyone else I interviewed. She was nurtured in her 'craft' – piano playing – from an early age and has been supported and confirmed by prizes and scholarships. In 1988 she won the Queen Elizabeth II Silver Jubilee young achiever's award, the James Hardie Industries special award and the University of Sydney's Albert Travelling Scholarship, which took her to Canada and Los Angeles. In 1991 she was granted a composer's internship by the US Academy of Motion Picture Arts and Sciences and the Society of Composers and Lyricists.

In 1995 her original score for *Hotel Sorrento* (1994) was nominated for best original music score in the AFI awards and won the Australian Guild of Screen Composers award for best original music score and the Film Critics Circle of Australia annual award for best music score. In 1996 she received three nominations from the Australian Guild of Screen Composers and won the award for best music in a children's television series for *Crocadoo* (1996). In 1997 she was again nominated for two awards and won best music for a television series for *Twisted Tales* (1996). Her recent credits include the feature *Kick* (1998), the television series *The Adventures of Sam* (1998), and the CD-ROM multi-path movies *Popeye – The Rescue* and *Popeye The Sunken Treasure*. She works from her studio in Gladesville, Sydney.

NERIDA TYSON-CHEW

Nerida began playing the piano when she was seven and the family inherited her grandfather's piano. From an early age she could hear music in her head and started writing music for fun. She went to the Conservatorium High School in Sydney.

When she was fourteen she saw *Psycho*. Finding it frightening, she turned the sound down and realised how much music could manipulate an audience's feelings. It was then she decided that she wanted to be a film composer. She had a piano teacher who had been a repetiteur with the Australian Opera and gave her a very rich awareness of the orchestra, so 'it became the most natural thing for me to write for the orchestra'.

She was supported and encouraged by her parents. 'They always said "we are so proud of you" and they helped me to become fearless.' Her mother was a couturier and her father is an accountant.

At the Conservatorium High School she picked up conducting from watching guest conductors conduct the school orchestra and she had plenty of opportunities to compose and get her pieces played. In her final year she won the senior prize for composition. From 1983 to 1986 she went to Sydney University and was preparing herself to write film scores. She was the only girl who did composition for honours. 'I was a bit of an oddity within that academic environment because I was wanting to write mainstream, publicly accessible kinds of music, rather than the intellectual, artistic kind.'

In her honours year she won a travel grant which took her to Canada for two weeks. Air Canada was one of the sponsors and when the representative heard that she wanted to write film music he gave her a side trip to Los Angeles. As a result of that visit she discovered that there was a post graduate course in film scoring at the University of Southern California (USC). She spent a year teaching in a private school to raise the resources to put together a recording session so that she could properly audition for the course.

She was accepted on her first attempt in 1988. Nine people were selected from all over the world, two girls and only three non-Americans. The course was very practical and drew on the whole of Hollywood. Bruce Broughton (*Silverado, Young Sherlock Holmes, Rescuers Down Under*), Buddy Baker who was the last staff employee composer at Disney, and Irwin Kostal who orchestrated *Chitty Chitty Bang Bang, The Sound of Music,* and *South Pacific* were course instructors while Henri Mancini, Jerry Goldsmith, Andre Previn and Leonard Rosenman were weekly guest speakers. The students had the opportunity of seeing how they wrote for the screen, the way they orchestrated and how they ran their recording sessions. Nerida also went to Jerry Goldsmith's recording sessions. Every two weeks the students had their own scoring sessions for films. 'All of us would be writing music to the same scene. We would have the experience of running a recording session, getting our point across to the musicians and then we would view everybody's piece of music and discuss it. It meant that by the time I was in a position to be doing professional work in a recording studio I already knew how it should be done.'

Nerida was then appointed as a soundtrack producer for a Japanese theme park. She lived in LA and supervised the budgeting and final production for the sound effects, dialogue and music recordings for various shows to be presented at the theme park. She also orchestrated a few of the shows. In 1991 she applied for a number of American scholarships and received a composers internship with the Academy of Motion Picture Arts and Sciences.

Bruce Broughton was, and still is, her mentor and she became his shadow. 'He basically said "Who do you want to meet? What do you want to do?".' She wanted to learn about music editing because music editors don't exist in Australia, so he set her up with one of the major music editing houses.

Through that internship she met Shirley Walker who was the only female composer she was aware of. Shirley Walker started by playing the piano as a session musician and then orchestrated scores. She is now a very busy Hollywood composer (*Memoirs of an Invisible Man, Turbulence* and supervising composer for several Warner Bros TV series). She is the conductor of choice for most composers who can't conduct. 'She is a very giving person and she was a huge inspiration and a mentor to me.'

During this period Nerida went to London with another composer and used a small portion of his recording time with the Sinfonia of London orchestra to make a professional recording of some of her music.

She then came back to Australia in 1992 and for eight months tried to get work. She wrote to producers and introduced herself to people in the recording business whose names she had got from Brian May when he was in Los Angeles. She wanted to build relationships with people in the industry which she hoped she would use when she got work.

She was 'going batty' with no work so she went back to the US and worked with Bruce Broughton again doing editing on DAT for the CD release of *All I Want for Christmas.* 'I was basically hovering around, doing little things, going to meetings not being obtrusive, but feeling I was keeping my ears at that professional level. That is what is so wonderful about living in LA in a composer community – you are invited to sessions and you get to be a part of the team.' She rang Shirley Walker who asked her to orchestrate for her and gave her writing opportunities on *Batman the Animated Series* (1992).

She came back to Australia and went to the Screen Directors Conference in 1993 to find out what was going on. Richard Franklin was speaking about his experiences in America and she told him that she had also been to USC and had been to Jerry Goldsmith's recording sessions (who had been Franklin's composer on *Psycho II*). Richard said he'd be interested to hear her music and she gave him a tape she had in her bag. As a result he asked her to do the music for *Hotel Sorrento*.

Once the film was released people knew who she was. She did *The Feds* (1995), nine telemovies for Crawfords which were purely programmed electronic music. Simpson Le Mesurier asked her to score for three of the *Halifax f.p.* (1994-5) movies. She then did the Japanese co-production *The Last Bullet* (1995) because Michael Pattinson, the director, had directed two *Feds* telemovies. She did a documentary and *Brilliant Lies* (1996) for Richard Franklin, all of Bryan Brown's *Twisted Tales* (1996) and the features *Under the Lighthouse Dancing* (1996), *Fern Gully II* (1997), and *Kick* (1998). She has also scored three multi-path CD-ROM movies in the *Popeye* series and the television series *The Adventures of Sam*, and is co-composer on the US production of *Flipper – A New Adventure*.

interview

HIGHLIGHTS

Under the Lighthouse Dancing which I scored in 1996 because I was able to do something poetic, emotional and lyrical rather than constantly dodging dialogue. Both *Hotel Sorrento* and *Brilliant Lies* were adaptations of plays and 95 percent of the music had to be carefully crafted under and around the dialogue. So it was a relief to be able to write music for *Under the Lighthouse Dancing* – music which could carry a scene without dialogue.

I think personally the internship was a highlight. During that period I gained a lot of experience in a non-threatening environment. When you are an intern people know you don't want something from them. You are allowed to observe things like the producer and director discussing who they will get to score the film and I also formed some very good friendships with people who I respected. That was a real highlight.

CHANGING TECHNOLOGY

I was well aware when I was coming back to Australia that if I wanted to be a working composer I needed to be able to produce my music in-house. The number of films that come out that have the privilege of using real musicians are limited. It is more important to me that I am working and being creative. So I have built up my equipment from when I lived in Los Angeles. My investment in electronic equipment is in the tens of thousands of dollars built up over the years.

▶▶ As a composer whose whole creativity comes from putting what's in my head onto a piece of paper, the equipment has opened up a whole new world because people can come in and hear and experience what I am trying to do before the final production.

There are two ways I use my studio – one is for the director to hear a simulation and the other is for a fully finished score to go to a mix. I use the same equipment; the difference is the time. If I am writing for something that real people are going to play I am not going to spend a lot of time to make it sound fabulous. But if it is not going to be played by real people I will spend a lot of time programming the equipment to trick the ear, as if the music is being performed by live musicians. I will program in a breath for woodwinds and brass and slight imperfections which take the music from being mechanical electronics, to giving the music life. But this takes time.

As a composer whose whole creativity comes from putting what's in my head on a piece of paper, the equipment has opened up a whole new world because people can come in and hear and experience what I am trying to do before final production.

On *Hotel Sorrento* the whole score was written out, pencil to paper, but I used the computer for the orchestra parts. It was my first film and I really wanted the director to be able to hear what the orchestra would play ahead of time. Although I know how to solve something at a recording session I just did not want to be in a position where I had to rewrite at the session because something did not suit the scene from the directors point of view. So I made sure that I had the equipment to be able to preview everything to him and I just had to teach myself as I went. When I am writing for an orchestra I know that the musicians can do things that I can't possibly pull off on a computer. So if you are writing for real musicians you are aware of what you can get them to do that you may not necessarily be able to play to the director ahead of time.

My whole method of writing is very different now. I still notate my ideas and think things through on the piano, but out of the need to be able to work very fast I have taught myself to use the computer as an electronic notebook. The old method where you sit at the piano and you play every part takes too long. I now play it all into the computer and then sit back and let the computer do the playing and make decisions. I can work a lot faster. That is the big difference for me. I suppose it was a bit difficult to learn but it is something that you just have to do and work it out for yourself.

When I did the *Twisted Tales* series I was contracted to write seven minutes of music for each show. It worked out that each show averaged 16 to 18 minutes of music and the only way I could do that on schedule and on budget was to fully produce a score in-house and deliver it to the film mix from my studio. Fortunately I was already set up to be able to do that. If I didn't have the equipment I don't think I could have accepted the job.

ISSUES FOR WOMEN

My being a woman has never been an issue for me professionally. Playing music is not a gender-based activity. I think that is a very interesting thing about music in general. Apparently at 20th Century Fox they had an all-male staff orchestra and when it became freelance and they started to employ women there were no ladies toilets near the recording stage. They were miles away because they had never built a ladies rest room.

It's a very tough industry for anyone to survive in. I wish in some respects that someone had told me how hard it really is – particularly the deadlines and the schedules. I would have had a more realistic expectation. It is very hard when I receive the directors cut late, the film mix cannot be moved and I have a compressed period to do my job in. I tend to have to work through the night because I've got to get the music on tape. I should insist on an extra week if they are three weeks late but I don't because it would impact on the film mix and their delivery dates for the picture. I think that is very female, that I would rather not be demanding.

The sound mix is a fairly male environment but as a composer I am so opinionated I just say what I think, maybe even if it's not appreciated. But I've never had a problem coming forward at a mix.

Bruce Rowland once said to me 'You know what is going against you Nerida? First of all you are only 5ft tall, and you are a girl, and you're young so you are going to have to...' and he was being very gentle with me, and he said 'You are going to have to work around that'.

Bruce is a tall man and I looked up and I said 'But you know what I've got going for me, Bruce?' he said 'What?' and I said 'I'm 5ft, I'm female and I'm young, that's what is going for me'. I think with anything artistic it's a journey of the individual pursuing their area of expertise. Gender is irrelevant.

I remember an orchestrator on *Batman the Animated Series* was very resentful when I started composing for the show because he hadn't had the opportunity and he said to me 'Oh, it's because you're a woman'. I was strong enough to say 'Well actually it's because I am a good composer, I don't think that these people would risk their reputation and sacrifice this production by having something cheesy just because I am a woman'. The other time was when I got the internship and some guy said 'You got it because you're a woman'.

It is difficult to promote oneself for work. I think that is a female trait. You don't want to be annoying, you don't want to be in people's faces and if you are being assertive it can be considered aggressive.

That's why having an agent is so wonderful. They represent you and promote you for work. I have a fabulous agent and we can talk quite frankly about things and she will support me when I feel there is something I am not really comfortable with in a deal.

I think with my generation we work with people who have daughters and they want their daughters to have careers and be successful.

Lack of women composers

I think that writing music takes courage. You are exposing yourself. I think that also there is quite a lot of responsibility, particularly if you are working with musicians. You have to know how to write for them. I think that sometimes a man can go for something and not really be fully equipped whereas a woman will not put herself forward unless she is fully equipped. I am not saying that that is why there are more men, I'm saying that is why there are fewer women – because we are a species that tries to be perfect. We expect that of ourselves. I am not saying that some men don't, but that is what holds women back.

There are more female composers now and I did have role models. Ann Boyd – Ann Carr-Boyd – and the older composers Miriam Hyde, Dulcie Holland, Peggy Glanville-Hicks. Although renowned and highly respected in the composer community, they are not necessarily household names within the general community. But I think part of it is that women composers don't necessarily want to be household names. We're not in it for the fame and the glory, we are in it for the pursuit of our art. That may be a generalisation. When I went to do my masters in America people would say 'Oh, Nerida, you're going to be really famous one day' and I'd say 'I don't want to be really famous, I want to be a working film composer who's having a fulfilling career'. I think that might be partly my being female. A guy would go 'Thank you, do you really think so'. Of course, I want my success and achievements noticed and respected, but 'fame' is not my goal.

Dealing with men

You need a sense of humour. When you are under tremendous stress and you may have someone who is being very demanding and it is stressful and difficult, I have learnt that I don't have to internalise and take responsibility for it. I don't have to blame myself, I have to be able to have a sense of humour about it and it makes it easier to cope with.

Because I work alone I've found that it is really encouraging to find out if other people on the team are experiencing the same sort of things. Or that a girlfriend is experiencing something similar at her work. Being able to talk about it – again that is a female thing, just to have a friendly word. If you have outside support, then you can laugh off stressful situations and be productive.

Sometimes people don't know when I am annoyed or frustrated. A couple of times with one director I've been in a position where I've had to really lose my temper because I had been pushed too far and I did not appreciate being put in that position.

In times of conflict I usually turn into Spock of *Star Trek*. I just back off and become logical. I get very non-emotional. I think people expect you to get emotional. I get detached and I use logic. I just say 'This is the situation and this is what is going on and I've only got this amount of time and this is what I have to do and you are going to have to give' or whatever. I just want to work in harmony. Maybe that is from being a woman. Wanting peace all the time.

To be very honest I have not experienced difficult men very often. I have really been very fortunate I've worked with wonderful people.

Sexual harassment and sexist remarks

I don't display my sexuality. I was asked on one occasion, by a woman, whether I was sleeping with someone and I found that shocked me and was very hurtful. My reply was 'Have you seen my husband? He's young and he's gorgeous and he's a hunk and I love him and I've been happily married for ten years'.

I only really recall one time when I met a producer who called me sweetie and I just let it go, I guess he saw me as a child or a pretty little fluffy thing.

ADVICE

Be the best you can. Go for it. Don't take no for an answer. If this is something you desperately want to do just make it happen because you can.

I would say get as much experience as a musician that you can. Play in bands, chamber groups and orchestras and sing so that you really get your musical skills together and then watch hundreds of movies. Watch them so that you are not experiencing the movie, watch them so you are observing the soundtrack, how things are done. Equip yourself and then go for it.

I don't think people have to go to university. I think the thing which is good about university or the conservatorium is that it gives you an environment in which you are playing music daily with other musicians. I found doing academic research gave me confidence. It was really fun and interesting and it helped me to develop my confidence. So that when I am not particularly inspired or feeling talented I can at least do a very good job because I have skills.

I think in Australia the best answer is to start scoring student films and shorts and really build up your relationships. Hang around the film school. You have got to build a portfolio of work.

Hanging out in recording studios would be a good experience. I don't know how you get access to equipment. If you are writing music and you are living within the musical world you have friends who can play your music. Which is what I did. I had friends play it and got things on tape. I rented equipment and paid people to play and they were recorded. Just build up a portfolio that way. It is really much easier now than when I was starting out. Technology is very user-friendly and it is not as expensive as it used to be.

Television is fabulous and it is a good way to start. Richard Franklin was quite disappointed when I started doing telemovies after having done *Hotel Sorrento* for him. He said 'Look you know you are a feature film composer not a television composer and other producers will look at you as a television composer and you won't get feature film work'. I said 'I think that's a bit passé because the reality of it is that, hopefully, people will look at my credits and think she's a working versatile composer'. It is more important to me that I continue honing my skills. Every job you do has different challenges and you are always learning something wonderful. So to me it is important that you are constantly working.

If I had chosen to sit around and wait for the one opportunity every three years to write an orchestral score for an Australian feature film I wouldn't be developing my skills to their full potential. I also think if you can cope with a television schedule then feature schedules will be more comfortable. So I think television is fabulous.

Try to find a mentor. But composing is unlike other disciplines because there is only one composer on every film and it is very hard to be in a situation where you are working as an attachment on a production, unless you have a composer who has the time on their schedule to be able to take you. Usually it is such a panic to get everything written in time that you don't even see your family.

The big thing about my experience was that in Hollywood there is just so much happening. There are movies being recorded every single week and because they are run by music departments in the major studios you know what is going on. In Australia I know that the recording studio can be empty for weeks on end and because they are all independent films that are being scored by individuals you are rarely aware when recordings are scheduled.

I went to America because I wanted to learn how it is done at the best. Most of the good composers in this country go to America to work. So I think it is a path that everyone ends up taking.

The other thing, particularly for women, is have a sense of humour and don't think that if someone doesn't ask you to score that they are rejecting you personally. It is because your work is not what they want at that time. It's true that part of the reason you get hired is because people probably want to work with you but if they don't it could be that they want completely different music to what you are offering. I think having a sense of humour is very helpful.

Finally, you have to be able to cope with the quiet times just as importantly as being able to cope with the hectic times. This is the nature of the business.

SOUND MIXING

A sound mixer is responsible for mixing all the soundtracks together to a final mix to match the picture. The picture editor, the sound editors, the composer and the director are usually all in attendance for the final mix. The sound mixer works in a sound re-recording studio and is also often responsible for recording effects and post sync dialogue. The sound mixer is employed by the producer in consultation with the director. They often have either their own sound mixing studio, or are attached to one.

Before computer automation, sound mixing was done by three mixers working at three separate desks. The most senior person mixed the dialogue, one mixed the music and the third mixed the effects. It was possible to start as effects mixer and work your way up to dialogue mixer. Today, with the computerisation of the sound desk, there is often only one mixer and therefore getting opportunities to learn is very difficult, particularly for a woman, because the sound recording studio is a very male preserve.

ROLE MODEL

Until very recently there was only one woman sound mixer, Annie Cocksedge. In 1982 she was the first woman to graduate in sound from AFTRS and for eight years she was a sound mixer at the ABC. After more than twelve years in the business she gave it away in 1990. The ABC has recently employed another woman. There are none employed in the commercial studios.

ANNIE COCKSEDGE

Annie comes from an extended family, she is number two, has one older and one younger sister, a brother and her sister's daughter who are both fifteen years younger.

Her mother is Swiss and her father English. She went to sixteen schools on three continents and came to Australia for four years when she was twelve. 'Adapting was my skill. Don't ask me what else I learnt at school but I certainly learnt how to adapt. I always just took whatever opportunities came up. I never expected things to be secure or permanent'. When she was seventeen she had appendicitis with nearly fatal complications. As a result of this experience she taught herself yoga and that has been a continuous thread throughout her life.

Her mother didn't work after she married but encouraged and expected her children to train for a career. Annie finished school in England in 1976. She had thoughts of being an actress but went to art college and worked part-time as a jewellers assistant, making jewellery.

After two trips to Israel working on a kibbutz where she was again impressed by the Australians she met, she went home to England and persuaded the family to return to Australia.

Annie is now the director of the Centennial Yoga Studio.

interview

GETTING STARTED

Within a month of returning to Sydney I found myself at a party chatting to an ABC sound recordist. That was the first time that film or television had ever entered my consciousness. I just thought, 'He is leaving that means there's a job going' so I said 'What's the boss's name?'

So I wrote to Fred Pickering, the head of sound at the ABC. It was a very short note – it was handwritten – all I said was 'I hear so and so is leaving, and I would like to replace him'. I hadn't asked what the job entailed or anything. I just saw it as an opportunity.

The next day I got a call from Noel Bolden, head of sound at the film school. Noel wanted a backroom person, had rung Fred and my letter was in front of him. Just luck. The ABC had a file full of eager qualified people but it was timing. Much later I discovered it was because Fred liked my handwriting. Fred is an intuitive guy, not at all your typical head of department. I went in for the interview and just laid it on the line and said 'You'll have to tell me what to do because I have no idea'. I was a backroom girl the next day.

I was eighteen and I worked at the school for a year on staff. I was shocked afterwards to realise how total ignorance had got me there because if you knew anything about it you wouldn't ever dream of doing what I did. I thought my career was then locked in. I'd got a job, Fred Pickering obviously seemed to like me and I thought I would go to the ABC after I'd done whatever learning I could do at the film school. I never saw myself as a student. I used to sit there watching their films go through, each one was a self portrait of some tortured soul and I thought 'God are these people serious, why don't they work like me'.

It wasn't until the very last minute at the end of my first year that I thought about being a student. As always, they were having trouble filling the sound places because there weren't enough applicants. They had never had a woman and I thought 'Ah, there's an opportunity'. I could also see that there was a lot more to learn and I was encouraged by all the right people to apply. By then I had a portfolio of work I'd done: mixing, recording, OBs [outside broadcasts].

I really enjoyed life as a student. Many people go to the film school and get inflated ideas but because I had had that grounding I had a different perspective. I regarded it as a great opportunity and from a technical point of view I thought sound was the only place to be.

The electronics side I found fascinating but it wasn't natural for me. I think that total ignorance was not a bad thing because every day I gleaned something technical and it was such a surprise. Some bloke who had done physics wouldn't have got the same enjoyment that I got.

Luckily I had the entire sound department and all the students behind me and the confidence that they had in me was a great help. They would spend time going through the various knobs and levels. They were very patient but I pick things up quickly and have a good memory, that's how I got by.

I listened to the rules, I was taught what to do and did it. It's a very regulated sort of business, and I followed the rules until I was quite sure I knew what I was doing. It wasn't that I understood what was going on behind the surface of the machines. But gradually as you get more confidence you play with the parameters and realise what goes wrong if you do step outside the rules. It was a very technical experience which I'd never thought I'd want to have, but when I was exposed to it I loved it, and then I couldn't understand why people would be afraid of it.

I became a technician overnight. I was suddenly in a technical job and everyone then saw me as a technician and if you had the necessary amount of confidence which I did, then everyone believes it. So it didn't take long for everyone including myself to believe that I was an eager sound person. I went from that one year as a worker in the backroom to three years as a student and my confidence and understanding increased enormously. After four years I came out not only with a full understanding from zero knowledge but also contacts – and that is what it does come down to.

I had been on attachment to United Sound, which was *the* mixing house at the time, and again I was noticed because I was the only woman there. Peter Fenton, the senior mixer kept an eye on me and bent over backward to get me there, when they were mixing *Gallipoli* [1980]. I was given not only the chance to watch but they even let me push faders around and participate in the intense experience that mixing is. And *Gallipoli* was particularly fabulous.

The day my grant came to an end at the film school I thought 'Well how am I going to pay the rent' so I rang United Sound. It was the logical thing to do. It was the time of 10BA and they had more film than they knew how to mix. So that very day, after the film school, I started a night shift at United Sound as the effects mixer. It was a Japanese co-production, a war movie, so there were massive effects, lots of guns and things like that. Straight away I was into the deep end and loved it and by that time I was known as 'Annie the Mixer'.

» ...by the time it comes down to the final mix everything is concentrated down onto one person's shoulders.

I had mixed and recorded, and enjoyed them both at the film school, but decided that I wanted to be a mixer. Mixing is more creative than sound recording which just involves running after a camera person trying to catch the best sound on the day, which depends on the environment and all those extraneous things. The mixer's job is much more about perfecting the sound. The fact that there were no women didn't worry me, I wasn't given a hard time. I was very conscientious and efficient and did the job. It was the height of the women's movement, late 1970s and the 1980s, so I was really aware of what I was doing and proud of it. I really did dedicate myself to sound.

That boom in the film industry lasted six months and all the films had just arrived into post production. I was moving from one film to the next, post sync recording as well as mixing. When the boom finished I instantly got jobs as a sound recordist, mainly documentaries, some dramas, and that kept me going for another six months.

In '82 I was a freelance recordist and was getting ready to go to Chile with David Bradbury, taking Spanish lessons, when Fred Pickering rang. He needed to replace Peter Miller who had gone there as a sound mixer after he left the school. I started work at the ABC the next day.

I was in the mixing chair there for seven years. Although the job itself never varied, the programs did. I was in demand and got a reputation because every time people turned on the ABC they saw my name go past. I did work reasonably hard but not nearly as much as I'm sure people thought I did.

HIGHLIGHTS

One of the good things about the ABC is that it was very comprehensive. *Four Corners* was at its best. In my time we made many of those programs that they refer back to now. I am very proud of those. I am not just a technician and that is why some people liked working with me because I was always interested in the content.

One works very odd hours on *Four Corners*, usually they would cut to the very last second and the mix would be literally just before they went to air. That kind of excitement is one of the reasons why people love the film industry. They are in it because of that amazing adrenalin buzz. I've had that, I enjoyed that but I think it is very addictive. A lot of film people are addictive people and that is not my style.

For me there was one highlight and it was *Scales of Justice* [1982]. At a technical level that was the most tricky thing I ever had to do. It was recorded on 2-track, on a stereo recorder, and although it wasn't stereo to air it had that feeling because there was dialogue going on in the background and dialogue going on in the foreground. It had a very live feeling. In those days, apart from an Altman film, you'd never hear that. Working on that program stretched me to my max, it was a fantastic experience.

MIXING

I always compared it to flying. It is like sitting in a cockpit. You are sitting at a control panel and everything is at your fingertips and whether it flies or crashes is your responsibility. It is a nice feeling of being in control when it works and it is an absolutely awful feeling when it doesn't work.

A film or television program is like a juggernaut that comes at you. Lots of people are involved in the shooting stage and in post production but by the time it comes down to the final mix everything is concentrated down onto one person's shoulders. In the other processes there is at least an editor, several assistants or a camera person and assistants and the pressure is spread across those shoulders. But when it gets to the mixer it all comes crashing through the door, everyone is totally exhausted, they have no money left and you've got less time than you thought because the budget's gone. It happens every time on features with sickening regularity. Each director comes in going 'this is the most important film you've ever seen, please do something with it' and then the next one comes in the next day. Everybody has got the impossible to ask of you. It's very exhausting.

The mixer has power but only in the mixing suite. Your job is to sit there and give the directors what they want and you are rated according to how well you do that job. It is your technical skills that give you the power to sit in the chair.

I really enjoyed the technical skill of being able to throw these machines around and make them work. But I also enjoyed working with people. It wasn't a solitary experience, you are working with intelligent people, the key creative people at that end of the production chain, and that could be a very pleasant experience.

LEAVING THE INDUSTRY

I was getting restless by '88. I'd done everything. We were going through a restructuring process and we thought times were really going downhill then. Budgets started to be reduced but those were still very much the good old days. What I observed in those seven years was a really vibrant film department, drama, documentaries, it was all film but gradually the shrinking budget started to take its effect. I was repeating myself after a while. It was no longer technically stimulating.

I had mixed features before I got to the ABC. Many people would spend their life trying to get to do them. I do not regard television as the lesser, I think they are both equally challenging and they have exactly the same problems. If you work on a 90-minute TV program, as some of the dramas were, they are the equivalent to features in technical challenges. Whether you are working on a feature film or an education program they still have the same problems and with mixing we are not just talking about the technical things, it is working with people too.

The new standards in volume for features means the mixer has to sit for fourteen hours a day, sometimes longer, under the most enormous sound pressure you can possibly bear. Often you are dealing with very harsh and violent soundtracks over and over again. The acceptable level of listening has got louder and they listen to it at the level that it will be replayed at Hoyts but in an empty room without the audience to absorb it – that is torture to me. So I have no desire to work with the fabulous new Dolby digital system.

Yoga was my one continuous thread and had been for ten years. I couldn't have got through doing that job without the inner strength that yoga gives me. As the job became less challenging for me, the more I got into yoga. I did a teacher training course while I was still at the ABC and I knew that that was really what I wanted to do; a mixers life is not healthy, stagnating in one position under a lot of pressure day in day out.

My final year at the ABC was part-time but it was unsatisfactory and that convinced me it was time to leave. In 1990 I went to India for a month of intensive study with the Iyengars in Poona, came back but never returned to the ABC.

I've got no complaint about the ABC or working there but I just think that anyone in any kind of high pressured job – and there is no doubt that mixing would have to be one of the most high pressured jobs in filmmaking – has a shelf life before you burn out and you turn into somebody you weren't originally.

I dropped into the sound world unwittingly. I was not devoted to being a filmmaker. Most people are, they are very hooked up on the image of being a filmmaker. I was very focused on the fact that I wanted to pay the rent and eventually pay the mortgage and make a living. Basically that was my reason for working in the film industry.

I wasn't somebody who would even go and watch films. I was not into the film culture. As I became a professional myself I would watch and appreciate the fine art, but if you spend all your day mixing film the last thing you want to do is sit down and watch another film at night.

ISSUES FOR WOMEN

The men have changed quite a bit. I was out there with the last of the old boys. It was like a rugby team that I was running with and I had no qualms about joining it. If they wanted me to play football I'd play football, I'd love it. I can relate to guys and you have to because, apart from some women editors, directors and producers that come through, you are in a man's world. You are with the men and you have to talk their talk and play their games.

It is a very macho business. At first I had to suppress my femininity. I was very much into the overalls as I didn't want anyone to say 'She's just getting this because she is a girl'. So you just have to be adaptable. It may not be comfortable.

But by the time I got into the ABC, and even before that in the feature world, I had a confidence in what I could do and everyone had respect for me, even if they didn't enjoy working with a woman. The job carries weight and I was in a powerful position. I would judge people on whether they could deliver the goods to me without having a major turn. If they couldn't – and some of them couldn't – they were the problem and they would know it.

People new to the industry might expect that every job is going to be brilliant, they eventually learn that this is not the case. I think the way you do your job is more important than the job itself. If you can work to that philosophy then life is interesting. That's how I was able to settle into the daily grind of mixing.

Lack of women mixers

I think it is a pity that I am the only woman who ever got into sound mixing. It was enjoyable, it is nothing to be afraid of.

Women do need to be encouraged. It is just the usual female thing of 'No I can't do that, because I've never done that, and because I've never thought of doing that'.

There is a resistance to doing something you don't know. I wouldn't have done it unless I had had all that support. I just decided not to be fearful of it. When you are confronted by something that you are fearful of, or you don't understand, your first reaction is to run away from it. But I think a better way is to face it, be exposed to it. People go for the obvious things like camera, directing and producing.

Women have got to get into the mixing suite. It's a bit of a mystery world. Unless you are already in editing or producing you don't have to go into the mixing suite, it is not visible, it's dark, almost esoteric. It's not visibly exciting, like being out there on a crew on the street where everyone sees you – but it is aurally exciting.

You have to do electronics – that's the donkey work as far as I am concerned. I hate reading electronics magazines and that was a problem. I did basic electronics at North Sydney Technical College as part of the film school course and it was really very difficult for me but it was really very difficult for the boys in my class too. I forced myself to do it because you couldn't get your certificate if you didn't, but one or two didn't.

I know lots of guys have trouble dealing with manuals. For every one who is technical there's many who are not, they cannot sit down, read the manual and then make that machine work.

What the men do better is what I was always very good at and that's bluff when you can't really work out why it's not doing what it is supposed to do. Many is the time you are faced with something on that desk which isn't doing what it should do, you just have no idea what's going on, and you have to talk your way out of it until some technicals come and fix it.

It's a very small fraternity and there are very few who really know what they're talking about. Probably only one and the rest look as if they do. They don't have the technical range and depth that everyone assumes they have. If all the women who dismiss the thought of doing sound heard me say that perhaps that will give them some encouragement.

I think a lot of women feel that unless you can do everything, lift up the desk lid and work out what all those wires are doing underneath, then you can't mix. In fact it is a very rare person who can look at the manual once and then be able to retain and recall all those vital points. I and most of the mixers stumbled along and that is the way we learnt. Press this button, if it explodes then it's not the right button. It's not something men do better than women, we women think the men do it better but they don't.

Finally, apart from this fear/timidity thing, I think the real reason women have not shown up in droves to become part of the sound department is that in the great hierarchy of people that form a film unit, sound is traditionally considered less important. Yes, it is seen as a skillful and essential position but it is not up there among the 'glamour' jobs such as camera, director and producer.

While I have said it involves being with and handling people, first and foremost the work requires technical and mechanical skills, so until women are prepared to face the challenge to become technically skillful you won't see them in the senior positions of the sound department.

ADVICE

Show willingness to do the job, even if you don't know how to do it. Willingness is key, because ability comes later.

Show initiative. If you want to do the job just go ahead. Do what I did. Write the letter, apply, push yourself. Just because someone has got a bit more physics experience than you don't let that be a reason for not doing it. Once you can fly your plane, whatever your operational job is, then your job is about getting on with people, getting through it with them, with as little blood on the floor as possible. I think women are quite good at that.

It is very important to go to the film school. From a technical point of view it is the best place to go because it has superb equipment. It was excellent training for me. It was having those four years, building confidence, that allowed me to rock up to United Sound and say 'I can start mixing tonight!'

PICTURE EDITING

The picture editor puts together the images and dialogue filmed in the studio or on location and adds visual effects and sometimes the music.

Feature films and single camera television dramas have scenes shot from a number of angles and out of sequence in order to maximise the most expensive elements in the production, such as the set and location, or the 'big ticket' actors. If the location is noisy the dialogue may be re-recorded and added later with the music and effects in the editing process.

Documentaries, on the other hand, often follow actions as they occur but have to be edited to construct a story from the material. Some of the sound can also be added later, such as a recorded voice-over commentary.

On a large feature the editing process is carried out by many people – the picture editor, who has overall responsibility, and various sound editors who are responsible for the dialogue, sound effects and music.

FEATURES

The job of picture editor has changed dramatically since the introduction of video and digital recording. Most film editing is now carried out using a digital image on different types of editing systems. The most sophisticated are non-linear and known by their brand names such as Lightworks or Avid.

The 'work print' is now a video copy of the film which can be accessed by putting the time code numbers (the video version of edge numbering on the print) into a computer. The editor or her assistant no longer has to handle the film or file the trims but rushes have to be logged so that the 'trims' can be found in the computer system. Changes to scenes can be made by changing the instructions in the computer, which means that non-linear (random access) editing equipment allows different edited versions to be constructed and viewed very quickly. Effects can also be generated electronically.

If the production is to be finished on film then when the editing has been completed the edit decision list (EDL) is given to the neg cutter, any optical effects are made in the laboratory, and the production is finished on film. With non-linear editing the assistant's job is to digitise the image and sound and to log all the necessary information so that the editor can perform her creative role. To minimise the cost of expensive computer equipment often the assistant's work is done after hours at night. Thus the assistant's apprenticeship role often precludes daily contact with the creative team.

When editors dealt exclusively with celluloid, and before the digitisation of soundtracks, the picture editor had total responsibility for the editing process. The soundtracks were dialogue, music and simple effects and the only major post produced sound was the music. In those days the career path of an editor was from assistant sound or picture editor, to sound editor, to picture editor. Today, however, there is an increasing specialisation and proliferation of jobs in sound post production to create the complicated soundtracks demanded by the sophisticated surround sound in the theatres, and sound editing is becoming a career independent of picture editing. For this reason the job of sound editor is covered in the sound section. Picture editors cut with the dialogue track and work with the sound editors.

On a feature film editing will usually take place in hired cutting rooms and if the film is shooting on location the editing department may not be anywhere near where the film is being shot. Some American productions which shoot in Australia are edited back in the US, although they view synched rushes on location. On the other hand if the whole of the film is being shot at a remote location a cutting room may be fitted out near the location to enable the director and editor to keep in constant touch as the film progresses.

DOCUMENTARIES, LOW BUDGET FILMS, COMMERCIALS AND CORPORATES

Productions which originate on video will be edited on a non-linear editing system similar to features. If the productions cannot afford non-linear edit suites they will use off-line machines using the time code to identify the shots. When all the edit decisions have been made an EDL is produced and the final edit is done in an on-line edit suite matching the original tapes onto a master tape.

Some digital non-linear editing systems, such as the Media 100, allow the editor to track lay, create the titles and do the on-line, as well as perform the creative editing role. These systems are often used for lower budget productions such as corporates and training videos.

Some documentaries are still cut on celluloid but most films are transferred to videotape with time code and often the picture editor is the sound editor as well.

ROLE MODELS

I have selected three role models whose experience covers the old and the new technologies and who provide a history of the film industry in Sydney and Melbourne.

Sara Bennett was one of the very few women editing feature films in the 1970s. She started in the film industry in the UK before the technology to edit videotape had been developed, when television programs were made on 16mm or 35mm film, and long before gender issues were discussed. Her attitude to being a woman in a male industry has changed over time. While it started as being typical of her generation, when women tried to fit into the male environment, her daughters and her long association with students at AFTRS have made her rethink issues around gender. Directors she has worked with include Gillian Armstrong, Shirley Barrett, Bill Bennett, George Miller and Jim Sharman. She is currently head of editing at AFTRS.

Jill Bilcock is arguably the most experienced Australian editor. Her career started with the resurgence of the film industry in Australia and she went to the first Swinburne film course. Fred Schepisi was her mentor and her first feature film was *Evil Angels*. She works out of Melbourne and used to run her own editing company working on anything that came along. She turned her house in East Brunswick into an editing suite for *Strictly Ballroom* and has edited *Romeo + Juliet* and *How to Make an American Quilt* within the studio system in Hollywood. She has worked with many first time directors and enjoys working on short films. Recently she has edited *Elizabeth*, *Head On* and the music clip *Until the Break of Day* which won the 1998 ARIA award for best film clip.

Dany Cooper is a younger generation film editor. She has had a fairly standard career path starting as an assistant on low budget films and assisting on features until she got her big break – and an AFI award – with *Angel Baby*. She has since edited *The Well, Self and Self-Bed*, which won the Dendy award for best short film in 1998, and was additional picture editor on *Babe – Pig in the City* and an American production *In Too Deep* which was cut in Australia. She has worked in the US but outside the Hollywood studio system.

SARA BENNETT

Sara went to a girls' school in Folkstone England in the 1950s where the headmistress encouraged her pupils to have a career. Her father died when she was seven and her mother, although not a career woman, was very supportive of her wanting to have a career and was delighted that she knew what she wanted to do.

At a school career counselling session Sara told the headmistress that she wanted to be a film technician so she arranged for her to meet Don Chaffey, the father of a new girl, and a film director rising through the ranks of Disney. In the school holidays he used to invite her to the studio when he was shooting and she went to a mix and into the cutting rooms. He advised her to go to the film school in Paris, got her information about the school and wrote her a recommendation. She started in 1961, having spent a year in Paris to learn French.

Don Chaffey also told her that women in the film industry end up doing continuity, production, hair and wardrobe but she should focus on editing because it has real creative potential and there was no reason why women shouldn't do it. 'That was the best advice I ever received, and he also said "the majority of editors in France and Italy are women but the majority in the rest of the world are men and if women can do it in France and Italy why can't they do it everywhere else".' Sara says that that was always in the back of her mind because in those days to have women editors was pretty unheard of in the Anglo-Saxon world and North America.

She left the Paris school after one year and went back to England. 'I wanted to handle film and wasn't really interested in the academic side.'

Her first job was in 1962 in a stockshot library at Rayant, earning £9.10.8d. This enabled her to get her union ticket, which was essential for working in the industry. She then got a job in a small documentary production company as an assistant editor making corporate films. She rose through the ranks and the first documentary she cut solo was *Treatment of the Open Wound* about compound fractures.

She was there for a year, when through an editor she was offered work on her first feature as a second assistant at Twickenham Studios. She then continued to cut documentaries and assist on features 'which were just unspeakably bad' until she got itchy feet and decided to travel. She took off in 1966 to go right round the world, stopping in Australia to have a working holiday and to see her sister. She did not expect to be able to work in the film industry when she got to Sydney but a Canadian man she'd known in London gave her a contact to Eric Porter Productions and she stayed there for about a year as an assistant and then as an editor cutting commercials. From there she got a job with Hans Pomeranz at Spectrum which was a tiny company where she had to do a bit of everything, including neg matching and sound editing.

She then went to Fauna and worked on *Skippy* (1968) with Don Saunders. Tim Read, who had been Don's assistant, had become sound editor and she took over from him. 'That was actually a good career move because I moved into drama which is what I wanted to do and there was a higher level of professionalism, bigger crews. It sounds a bit odd to say it now but *Skippy* was a pretty desirable thing to work on, so I did the last thirteen episodes as Don's assistant. There were two crews so there were two editors, Don and Ernie Hilton, and two sound editors. A huge number of people went through Fauna. It was probably the classiest act in town at the time. It was a bit elevated over Crawfords. John Seale was [camera] operating and Gerry Letts was first assistant on the second unit.'

After *Skippy*, Sara assisted on the first two episodes of the *Barrier Reef* series (1970) and then she took the job of sound editor. She was sound editor on 36 episodes of *Barrier Reef*, which was shot on 16mm.

'That was really good training working with Don, who was an absolute stickler for discipline and professional standards. I learnt a lot from him about running a cutting room, scheduling and time and management organisation. I don't think he was a great editor but he was a very good manager. I was quite loyal to him and subsequently when he went to the film school he used to bring me in to do things at the school. I gave some sound editing courses in '73. In the meantime I got involved in the union.'

She was sound editor on the *Spyforce* series (1971) and a couple of features and married in 1972. She was sound editing *The Cars That Ate Paris* (1973) when she was pregnant with her second child. 'I took a little bit of time off for each child.'

»I never saw myself as being disadvantaged by being a woman. I think that is probably the key factor. I had chosen to do editing, I had a natural facility and ability as an editor, I enjoyed doing it and there was no earthly reason why being a woman was going to be a disadvantage.

Her first job as a picture editor was *Education* at Film Australia. Chris Noonan was director and Tim Read was producer. 'I suppose I had been on the edge of picture editing for a while and Tim actually pushed me into it, he said "do it, do it".'

The first feature she picture edited was *Summer of Secrets*. 'We'd had the first major public screening of *Caddie* and we'd all gone to lunch in Chinatown to talk about the film. We were given a big table upstairs. I think it was about 2 in the afternoon and there suddenly in the doorway was Michael Thornhill. He had been downstairs having lunch with Jim Sharman and heard Tony Buckley's [producer of *Caddie*] laugh. As the afternoon progressed the faces changed and I found I was sitting next to this quiet person who turned out to be Jim Sharman and somewhat drunkenly I raved on about his production of *The Threepenny Opera* which I'd just seen. We sort of clicked and a few days later Michael stumbled into my cutting room and said 'Do you want to cut a feature?...', I said 'I'm not a picture editor, I'm a sound editor.' 'Oh no, no, anyway read the script...' It was the thing he was about to produce, with Jim directing – *The Secret of Paradise Beach*, which eventually became *The Summer of Secrets* [1976]. So that was my first feature as an editor, me protesting "I'm not a feature editor" and them saying "come on, yes you are". It was one of those totally unpredictable kind of things which you couldn't possible have made up if you'd wanted to. Gilda Baracchi was continuity, Jane Norris was art direction, it's quite funny that we were on that together and then we were at the film school together fifteen or so years later.'

Sara did one more job as a sound editor, which was *Eliza Fraser* (1976), and then edited *Summerfield* (1977) and went from one picture to another as a picture editor pretty constantly on features, series and documentaries. Finally in 1992 Sara decided to drop out of the film industry. 'I suppose I just got worn out and fed up after I did *Who Killed Malcolm Smith* [1992], which was not a happy experience. I just realised that there must be something more to life than working in little rooms at weekends when everyone else was enjoying themselves.'

'I also suddenly saw myself like Don Saunders in his last years when he was getting bitter and cynical. It came from the fact that he thought he was smarter than the producers and directors. I thought "My God, I'm turning into a Don Saunders. I've got to get out of this." It's inevitable if you're dealing with inexperienced people but then you realise that they are actually the risk-takers, they're putting their necks on the line and you're being quite conservative. And I think there is a regret that you are no longer a risk-taker. I think when you're younger you do take risks and then you look for security and you start resenting those who have power over you and those who are actually taking risks.'

Sara left the industry and went overseas but returned in 1994 and is now head of editing at AFTRS.

interview

HIGHLIGHTS

Working with Jim Sharman on *The Night the Prowler* [1978], which was from a short story by Patrick White, who also wrote the script. It was a good script and a good idea and had wonderful confrontational qualities about it. But it was working with Jim again, I already had a rapport with him and a degree of confidence and it was just altogether a good creative experience and very exciting. Jim respected me and he is a bit of a risk-taker, like Bill Bennett, neither of them are precious, there's a confidence about them, you can make suggestions and they don't feel threatened, you can be a bit outrageous and they like it. They actually want you and encourage you to be outrageous. I remember towards the end of the cut I saw *Bonnie and Clyde* on the big screen for the first time, I'd only seen it on TV before, it's a legendary film with editors. I was blown away and I came in next day and I said to Jim 'I want to recut the whole film. I saw *Bonnie and Clyde* last night' and he said 'Okay' and we spent that day going through all the reels and just looking at the transitions.

We didn't recut the whole film but we just looked at getting from one scene to the next, which was what was so exciting about *Bonnie and Clyde.* There was an audacity about story telling, a sort of confident shorthand that they used. You could do that with Jim. You couldn't do that with a lot of directors, they would be too cautious. Jim was also terribly demanding but also very rewarding. The two are sort of synonymous. He'd give you a push that made you grow as a filmmaker. He always pushed me further than I thought I could go and that of course is terribly rewarding.

The *Working* series [1979] for Robin Hughes at Film Australia was another highlight. That was a really important learning experience for me because it was a sort of cinéma vérité observational series of documentaries, and I'd never done that before. It is very much harder to cut and I found working with

Robin, and getting the story out of the cinéma vérité material with big shooting ratios, was a really important learning experience. There were lots of different directors – Gilly Coote, Stephen Ramsey, Curtis Levy – and Tony Wilson and Paul Tait shooting. It was quite a class act. I think there were eight in the series. They were quite modest, 15-16 minute discussion starters for high schools about attitudes to work.

Robin was a terrific producer, a very strong storyline producer who defended her crews' efforts wonderfully in that melting pot at Film Australia. I respected her a lot and I found her terrific to work for.

That series was important for me in doing documentary work, as I discovered later when Bill Bennett asked me to do *Mortgage* [1989]. *Mortgage* was one of the hardest things I cut but also one of the most rewarding. I loved working with Bill – he was nurturing, stimulating, rewarding, a fun director, wonderfully decisive and a good guy. He is the most encouraging director for the creative juices of almost any director I've ever worked with. He is completely free of any hierarchical bias. You feel that if the clapper loader or the driver of the catering truck have got a suggestion, it's valid. He's got a nice sense of larrikinish humour. But it was also that *Mortgage,* like *Malpractice* [1988] and *Custody* [1987] were drama documentaries, or docudramas – they were mixing the two genres. Bill didn't actually have a shooting script, he only had a treatment and would then workshop before shooting. The actors improvised their backstories and he then shot the films like a documentary. Steve Arnold shot handheld 80 percent of the time and so the editor ends up with an absolute hybrid. You need to be a drama editor and a documentary editor and you need equal skill in both departments to deal with that kind of material. You have got the challenges of both and the limitations of both; you get the freshness and urgency of documentary but you have the structure of drama, although it is much looser than scripted drama. You've got a double lot of problems, but you get double rewards.

The Dismissal [1982] was another absolute key thing that I did. Working with George Miller was again a giant learning experience.

Probably more with George than anybody else because of the way he works and the way he talks to you. He is a very, very generous person who doesn't ever say 'Do that because I want you to do it'. There is always a reason why. If ever he wanted to make a change he would explain why he wanted it. It's because he was briefly an editor himself. There is no director I have worked with who is more precisely interested in the editing, to the half frame, than George. Incredibly picky about it and knows he's picky about it.

I had a very funny interview to do *The Dismissal*. There were six episodes and five directors – Carl Schultz did two episodes. There were two editors – Richard Francis Bruce was on board and I was going for the second editor's position. I'd never met George before but I'd seen *Mad Max* [1978]. *Mad Max 2* [1981] wasn't finished at that stage. Tim Wellburn had edited *Mad Max 2* so I rang him up and said 'I've got this interview with George, what should I know about him?' Tim said 'Oh he's lovely, he's gentle, a very creative person but he sits there and watches every single cut, every single frame. If you don't want somebody breathing down your neck forget it, but he's a lovely person'.

Anyway I was having this interview with George and we were chatting away and then he said 'Now there is something you have got to know about me as a director. I'm one of those people who actually sits in there behind you and watches everything you do and I change things by the half frame, I drive most editors completely mad.' I said 'Yes I know'. By this time I was completely relaxed, and he said 'Oh you've been talking to Tim have you?'. I said 'Of course' and he said 'Okay, you've got the job'.

The Dismissal was the first of quite a few historical series... *Allies* [1983] and *The Last Bastion* [1984]. They had a lot of commonality and I enjoyed the subject matter enormously. It is so important that the subject matter is something you enjoy being involved in because you are working so intensely and for such a long time with the film that if you get something that doesn't appeal for one reason or another it is very hard to stay with it.

Probably one of the worst experiences was *Eliza Fraser* [1976], the last film I worked on as a sound editor. It was a really weird situation. They cut it in Melbourne and shipped it up to us in Sydney; I had one screening, didn't meet Tim [Burstall, the director] who was off in London. Ted Mason was picture editor, I had about a five minute brief with Ted and then he was off somewhere and I was left high and dry with the film. There were boxes and boxes of trims and stuff and three things I'd been asked to do. I'd been used to working with Tim Wellburn, Donald Crombie and Tony Buckley where we would spend hours working through what we were going to do, what we were going to post sync, and these people just all vanished. But that is the exception. I have had lots of really good experiences.

ISSUES FOR WOMEN

I think it is an attitude, it's your own self image which determines what you do and I think that that initial advice from Don Chaffey, that there was no reason why women couldn't be film editors, was really important. I never saw myself as being disadvantaged by being a woman. I think that is probably the key factor. I had chosen to do editing, I had a natural facility and ability as an editor, I enjoyed doing it and there was no earthly reason why being a woman was going to be a disadvantage. I never really took that on board. I never gave it any thought.

The other side of that coin is that if you go around saying 'I'm disadvantaged, I'm a woman and I want to do a man's job' then you are actually going to find all the disadvantages and all the problems and I never did that.

I think that there were occasions when I got a job as an editor over a man because they thought that I would not be too difficult and I would actually do what they wanted me to do. If that's true then that is a very silly reason for choosing an editor.

Having a family *has* been a disadvantage but I don't regret it. When you have kids you have got that other role to play, you can't be as single mindedly devoted to the professional role of editor. It was very hard too for me to give 100 percent focus on the professional role when you've got that domestic role as well. I am not just talking about the times when kids are sick – and that always happens at the worst possible times. I think it is the fact that there is something else in your life that means a great deal to you as well as your profession and a woman who doesn't have children, doesn't have those other responsibilities. There is nothing to stop her spending 23 hours a day in the cutting room. Whereas if you are a mother with children there are other things not only to stop you but other things that you want to do. You are perhaps more rounded as a person.

But you can't go on location and I have lost a few jobs because of that. Not often, but sometimes, if the film is Melbourne-based and they want you to cut in Melbourne. Ann Turner approached me about *Celia* which was a terrific script and I would have loved to have done it but they were shooting in Melbourne and they wanted it edited in Melbourne. We tried to negotiate doing it in Sydney but the producers were in Melbourne, so I missed out on that. I was approached to do *The More Things Change* [1985] but again it was a Melbourne-based feature and I couldn't do it for the same reason.

But there are advantages. Sound editing *Caddie* is an example. It is such a woman's and kid's story that I think there was an identification, an engagement I had with that film that was to my advantage. There are more disadvantages than advantages but there are advantages.

Child-rearing

It was very difficult. There were not many kindergartens in those days and the hours I was working made it difficult. My kids were born in '72 and '74. I was sound editing all through the child bearing process.

My husband was a very good cook and the deal that was struck was that he would cook so long as he had nothing to do with nappies. I managed to keep the children in nappies for years and by that time the pattern was established and he stayed as the cook!

He was never the kind of father/husband who took child minding duties very seriously. If I left him child minding he was just as likely to have headphones listening to opera while both children were crying upstairs. He was good in other respects but not in that area. Also with the sort of hours that he worked and the level of responsibility he had it was not an option for him to be home at 5 o'clock. So clearly if I was going to work I had to have somebody come to the house early in the morning and stay till late at night. I had various people, lots of short-term ones that didn't work out but two or three long-term ones who were wonderful. I never had people living in.

The good thing about freelancing of course is that there are always gaps in between jobs so that there were periods when I wasn't working. When the family was aggro about me never being home and working long hours I could always say 'It will be over in two weeks time. I'll be home'.

Being an editor you are usually in one place. It wasn't until the kids were older that I did do a feature on location, in 1983. It was a wonderful location, a great experience and I was away for six or seven weeks and at one stage the children came up on a long weekend.

Dealing with men

My mentors have all been men. First there was Don Chaffey and then Don Saunders and Tony Buckley. They have all been very good to me. Editors tend to be mostly pretty friendly and supportive of each other, because you are often working in a place like Spectrum or Frameworks, unlike crews where the DOPs hardly know each other because they never work together. They're never in the same space. Whereas editors are often working in the same studio and there are a number of productions going through. Or on something like *Spyforce* and *Skippy* there are several editors. I still think of all those people like 'family'.

But there are some terrible misogynist men out there who can be absolutely vile. I worked with one director who was so vile and abusive to me in the mix that the mixer stopped the mix and got him to apologise to me.

The editor is a position of some authority and some directors have a problem with that and feel threatened, particularly if the editor is not compliant with what the director wants. I see one of the editor's roles as being the critic, a constructive critic, but nevertheless having an analytical contribution as well as being creative and collaborative. It's a very complex role. There was an idea back in the '70s that the editor's role was really not a critical, analytical role but an interpretive one. I think that has changed. Now I think there is much greater awareness of the editor as having a greater role to play.

Working with male directors

One of the key things is being up-front and setting the parameters at the beginning. For instance, say to the director 'Look, the first few weeks I want to work on my own and you can come in and have a look now and then but this is my conceptual period, looking at the material and doing first cut as per our notes. Then you can be in the room once I'm confident with the material and we are more on an equal footing. When we both know the material.' I encourage students to set up the working relationship right at the beginning and to negotiate and not be apologetic about it. If you say to the director you don't want him in the room after he's been sitting round for a few days, it could be offensive but if you say it right at the outset, 'This is how I like to work', nine times out of ten they'll say okay.

If the director is difficult, try to work out what it is that is difficult about them and then work out different strategies for dealing with it. If it is a gender-based thing then the only answer I can come up with is to actually bring it out in the open, identify what it is, talk about it and open it up for discussion and point out how difficult it is for whatever reasons. The old me (I'm a cured person now) tended to try and suppress problems and ignore them and of course that doesn't work. But the younger women these days are very articulate, very clear in expressing themselves and assertive without being aggressive, particularly once they have got a bit of confidence and got a few titles up there on the screen. That is something that my generation on the whole is not very good at. Lack of assertiveness is an issue with my generation.

Today's younger women have a nose for the sleaze director. They are very quick to pick up on sexism and sexist attitudes. They are much less tolerant. My daughters can smell it a mile off when I haven't even noticed it. They are much more assertive and they just don't put up with things we were conditioned to accept but then resented and suppressed – which is a very negative and uncreative way to work.

I like to think that here in the editing department at AFTRS we consciously try to empower the students, to actually make them assertive, to make them articulate. I think one of the roles of screen studies here is to give the students the vocabulary to recognise the stereotype in the script or recognise it in the people they are dealing with. They are trained much more than we were and they are much more perceptive. In this department we consciously encourage them to speak out and express themselves. They often come here from industry backgrounds having been assistants or tape operators and are very shy to express themselves in seminars. They sit back and take notes but by the end of the year we can hardly shut them up!

But the important thing to remember always is that it is the film that counts, you are engaged to cut the film and all the other things are unimportant. You have to be a professional and not let personal things get in the way.

Working with female directors

It is different. I think working with a woman there is a lack of hierarchy. Men tend to assume superiority, assume control, assume the power position. Not always – and there are obvious exceptions like Bill Bennett – but women don't do that. Although some women producers certainly do. On the whole women have a better sense of unstated equality. I suppose in my case, speaking as a lesbian, I find it easier to work with women even though they are not lesbian, which 90 percent aren't. I suppose I feel more comfortable.

I have had some very happy working relationships with women, Shirley Barrett [*Chainsaw*, 1990] and Nicola Woolmington [*Searching*, 1991] are recent ones. Both are very different people but wonderful to work with. They worked much more as equals, which was terrific. Shirley Barrett said 'We haven't got the budget for a full-time assistant so Tris [Tristram Miall, producer] wants me to be your assistant. I can just remember how to lace up a Steenbeck!' There was an unpretentiousness about her, she was very up-front.

She transcribed all the interviews off the Steenbeck and we talked about the best way to work, to concentrate on structure, not worry about the details, just bang the stuff together and concentrate on the structure first, then we start refining it. She said 'Well that is exactly how I write' so she understood perfectly, and the association between writing and editing was absolutely transparent. She has an enormous sense of humour and we very quickly giggled our way through the cut. We had two Steenbecks and she used to work on the second one pulling out bits. It was a really good relationship.

Objecting to content

I've objected to very male dominated macho action type things. I turned down Kennedy Miller's *Cowra Breakout* [1984] because of the subject matter. I read the first draft of the first episodes and there was so much about blood and death and cannibalism and suffering I just thought I couldn't live with this for six months. You do become engaged with what is on the screen and sometimes that world on the screen of the Steenbeck is more real than the world you are actually living in. If you don't like the content you don't have the emotional rapport. It wasn't a popular decision as far as Kennedy Miller was concerned but I just knew I couldn't live with *Cowra* for six months, it was not my sort of subject matter.

Feeling vulnerable

I deal very badly with conflict situations if I find myself working with someone who actually thrives on conflict, someone who wants conflict, whose whole modus operandi is through conflict, I deal with it very very badly. I hate conflict. I shut down.

Criticism

It depends where it's coming from. Sometimes you know it's an overt agenda, sometimes a hidden agenda. When there is criticism from a producer and it's unjust criticism that can make me quite angry and overly assertive.

I usually cope pretty well with criticism, at a professional level. The editing process is a process of criticism, not only with the director, it's the producer as well. You welcome that criticism and when it's not there you miss it. In post production when you and the director have been working together for a long period you get to a point where you can no longer be objective and you are begging for feedback. I welcome that process and find it incredibly stimulating. That was one of the joys of working with Bill Bennett. He is very secure in the way he works. He invites criticism all through the process – from the crew while he is shooting and from the post production crew, and then when you're editing he very deliberately invites people in to see the cut at various stages and very seriously reacts to their criticism. I've certainly done that over the years too.

Some directors are very threatened by that. Here in the editing department at AFTRS we encourage the students to comment on each others films, which is actually a very constructive way of working, and because they have got to know each other they don't feel threatened by other editors offering their comments. It's a very important part of the teaching process because by nature editors are fairly unassertive people. One of the things I've done since I've been here is to initiate the editors picnic. We screen something and editing students get together with a guest editor and talk editing. It's editors talking to editors about editing. It's very important for editors to have that experience in a non-threatening way so, in turn, that they can give feedback to the director in a non-threatening way. During the shoot directors are often very stressed and very vulnerable and you have to find the language to convey those constructive criticisms to directors.

FUTURE

I am not saying I would never edit again because I have actually got seduced into something in the early stages of production. But I don't want to go back into the pool of freelancing. I don't want to do things I don't want to do. It's very hard work editing. It's very demanding. If I could just pick and choose that would be fine. What I think I want to do when I leave AFTRS is research and write about editing.

Post production has changed a lot. When I was doing a lot of feature films it was fantastic for the editor to stay on right through the post production process. You probably worked fifty hours a week and then went right through to the final mix. You did other things like titles, opticals and music. Now picture editors are often laid off at lock off, and the sound crew comes on, the opticals and titles come through and then the production office doesn't know what to look for, they ring up the editor, who is not on the payroll. So the editor no longer has any kind of total responsibility for the final picture.

ADVICE

The most important thing is what Tony Buckley said to me when I was at a crossroads in my career, not knowing what to do. And I say it regularly to people: 'You've got to focus on what you want to do. If you want to be an editor, then you've got to edit'. I get quite frustrated by students who leave AFTRS and then go back to assisting. I know why they do it, they want the security and they want the income but really after they have studied for a year of two, we are teaching them to be editors not to be assistants. When students finish at the school they should say 'I don't mind what I cut so long as I'm cutting. I am an editor not an assistant. I don't want to assist. I don't mind if it's a corporate as long as I cut'.

The role of assistant has changed completely. In my day there was a clear career path but now with digital editing the assistant's role is a computer role, a digitising role. Once the digitising process is complete, on a lot of productions the assistant is no longer on the payroll, they are not around or they're around at night and in a separate space to the editor. So that the traditional way of training where you learnt by being assistants and actually being in the room with the editor filing trims, learning by osmosis, sitting in on discussions, being there at the screenings and listening to the observations, is now not possible. With digital editing you don't need anyone filing trims so that informal apprenticeship system has vanished.

In France assistants are not just working on one film at a time, they are working on three or four films at a time, just like tape operators. They are so remote from the editing process, and I suspect that is going to happen here too.

The irony is that digital editing provides a wonderful opportunity to learn because you are not actually cutting up the rushes. It is a wonderful opportunity for an assistant to 'have a go', but the opportunity does not exist in current situations because of the cost of using the equipment.

A lot of people applying to AFTRS now are what I call refugees from non-linear editing. They got jobs as assistants and thought they were going to learn how to be an editor but they ended up working the night shift and learning absolutely nothing about editing, nothing about the rapport between the editor and the producer, the editor and the director, the editor and the laboratory. So I suspect film schools are going to play a much more important role in training editors and if you take the creative role of the editor seriously then film schools are going to be the only place to learn.

JILL BILCOCK

Jill Bilcock was born Jill Stevenson and grew up in Melbourne with two older brothers. She had a very political mother who was the first female principal of a co-educational technical school, and was the first female union leader in the Technical Teachers Association. Jill went to Nunawading High School. Her mother encouraged her to go to a technical school so she left school at fifteen and went to art school at Swinburne.

In 1966 after she had done the two-year certificate course, Brian Robinson started the film course and Jill was one of the first students. There was very little equipment but Jill got hold of a 16mm Bolex during the 1966-67 summer vacation, when she was eighteen, and went to China during the cultural revolution with a group of 60 students. When she came out of China into Hong Kong she realised that she had footage that the world had never seen. 'I was rushed at by journalists, foreign press, CBS, NBC. They knew how tall I was, the colour of my hair, the colour of my eyes, they had all this information on me and telegrams offering me $1000 for the film unseen. My mother, back in Australia, was saying "Don't give them anything. Don't show them a foot of that film, they will do something terrible with it".' Jill stayed in Hong Kong for a week and made a small film for CBS and did the commentary herself.

Jill's final exam film at Swinburne was on Aboriginal human rights issues. She cut it and stuck it together on the kitchen table using the original reversal because Swinburne had only got a Steenbeck in the last three weeks of the course. It was accepted for showing at a number of film festivals.

When she graduated Fred Schepisi chose her, with another graduate – Graham Jackson, an animator – to work at Film House as a general dog's body for $30 a week.

Fred said she could try anything she liked. He suggested she became a cameraperson because she had done still photography but she didn't feel she was physically strong enough. She decided to do some editing and cut some 16mm and 35mm commercials and a surf film. After eighteen months she was getting impatient and left Film House. She assisted Brian Kavanagh on *The Naked Bunyip* (1970), which was the first and last time that she has ever been an assistant.

Jill then went overseas for two years, including a year in India. She supported herself by doing small parts in Indian movies in Bombay. She was the bad guy's girlfriend because she had a wardrobe, high heels and a coat, ready for London. She came back to Australia to get married and was caught by the Education Department to go to teachers' college because she had had a scholarship. It took three years teaching to get out of her bond and she worked on and off at Film House editing during that time. She then went to South America for a year travelling, taking still photographs and sketching.

She came back to Australia in 1976 when *The Chant of Jimmy Blacksmith* (1977) had just started production and worked on it with Brian Kavanagh, the editor.

She then worked as a freelance editor with Mike Reed in his post production company cutting commercials. Here she met Richard Lowenstein, who had just graduated from Swinburne and had been taken on as her assistant. Jill later cut Richard's first film, *Strikebound* (1983). She then cut *The More Things Change* (1985) for Robyn Nevin and *Dogs in Space* (1986), again for Richard Lowenstein. During this time Jill set up her own company in a tiny room in South Melbourne. She sold her little terrace house and bought a six-plate Steenbeck for $85,000 and a four-plate from a Sydney editor. She cut the musical *Australia Made* (1986) and a lot of music videos with Richard Lowenstein – INXS, and the Little River Band.

Fred Schepisi recommended her to be a co-editor on *Evil Angels* (1987) with either an English or an American editor. She'd worked with both of them before but 'neither of them wanted to share the credit with me so Fred said OK I could do it'. She then worked with John Seale, who was directing for the first time on *Till There was You* (1989). The film was edited on location in Vanuatu, and in Sydney, and this introduced her to Spectrum Films and the Sydney editing scene. She then started to cut commercials in Sydney and met Baz Luhrmann. 'I went over to meet him when he was setting up *Strictly Ballroom*. He interviewed lots and lots of editors. I had gone to see the first opening of *La Boheme*, the opera which he directed. It was such a coincidence because it had only played for a few nights and had been on when I was in Sydney. I was very impressed by the opera. We talked and we made tea together, and discussed tea cups. Baz and I got on incredibly well and as I left he said to me "Really nice to meet you because what I need is a mature person with a young outlook because I'm a young person with a mature outlook".'

>> **You need to concentrate over and over and over on every line, every performance, check it, think about it, whether it's in the right place in the film, whether it's happening at the right time in the film. There is no way the first cut is anything like where you want to end up.**

'That was the start of a very special friendship because I hadn't even read the script and I said yes. I just knew he'd be able to do it.'

After the success of *Strictly Ballroom* (1991) financially she had the worst year of her life. 'I don't know what happened. I ended up having to go to Thailand to cut commercials, earning money and bringing it back in paper bags to survive.'

Say a Little Prayer (1991) with Richard Lowenstein was the next feature and then *Temptation of a Monk* (1993) with Clara Law. She got that through Roger Savage, a sound mixer who runs Sound Firm in Sydney and Melbourne. 'He was clever enough as a businessman to realise that a lot of work would come out of Asia, so to keep his business going he was talking to people who were going to China and Hong Kong. He introduced me to Clara and said "Can't you get one of your girls to cut this Chinese picture? I'm doing the soundtrack for it". I said OK and thought it was one of those terrible, crazy things. Clara shot it in China and used Andrew Lesnie as the DOP. The rushes were beautiful, absolutely gorgeous. So I said "Right Christina, off the machine, I'm cutting this". Clara had to translate the script, which was in Mandarin, and we cut that whole feature in four weeks in a language I didn't speak.'

She cut *Muriel's Wedding* (1993). Lynda House, the producer, had worked on *Dogs in Space*, and PJ Hogan, who directed it, was another first-time director.

IQ (1994) for Fred Schepisi was the first film she cut non-linear on Lightworks, using the Lightworks manual as she went. Fred Schepisi had already used Lightworks on *Six Degrees of Separation* (1993) and wouldn't go back. 'I just picked it up very easily, no problem at all once I started. The first couple of weeks it took a while to cut things but after that it was second nature. By the time I got to *Romeo + Juliet* [1996] I was just making millions of cuts constantly.'

Jill had planned to edit *Shine* (1995) but then Jocelyn Moorhouse talked her into doing *How to Make an American Quilt* (1994) with her. She had worked with PJ Hogan, Jocelyn's husband, on *Muriel's Wedding*. She edited *How to Make an American Quilt* at Amblin, Stephen Spielberg's company in Los Angeles, and wanted to use Lightworks but Michael Carne, his editor, said it had to go on film. 'It looks like it's cut on film, it's got a gentle soft look to it, as opposed to the non-linear instant headache editing of *Romeo + Juliet*.' Jill was meant to come back to Melbourne with *How to Make an American Quilt* at the end of shooting but Jocelyn didn't want to move her son from his school so she had to stay in LA.

It was while she was editing *How to Make an American Quilt* that Baz Luhrmann came over with video footage he had shot with

Don McAlpine in Sydney to try and sell *Romeo + Juliet* to the studio and show that Leonardo Di Caprio could sell the language with an American accent. 'He came over with all this material and for two or three weekends I edited the thing together as a promotional video which the studio loved and it got the green light.'

Jill went to Mexico for *Romeo + Juliet* and set up two Lightworks and put half the film on one, and half on the other – which meant she could have somebody working on one independently of her. After the shoot they came back to Melbourne and worked in her house in East Brunswick. She had built a studio out the front which had the Lightworks that they had brought back from Fox in America and she part-bought a second, which she put in the living room.

They worked there for a few months, conformed the picture and did test opticals in Melbourne, then picked everything up and went over to America to Skywalker Ranch, George Lucas's company, just outside San Francisco, and kept editing while the soundtrack was being put together. 'There was not a lot of time to do *Romeo + Juliet* because they had run out of money and it had a release date of 1 November 1996.'

interview

HIGHLIGHTS

Evil Angels because I loved the idea of doing a true story. I've always liked that, so I felt emotionally involved in the process as it was so demanding but I felt very happy with the result.

It was huge, there was so much TV stuff to organise for that film. It was the biggest job by far that I had done. Getting everything ready to put it on the TV, editing it, it was pretty tough that one. I had up to three assistants and an assembly editor at one stage. It was the first international picture I'd done but Fred had confidence in me, he was a tough man, he would do anything for anybody and if he believed in you that was fine. He was a great believer in talent, giving young talent a lot of leeway. He'd do anything to get you ahead or a start. He had no qualms about it, he was very, very generous like that. In fact, he recommended me at a very early age to George Miller to cut *Mad Max* [1978] but at the time I said it was too violent.

We did the post production in Melbourne but it was my first experience of having to go over [to the US] for the preview system and my first experience in seeing a director fall apart. We took twenty minutes out in a couple of days and Fred lost his memory. He had a complete block and had to go to Cedar Sinai Hospital and have tests. His memory came back next morning but it was a very dangerous time. He didn't remember he'd made *Roxanne* [1986], he didn't remember why he was in LA or what the film was about. His long-term memory was fine so he remembered me but he couldn't remember anyone else in the short term. We edited on the lot at Warner's on the most terrible equipment I'd ever seen, scummy room, I couldn't believe it. I was on my own doing it all and that was very scary. I was overwhelmed by the bigness of everything, having to sit in a meeting with the head of Warner Brothers and fight for the opening and speak up. It was a fairly exciting experience.

Strictly Ballroom was also a highlight because I had such a lot of input and I felt in control of what I was doing. It was just creatively very rewarding. If I wanted to go further Baz was there and wanted to go further too. It was hard but it was fun and then it turned out to be the success it was. I knew while we were shooting it that it was going to be something special. It is probably the best thing I've done, the most complete work that I've done. It's a film I can still watch. There are not many that I want to watch again.

I had to beg a lot. Atlab was fantastic. I'd say 'I've only got $14,000' and I'd want almost twice that amount for opticals and they were just amazing. They'd say 'What do you mean you are going to get this, or you want this done, it just won't work. You haven't got the money or the time' and in the end we always got it, I think through perseverance, and because it was on film. Peter Willard [General Manager] was exceptionally generous. They were so thrilled with the end result, too, people were just overwhelmed by the fact that they had stuck their heads out. Also, nobody expected anything of you, there was no studio interference; you had an opportunity to do it the way you wanted.

It was the same on *Evil Angels*. I remember being stuck at Colorfilm during the Xmas break. There was no staff there and I was answering everyone's phone for them. I was still trying to get the colour grades right and I felt so alone. There is such a lot of carry through in editing – a lot of things people never realise you do. I must have checked hundreds of prints and just changed the colour a bit here and a bit there. People appreciate it – Verity Lambert [the producer in the UK] and Fred just knew that I wasn't going to go home until it was right, even if I slept on the doorstep. You go through these experiences where you become totally attached to a project and you won't let go until it is right.

AMBITION

I'd like to do some more small films with first-time directors. I like working on films about real people. That was my attraction to *Shine* and *Strikebound*. I'm looking at a couple of things at the moment. I am very shy of getting back into the studio system after *Romeo + Juliet*. I find it repulsive. You just get interrupted all the time while you're working. There are constant requests to get a bit of material dubbed off. There are always different departments that need to see a bit of film for one reason or another so the machine is constantly spitting out extracurricula tapes for everybody. I hate the way they publicise things and their marketing ideas, it's towards money and it just seems to interfere with the soul of the film.

There are too many other people around and the creative stream of consciousness gets interfered with so you often tend to lose your way. At home you tend to get in your room and get the job done in much less time because nobody is really interested.

On *Muriel's Wedding* PJ [Hogan] and I really scoured the material. We had a lot of fun doing it, getting that character Muriel right. The first time it was cut she was hideous, you wouldn't like her. The same with Baz on *Strictly Ballroom*. We would go through everything and we'd try things, and we'd move stuff around, we'd trick people with bits and pieces. It's a complete mind exercise and it is so satisfying, but if it gets interrupted you tend to get the scrappy bits in the film and then the time runs out. You need to concentrate over and over and over on every line, every performance, check it, think about it, whether it's in the right place in the film, whether it's happening in the right time in the film. There is no way the first cut is anything like where you want to end up.

Editing is only an accidental career. I think that if you have an art background you can pretty well adapt it to anything you like. I would like to do more drawing.

ISSUES FOR WOMEN

I think I've been luckier than many because I came through in that '60s and '70s period when just being young everybody loved you, so getting work and being a woman was not a problem. I can't think of a time when I actually had any problems. We were respected as being young and wanting to do something new as opposed to today where everybody talks about the problems of being a woman.

I don't think I've ever been victimised for being a woman but I think that comes from my mother being so strong. I've never stopped to think that it was a problem. I've never had a problem speaking out. I am a nagger, I just won't stop until I get what I want.

Working with male directors

I don't think I've ever worked with a director who hasn't already respected me creatively, so I don't think I've ever had a problem. Most of the men I've worked with, like Richard, Baz and even PJ are all quite feminine, they are creative and I'm older than they are. Fred is very chauvinist and he will say dreadful things but I am used to it. I don't take any notice. It is probably offensive to a lot of women but because he has been around since I was eighteen I have a long history. He married my best friend, so he's part of the family.

Sexist remarks

I just bite back usually if I find them offensive. When they come from somebody like Fred, which is his era, it is hard to stop him. Now I just speak up for myself and I don't make a big issue of it because I think then it just becomes worse. I say some pretty nasty things back and he's got used to a few of those.

Most men I work with don't make sexist remarks. You have more trouble walking past a building site than you do in the cutting room. I think it probably affects younger girls. They feel that they are not getting the respect that they should and that probably happens quite a lot. But I've always come from a position of 'don't mess with me or otherwise I'm leaving'.

When I was eighteen I was asked to do some pretty terrible things like go over to the police and chat them up so we could go on shooting. That was a transitional period before you realise that you are being used. If I was asked to do that now I would probably say 'no way' but I don't think that I knew any different at that point. They were always commenting on how pretty you were, how clever or good looking. It's a backhanded insult half the time.

Working with assistants

I look for skills mainly, intelligence, personality and that they know what they are doing, and are not going to irritate me. I only once employed somebody without meeting them and it turned out to be a disaster. I'd rather meet them, talk to them and see what my instincts say, see if I'll get on with them. I've had great girls working with me throughout my business. We just laugh and laugh and laugh and work incredibly hard. On *Quilt* I had three men and they were fantastic, just amazing. One was English, the other two were American. They looked after me and got the coffee and so on. It was a very happy time because there was no in-girl fighting. The three were incredibly different personalities and because they were busy they never bothered to get into each other's space.

Women are companions, they are great to have around and they are very good at their job. I've worked with Jane Moran a lot and she looks after me, she knows when I'm really stressed so she'll just pick me up and put me in a car and drive me down to Palm Beach or something and then bring me back. I am fairly close to the people I work with, so we need to get on very well.

Domestic arrangements

I've been married twice but now I live alone. I have a lot of people come and go and stay. I was not able to have children, I would have loved lots of children and I would have had a completely different career.

I like to stay in Melbourne. This is my home and where I live. All my friends and family are here. *Strictly* was shot in Sydney and then we did post here and Baz lived in this house and we worked in a terrace house in South Melbourne. Everybody ran out of money so I was feeding them, housing them. That was a pretty tough time but we did have a lot of fun too and then it turned out to be the success it was.

When I have a job overseas I just tend to get up and go and I get somebody in the house.

Feeling vulnerable

Every time I start a new job I feel terrified. Sometimes I lie in bed and I think editing is such a hard job, it's just so hideous. Before you start a new project you know you've got to set it up and prove yourself again to somebody else and there are all these new people. It doesn't matter if you've worked for the director before. I think every job is so hard, even the smallest film. *Romeo + Juliet* and *Strictly Ballroom* were almost 24-hour commitments but *Quilt* was a wonderful film. I used to walk to Universal from the horrible apartments and because Jocelyn had a child she would be out of there by six, I worked proper days and we had weekends off. That was a properly organised, scheduled film without any major deadlines, whereas on Australian films you've only got so much money so you can only work for seven weeks and then after that you work for no money. I don't usually book the next job because I know they never finish on time.

Crying

I cried a couple of times on *Romeo + Juliet*. When I was not getting on with the director, when we were having a row over something stupid, never anything creative, just human issues. Although I did cry once over work. I cried at Atlab on *Strictly Ballroom*, I was so horrified. We had been doing the *Strictly Ballroom* lettering, and we'd been painting the cells and setting them out, doing the whole thing ourselves and I took it up to Atlab in Sydney because I was going up to discuss all the opticals. I got up there and I was met by Ian Russell and I said 'How did the animation turn out' and he said 'There is nothing but black film' and he laughed. It turned out that the guy who had shot them on the animation camera had broken out the unexposed section, the wrong piece of film, so there was just black film and no titles on it. I then went in to see Roger Cowland about the opticals and he said 'Well how do you expect to do that, you can't do that.' I'd got on a plane, I'd paid my own ticket up there, they didn't understand that I was investing everything in the world to try and do these opticals and they couldn't be bothered. They didn't have time for a silly woman from Melbourne. I just started to cry. They felt terrible and after that they couldn't do too much for me, they were just so incredibly good. Roger Cowland became personally involved and developed the stars using the Atlab leader.

Coping with criticism

I'm pretty sensitive to personal criticism and I tend to take quite a bit of notice of criticism when it comes to dealing with something I've done. I take it and I reinvent it because I try and work out what it is they're after. I have been lucky with criticism. I don't tend to get a lot. I don't like to read lots of reviews and things after. I find them irritating because there is a lot of negativity.

ADVICE

If you really want to be an editor you should take a video camera and shoot something and try and cut it. Or write a little story and shoot it. It is so easy nowadays, equipment is so accessible and you can see whether or not you've got the ability to do it. You can go in and help people, do things for nothing, which is the only way you get noticed.

My experience has been that you just have to get into the workplace and you have to be noticed and liked and found indispensable.

You have actually got to show that you can use the equipment, and have an ability to put a story together. It is being around people and in the environment and showing something you have done yourself. You can easily take stuff off the TV and cut it together.

On non-linear editing you get a lot more opportunity to show that you can do something. With film you can't go round chopping up other people's rushes and they don't like assistants to have a go at a scene because of the unintentional cuts, but with a non-linear situation, if you've got drive and you want to get on you could be recutting the movie at night.

When you are editing, listen to what people say to you. Even if you disagree, try and work out what it is they are trying to say because the director is the boss. But try and maintain your individuality, you have to stick up for yourself and you do have to try things. The problem with editors is that sometimes they fight the director and that is not really very good for you. You can get your own way by other means, you do have to get respect and then use your influence. You're not always right, they can be right too and they can be wrong. So you should be prepared to try and then see what it is that they are getting at. If they are completely wrong and they are any good you'll work it out between the two of you. Try not to be too temperamental because there is nothing worse than a director dealing with somebody who is on the attack. It is not your job to attack, your job is to translate an idea. You are not the most important person in the world even if you may think you are. The director takes the blame in the end, not you.

DANY COOPER

Dany comes from an artistic family and has one younger brother. Her mother is involved in craft and her father was an administrator for the Arts Council of Australia and a director at the Australia Council for thirteen years. As a child she was taken to opening nights and mixed with people who were in the performance side of the arts. She was also taken to a lot of arthouse films but never thought of filmmaking as a career. Her mother brought her up to be financially independent, saying that she should never depend on anybody, whether man or woman, for money.

Dany completed the Higher School Certificate at Hunters Hill High School in Sydney when she was sixteen. As an aspiring violinist she played in the rank and file of the Sydney Youth Orchestra. She went to the University of Sydney and majored in fine arts and anthropology. In her final year she did a film theory strand with practical elements and was introduced to editing. 'It was like a combination of music and art. I could combine musical phrasing with layout and arranging and I really loved it.' She was also inspired by Gilly Coote (documentary filmmaker), who was a friend of the family. 'One day I told Gilly I wanted to work in the film industry and she said "you should be a film editor with your musical background". So I went to North Sydney Tech and did the four-year part-time course.'

During that time she worked as a sales clerk at CBS Fox Video until she got her first job as an assistant editor with Denise Haslem on *Out of Darkness: Rithy's Story* (1984) a documentary for SBS directed by Gilly Coote. 'I didn't get the job because of Gilly. My name was on a list that Denise had, of people wanting work, but maybe Gilly had put my name there. It's hard to get into the film industry without knowing someone.'

Dany went on to work with Gilly and Denise on *A Singular Woman* (1985) a documentary about Marie Byles, the first woman solicitor in Sydney, again a friend of her mother's. She then worked at Film Australia on documentaries as a picture and sound assistant while she finished her tech course. 'I guess I thought it was worthwhile continuing. There were about five of us who stayed for the whole course. They taught us how to use a splicer, and other basic techniques. The staff was all male, apart from one woman who taught film theory.'

Her first drama was a telefeature. Denise Hunter (the editor) rang her up looking for an assistant. She went on to work with Denise on a community service celebration for *A Decade of Women* (1985), directed by Gillian Armstrong, and a series of Bill Bennett features – *Backlash* (1986), *Dear Cardholder* (1986), *Jilted* (1987), and a documentary, *The Banjo and the Bard* (1987). Her career as an assistant on dramas also involved work with a number of other editors – Sara Bennett, Liz Goldfinch, Ted Otton, Frans Vandenburg and John Scott.

The first picture she cut was *Beyond El Rocco* (1989). It was a 100-minute dramatised documentary on the history of jazz in Australia, directed by Kevin Lucas and produced by Aanya Whitehead. 'Kevin was a friend, a fellow filmmaker. It was his first film as a director. We had five-camera coverage, 16mm footage and cut it on an old four-plate Steenbeck. It got a theatrical release at the Valhalla Cinema in Glebe.'

After *Beyond El Rocco* she thought 'Great, I'm a picture editor, no more assisting', but then she couldn't get any work. So for the next couple of years Dany was a picture assistant on numerous features for a variety of editors. *Map of the Human Heart* (1991) was the biggest and last picture she assisted on.

In 1992 Barbara Bedford from the ABC rang her and asked her to edit an episode of *A Big Country* (1992). 'I was really pleased because this was different from the other work. I had never met

Barbara and Stephen Burstow [the director] before. I think she had seen and liked *Mr Neal*. I was very grateful to Barbara.'

Dany learnt non-linear editing through the support of Bill Bennett who produced *The Gadfly* (1993) with Corrie Soeterbeck, which Lewis Fitz-Gerald directed. 'Bill decided I was going to learn Lightworks. I had edited *The Last Man Hanged* [1992] for him and Lewis on 16mm and he included a Lightworks learning period in the schedule. It was a wonderful thing to have done and meant that I was able to learn non-linear equipment early in my career'. She learnt to use Avid on *Ladies Please* (1995), a television documentary directed by Andrew Saw.

>> **When I am working particularly well with a director we finish each other's sentences, it becomes a form of shorthand. We don't need words to communicate.**

I think it is harder for women to become editors than men. Women fall more easily into support roles. I think women are sometimes passive in the way they seek work. We make rejection personal.

Angel Baby (1994) was her first feature and won seven AFI awards in 1995 including best editor. It was edited in Melbourne. The producer Tim White was co-producer on *Map of the Human Heart*. 'I got a call from Tim, who has always been very supportive, saying "Lewis Fitz-Gerald has told Michael [Rymer, the director] about you and he wants to meet". I had nothing to lose as I knew he was seeing everyone in town, so I was relaxed. We got on well. I guess I was in the right place at the right time.'

Dany has gone on to edit television dramas, documentaries and other features, *Allie and Me* (1996) which she edited in Los Angeles with Michael Rymer, *The Well* (1997), directed by Samantha Lang and which was chosen for Official Selection into

Competition at Cannes, 1997, *In Too Deep* and additional picture editor on *Babe: Pig in the City* (1998).

interview

HIGHLIGHTS

The Last Man Hanged because I loved the working relationships and what we did with the film. Bill Bennett was really fantastic, he was like a mentor to both myself and Lewis Fitz-Gerald. We experimented with different editing techniques and developed a new way of overlapping dialogue as a result.

Black River [1993] because it was fantastic to do a second film with Kevin [Lucas]. It was an opera about black deaths in custody, and had never been done before. Visually it is very beautiful, and if editing is a relationship between light and sound then this film was one of the purest experiences I have had so far.

Angel Baby because it changed my life. It was my first feature and that was really incredibly exciting and I won an AFI Award for it.

Working with Michael in America was fantastic. *Allie & Me* [1996] was great fun. There are thousands and thousands of editors over there. They seem to be set up like big family groups. Very male, very father/son/grandson lineage stuff. You'll get the father as the supervising editor and the son as the second editor. I found it fascinating.

The Well [1997] forced me to re-evaluate the changes in my life. It's a beautiful script by Laura Jones and I love the two women leads, Pamela Rabe and Miranda Otto. I used to say to Samantha Lang [the director] that it was fantastic to come to work to see them. It was like entering another world and it was great to work with those characters.

FUTURE

I just want to go on cutting better films. I think filmmakers in Australia tend to drop out at a certain age, but overseas, they work well into their 60s and 70s. I think we need more respect paid to tradition and experience. There are a lot of father/son teams in the US, so traditions are passed down in a way that is rather wonderful.

Here it's a problem of ageism, and not special to the film industry. The cult of consumerism has somehow got it all mixed up, creating the 'first-timer', in whatever position. The problems begin when a film isn't perfect. We throw out the new and get a newer – it becomes self perpetuating because we need to find someone who can hit it first off, the perfect film, first time, by the perfect director and crew. I don't think that is a good thing for the industry. It denigrates experience and wisdom in favour of youth and newness. I think we are culturally confused as to why we make films.

SELECTING ASSISTANTS

Loyalty is very important. When you are editing you need to be surrounded by people you trust, you need to know that they will carry out what you have asked for correctly, and that while they are working on the film they will be on a similar emotional level to you in the amount of care and respect that they will give to the film.

They have got to be completely loyal to the picture editor and to the film. Not talk about the film to anybody, not bad mouth or repeat anything. With editing you're locked in a room for a long time, you get quite intense. Quite often you say things that you don't mean and you say 'Anything that happens between me and the director I don't want repeated'. I can forgive mistakes but I can't forgive disloyalty.

To be a good assistant you need to develop foresight. You have to understand the people in the editing room so well that you know what they want before they know it themselves. It's great training for becoming an editor. When I am working particularly well with a director we finish each other's sentences, it becomes a form of shorthand. We don't need words to communicate.

STYLE

As an ex violin player I relate to images rather like musical phrasing. I see pictures not as pieces of filmed dialogue, but as excerpts of light and movement. Sound is very important to me. I think editing is about rhythm, and the rhythm I create with a set of images is influenced by the sound effects and music that go with it.

I respond to rushes as a brand new thing each time. I don't cut a film with a preconceived idea of style, or look. The raw footage has its own integrity. I only force a style onto a film when the original material demands it. Of course that can be exciting.

As an editor you are trying to get the best out of yourself, the material and the director.

ISSUES FOR WOMEN

I think it is harder for women to become editors than men. Women fall more easily into support roles. I think women are sometimes passive in the way they seek work. We make rejection personal. I've always found it very difficult to approach someone about a new job. It took me eight years to start editing. No-one held me back, there just weren't many job opportunities. I don't regret this now because I was able to learn about many different areas.

Women sometimes knife each other when they should be supportive within their own ranks. The industry cultivates a sense of desperate competition which is detrimental to the process, which should be one of interaction and collaboration.

Sexism

When I worked in marketing at CBS Fox Video the company was run by men. The women were always in the support roles running around looking after the men, which I thought was pretty sexist. But my experience as an assistant editor never placed me in a position like that again.

In the cutting room there is really no problem. When I was an assistant there weren't many women editors but I was lucky enough to work with most of them. As an editor the director has hired you anyway so there is not likely to be a problem with him.

An editing relationship on a feature is a bit like a marriage for a short period of time. It's one-to-one and it's very volatile. You are very intense with that person and you get very close to them. I've never really had that exploited. Not in a way I couldn't handle immediately.

But within the walls of a cutting room I have found that the relationships pretty much remain the same no matter what gender is involved. It's when you leave that environment that problems may arise.

Men in technical roles sometimes assume a patronising manner which can be offensive. When I was an assistant I found men in big groups intimidating, particularly in sound mixes where a sort of locker room mentality grows. On one occasion the mixer kept turning to the sound editor, both men, after I had politely requested changes, asking 'What did she say?'. He was unable to deal directly with me. As it was only a short mix I didn't see the point in politicising it. Sometimes it's just simpler to get on with the job so you work out a way not to rock the boat. Of course I never worked with that mixer again.

I think women discuss who they will and won't work with, more often than men do because they are forced into a position of having to pay closer attention to interpersonal relationships. I know we did on *The Well* and the result was great.

I felt working in the US was more sexist than working in Australia. I was cutting in a place called Big Time in west LA, there would have been about forty cutting rooms, and there were only two women cutting there including me. I had a number of assistants and they were all male and they were fine.

I had two women producers working for me and they got results. They would ring up and let blast if something wasn't going to plan. I don't know how to ring up and just yell. I wish I did. I don't think Australian women know how to do that, and they generally don't get results when they do but are labelled as over aggressive and bitchy.

Content

You put six months of your life into a film and it's essential you are happy with the choice you make. I try and choose films that I know I will learn something from. A new style, a great script, a new producer, but I also love working with the same people more than once. A relationship that has been developed creates a better film the second and third time because you can cut through the stuff that occurs when you don't know someone. Trust is built from shared experience. I don't want to label myself as an editor of a certain type of film. If the script is good then I am interested.

Working with women

I have had very strong women role models who have always been supportive. Gilly [Coote] was fantastic, and both the Denises [Haslem and Hunter] looked after me when I was an assistant. Jan Chapman and Helen Bowden on *Naked* were both wonderful.

I've found women tend to respond to situations more emotionally than men. There is no value judgement here, it's just a different way of working. *The Well* was mainly headed by women and I found there was a relaxed atmosphere at meetings – perhaps it's because some women are less afraid to display vulnerability.

Feeling vulnerable and crying

I used to feel depressed when I had no work because the nature of the industry means that there is no such thing as a holiday, only being in work, or waiting to start work. Now I think it's a great opportunity to enter the real world. My partner is very supportive and it helps that he is not part of the industry but he understands it. I only cry when an injustice is done, or when something is very unfair. I prefer to solve rather than cry.

ADVICE

Filmmaking is narrow and extremely obsessive. Editing isn't a 9 to 5 job. I sometimes start work at 7.30am and finish at 9.30pm and 7-day weeks are becoming more common. At the most intense period of cutting, the film takes over your life. Total commitment for short periods of time can be difficult.

Working as an assistant nowadays is not the straight career path I followed. Non-linear editing has changed the assistant's role. You need to be computer literate and be able to do shiftwork. You may find you won't actually be working with your editor but on a night shift when they have left for the evening. There isn't a lot of room for learning or exchange. This won't change until we increase post production budgets and don't have to share computers.

Going to film school will introduce you to your peers. You will learn by doing, and by being the editor not supporting an editor. It is perhaps a longer road unless you affiliate with some brilliant director or producer. But nothing beats industry experience.

You should contact already established editors and assistants. Be prepared to go and spend time in a cutting room. This is a great way to get known and observe the editing process. I think if you are interested in film you will do anything to get started. My first job was a continuity person on two films at the film school and I worked for free.

Try to be incredibly brave and believe in yourself because a lot of people will try and persuade you otherwise. The first film I cut I just believed I could do it, I didn't have any doubt that I couldn't do it. I think if you believe you can do something you can. But self criticism is a useful tool also because you need to understand other points of view.

Don't become an editor because you expect glory, the directors and stars get the fame. You have to love doing it because you love editing. Be acutely sensitive to everything that is happening around you. Relationships between characters, relationships between people, the relationship between the person you are sitting with and the footage. Our job is to interpret.

VISUAL EFFECTS

The area where computers have made a great impact is in visual effects. This has taken over some of the work of the art department, which used to provide models and physical special effects, and the editing department, which used to supervise optical effects through the laboratory.

Now on large features there is sometimes a visual effects producer and a growing effects department which is being brought into the pre-production phase when virtual sets and digital special effects are integral to the production.

The introduction of computers into the design process began in television with the character generator to make captions. Expensive computers and sophisticated software packages followed, providing powerful painting and animation tools, and many graphic artists took up the challenge to learn complex new programs.

As computers became more accessible and affordable, the demand for special effects increased and graphic artists took over a lot of the work which had previously been done by special effects departments in the processing laboratories. Computer packages were also developed for both 2D and 3D animation.

Production houses invested in computer equipment and an increasing number of TV commercials and corporate productions are now made with the aid of computers. Many graphic artists have developed computer skills, either through self-training, or as part of art school courses. But at the high end of the market the equipment is too expensive for many of the schools, so that hands-on practise is only possible in television stations or production houses. More recently the AFTRS has offered training courses in high-end graphics.

While the emergence of digital media has created an entire new industry – the multimedia industry – in film production, the impact of digital technology is most significant in the areas of editing and in special effects and animation, both 2D and 3D.

SPECIAL EFFECTS AND ANIMATION

Most feature films now include some computer-generated imagery and/or manipulation, even though it is not always immediately apparent when watching a film.

It may be retouching, getting rid of a boom shadow or reflections of the crew in a shop window; modifying real locations for period shoots or getting rid of unwanted power lines on a location; rebuilding a location or a whole city for a sci-fi spectacular; making animals or creatures talk; inflicting all kinds of damage on actors; resurrecting dead people – the computer and powerful programs provide endless possibilities.

Therefore it is important for any graphic artist wishing to enter the film industry to pursue training on high-end Silicon Graphics computers equipped with software such as Alias and SoftImage (for 3D animation and special effects) and Flame, Matador and Illusion (for digital video editing and special effects). Some of these high-end programs have also been developed to run on PCs; for example, SoftImage has a Windows NT version.

2D work consists of designing, using existing images gathered from a number of sources, layering graphics, and compilation work. 3D modelling is building 3D objects, environments and scenes from scratch, animating the models and choreographing their movements, setting the cameras and adjusting the lights and determining the surfaces and shading characteristics. When there is live action the animation has to match the appropriate colours, shadows and reflections.

Any 3D production house will value animation skills. Some will employ people with no computer experience if they are good 'traditional' animators. While it takes time to learn new software and hardware – and sometimes production houses have proprietary software developed in-house for their use alone – digital artists find it an exhilarating experience which offers the opportunity to 'push the boundaries' in new and exciting ways.

Both 2D and 3D animators will normally work to a storyboard with a designer who knows exactly what any live action looks like. Sometimes the 3D animator will go to a shoot to make sure that it has been set up properly for the special effects and take note of the lighting and the camera lenses. Lenses and computer-controlled camera movement can be accurately matched in settings in 3D animation software.

While the majority of 2D and 3D work is for commercials and corporate videos, there is a growing amount of 3D special effects work required for big budget feature films.

In the large production houses there tends to be specialisation. On large jobs the 3D tasks are often divided up, whereas on smaller jobs one person may do all the tasks. Some production houses may specialise in particular areas and, in some of the larger houses, the levels of specialisation can almost reach the level of a factory production line. The skills required by each production house depend on what type of computer equipment and software they use.

In this new area of computer graphics, women tended initially towards 2D animation, painting, titling and illustrating, and less towards 3D animation. Linda Dement, a revered innovator in the field, and a teacher of computer graphics, says this is beginning to change.

Matthew Gidney, a lecturer in animation at AFTRS, observed that his male students come from the world of game parlours and computer games – 'they live in a virtual reality head space' – and tend to push the equipment to see what it will do, whereas his female students have come from the art world.

Linda Dement questions the perspective that women do not experiment, observing that her young female students – who also have game parlour and computer games backgrounds – 'push equipment all the time', as does she.

While it is generally acknowledged that higher end programs are difficult to learn – they are not yet as 'user friendly' as some of the better known desktop programs (eg, Illustrator, Photoshop) – those who have tried and conquered say it is incredibly satisfying to tackle a difficult program, push the outer limits and create new and wonderful images. On the other hand, newcomers to the technology can be severely frustrated by the steep learning curve required.

A common notion is that 'programs and computers are made by men for men', hence creating an alienating environment for women to work in. This is an interesting perspective, given that the first computer was developed by a woman, Ada Lovelace, in collaboration with a male partner. The first programmers were women who, during the second world war, used computers to develop firing tables. And in digital arts, Australian women have a high international profile with a reputation for producing 'cutting edge' and 'risky' work (Plant, 1997). This begs the question of why there is a paucity of women digital animators and special effects artists. Recently, a woman producer actively tried to employ women to do 3D for an animation series but found that there were very few who were interested. At the same time, younger men working in this new area say that they would like to have a mixed gender workforce but find it very difficult to find women.

The AFTRS ran its first three-month certificate 3D course in 1997 for professional editors, graphic artists, compositors, animators and effects artists. Among the fifty applications for the ten course positions there were only three from women, one of whom was successful in gaining entry. The experience of the AFTRS, in terms of its film and television training, is that women – perhaps through lack of confidence – were slower than men to take up the opportunity of training, but once they did so they were extremely successful in their applications. For example, although there were still fewer applications from women (163) than men (187) for 1998, a slightly higher number of women were successful in getting places.

ROLE MODELS

Because digital imaging is a new field there are not many well-known women at the top. I have selected four who represent different aspects of this new area, and it is interesting that three of them have come from a combined arts science/practical background. Sally Pryor and Kit Devine both have science qualifications. Sally studied science and then moved across to art, whereas Kit started in design. Carolyn Reid has no formal qualifications but started in a design company and has done practical courses in panel beating and welding, far removed from computers but illustrating a very practical hobby. Lynne Cartwright, with graphic design qualifications, came to computers in the course of her work as a graphic designer.

Sally Pryor describes herself as an artist/programmer/animator, and independent multimedia developer. She was one of Australia's first 3D computer animators. In 1984 her student film *Dream House* was the first Australian piece ever selected for SIGGRAPH, the major annual US computer graphics/animation conference and festival.

Sally spoke at most of the early national forums about women and technology and ran a women, art and technology project while artist-in-residence at the Performance Space Gallery in 1989. She has lectured widely and in 1991 published a seminal paper, *Thinking Oneself as a Computer*. She was lecturer in computing and multimedia at the University of Technology and produced *Postcard from Tunis* (1997) which won a number of international awards, including an award for excellence at Invision (US). In 1997 she was awarded the inaugural Elektra award presented by Fox Studios for outstanding achievement in the area of new technologies. In 1999 she was awarded a two-year artistic fellowship from the New Media Arts Fund of the Australia Council.

Carolyn Reid is one of the top computer graphic artists. Hers is a true story of the junior in the design department becoming its head. She was one of the early users of computers for graphic design and became the Australian demonstrator of the Image Artist

System. In 1986 she won the Certificate of Special Recognition for Creative Use of Computer Graphics and Animation at the Penguin Awards. She has worked in London, New Zealand and South East Asia, training on Quantel equipment. In 1994 she set up her own production house, CAR Productions, investing over $300,000 in computer equipment. She produces graphics, special effects and 2D animation for top-end TV commercials and programs.

Kit Devine and Lynne Cartwright both belong to that very small number of women 3D animators and work in different commercial production houses. They work on a very high throughput of commercials and corporates and have far too many credits to identify.

Kit Devine works at Garner MacLennan Design, a production house which specialises in design, animation, computer graphics and visual effects for film, video and multimedia. It is the second biggest production house doing 3D animation. There are eight 3D animators and one other woman who has recently joined the company.

Lynne Cartwright is senior computer animator at Animal Logic, a production house providing high-end visual effects for film, television and commercials. There are three women out of twelve who work on 3D animation. As well as commercials and corporates, Lynne works on the growing number of features that are now using visual effects.

SALLY PRYOR

Sally grew up in Ballarat. She liked art but was encouraged to do maths and science at school and did not continue with art beyond fourth form. 'It was a great loss for me and it took ten years to find a way to come back to it.'

She is the eldest of ten children and was encouraged to be a high achiever. Her parents were professionals, her mother a microbiologist and her father a surgeon.

Sally left school in 1971 and went straight to university to do science, where she was desperately unhappy. Her first job was as a dietitian's assistant, and she then became a hospital biochemist. She went overseas and lived in Jordan for four months, working in a hospital.

She returned to Australia to do a Master of Science in biochemistry. 'I was desperately wanting to integrate cold, abstract science with something more personal and I thought nutrition was one way to bring biochemistry and self together. I liked science but it always felt wrong. I was bored, frustrated and angry and it wasn't enough. I used to walk around and think how can all these people be satisfied? It just wasn't the place for me.'

It was by chance, a few years later, that she found she was good at computers. There was a programmable calculator at work and she realised that it was really easy. So she looked for a job to train on computers. This was the late '70s when computer companies were desperate to get computer people and they took any graduate who passed their aptitude tests.

'I always liked IQ tests at school but I got out of the habit over the years and when I went for my IBM interview I got lost and I didn't do very well, so they said that I might be able to sell office equipment. I went home and got hold of Eysenck's book, *Know Your Own IQ*, did all the examples and trained up again. I went back and resat it and they were so shocked they couldn't quite believe it.'

Sally finally chose to go to Burroughs (now UNISYS) and learnt programming. She was still frustrated because her artistic self wasn't being expressed. So she took art lessons with Jenny Watson, an Australian painter, and learnt to use pastels rather than watercolour, which she had had trouble controlling at school. Through a boyfriend who did collage she found another medium which she could control. She started to bring together the two aspects of science and art in herself.

She was then looking for a way to bring art and computers together. There were no PCs, no paint programs and few word processing packages but an old boyfriend told her that Swinburne Institute, which is now the VCA (Victoria College of Art), was starting a computer animation course and they were looking for people to be their first students. So in 1983 she and a male friend did the one-year course and, using 3D wireframe shapes moving in space, made *Dream House*, about a woman's dreams as she looked at all the things in the house which represented aspects of herself. It had international success and was the first film from Australia ever selected for SIGGRAPH, the major US computer graphics/animation conference and festival. 'At least twice, men after me have claimed that they had the first film in SIGGRAPH. That is really irritating. I have to be really alert otherwise I am going to be written out of history.'

When she finished at Swinburne in 1983 there were no jobs for computer artists in Australia. She was a student volunteer at an international conference and one of the speakers was from a prestigious American 3D computer animation company and mentioned that they were having trouble getting people who had both an art and technical background. She took the initiative and after his talk, when he was surrounded by other high powered men, she used her technique of butting into a conversation, honed from coming from a family of ten, and invited him to see her work. He came to the college and when he saw what they had done on very basic equipment he offered her and her colleague a job on the spot. They went to Columbus Ohio to extremely prestigious 3D animator jobs which were very well rewarded, but had extremely high stress. She stayed there a couple of years and came back to Australia in 1986 and did commercial work and television IDs at Video Paintbrush Co. Again she got bored because she was making things which she regarded as totally meaningless. 'Usually you were asked to do 3D to give a veneer of hip happening and up-to-date sort of thing. It was all very surface – nothing about ideas.'

Then a company on the central coast, Integrated Arts, got a large government grant to build a custom designed computer and software. 'It was a very ambitious project. It was run by a man who had achieved fame with the Fairlight.' Sally was one of two women (the other was Kit Devine see p188) employed on the user interface team but eventually they both realised that the project was not going well and left.

By this stage, PCs were around. Sally had brought one of the first Amigas back from the US. She was doing a lot more art installations and was starting to exhibit and talk in public. She was making the change from thinking of herself as a commercial animator to thinking of herself as a computer artist. She got a part-time job lecturing at the College of Fine Arts (now located at the University of New South Wales) and had one more stint at commercial animation at XYZap because she ran out of money.

She did one of the earliest residencies at the Performance Space in Sydney and ran a workshop called Women Art and Technology. She was one of the earliest computer artists and got grants from the Visual Arts/Craft Board of the Australia Council with which she bought equipment.

In 1989 she joined the staff of UTS and started two intense years lecturing full-time and doing many public appearances here and lectures overseas. She also wrote a seminal paper called *Thinking Oneself as a Computer*, which explored what it means to think about yourself as a computer from a gender point of view. She presented it at SISEA, in Amsterdam, one of the first art and technology forums. 'It was a very good paper and I think it is only actually ready to be heard now. I am just starting to get email about it but I'm always ahead of everyone else, which isn't always a good thing! I was also always dragged out as a female role model and did practically every woman and technology and virtual reality forum in Australia.'

>> **Computer art is a certain kind of mix of technical and creative. So I see it as a challenge in the creative process, just as a lighting person is a creative person working with technical things to get a solution. I've been really lucky. I think gender has been a plus for me. The only negative is my own lack of confidence in myself and my abilities and that has been a major thing.**

In 1990 she burnt out and decided to go to Tunisia. She married a local man and built a strong relationship with his family. She changed her Master of Arts topic, which was going to be *The History of Women in Computing*, and started working on language learning through images which sowed the seeds for *Postcard from Tunis* which is now a CD-ROM and won an award for excellence at Invision (USA).

She came back to UTS and multimedia, which integrated her interest in graphics and computer animation and computer programming. She and Megan Hayward, a media lecturer, taught themselves how to author and have each produced projects – *I am a Singer* and *Postcard from Tunis* – which were the only Australian entries picked for the prestigious New Talent Pavilion at Milia 97 in Cannes.

This is Sally's second time round being a star. When she went to America she had a lot of press and now *Postcard from Tunis* is starting to be very successful. It is an interactive artwork on CD-

ROM, a personal portrait of Tunis, also about ancient writing, contemporary writing and what writing might mean at the human computer interface. Through its unique interface the user learns some Tunisian words and can start to read written Arabic. She did the programming, the artwork, everything except the music.

interview

HIGHLIGHTS

Getting into computers, combining that with creativity and making things that are really interesting. Also saying something that is worth saying in a way that combines the analytical side with the creatively delicious. Things like exploring roles for women, representation of Arabic cultures, or how interesting reading and writing truly are and how they might relate to user interface.

I've written about dualisms, self-other, mind-body, female-male. One of my themes is if you think you are a computer you identify with the code and the body is thrown out as if it is not really an important part of your identity. That is usually what women get thrown out onto.

So dualism and an awareness of it started to be a really interesting topic for me. I got that from being at UTS. I don't have an arts degree, I got one through hanging out there and absorbing ideas everywhere.

Going to the Arabic world, I'd always been drawn to it, and I had put off going for ages because of the gender thing and the feeling that as a woman why would I take an interest in a culture that is going to make it even harder for me than it is here. But in fact that is not a black and white issue either. I think the western thinking, that we have freedom and that they don't, is insulting and simplistic. It's a lot more complex and much less one-sided than that.

I love solving technical problems. It does interrupt the creative flow but it happens to be something I enjoy as well. I have always loved bugs in computer programs; it happens for a reason and you just haven't found it. You accept that there is going to be a solution and you have just got to find it. It's like Sherlock Holmes. It's patience with a methodology, because it is some stupid little thing and it's never any great brain power.

Computer art is a certain kind of mix of technical and creative. So I see it as a challenge in the creative process, just as a lighting person is a creative person working with technical things to get a solution. They're solving problems too.

One of my themes in *Postcard from Tunis* was to develop a different kind of interface. For example I think that interesting interfaces let you write as well as read. I find just pointing and clicking really dull, just click, click, click and consume, consume, consume. So I had to actually dream up other ways and then program them myself and I loved that. I have always liked abstract structures – how they work and how they fit together – which is why I like science and physics and all those things. So it has actually worked beautifully for me.

ISSUES FOR WOMEN

I had a really classic upbringing where I thought of myself as a girl and what things were appropriate for girls. My mother is a very active, achieving person but a deeply female role model. There was nothing in my background other than science and maths which encouraged me to get out of that classic model. I was encouraged to be attractive and date, do well at school, go to university, get married and have kids.

I've always had gender awareness. Gender follows you around the room. When I went to university in the '70s it opened my mind to feminism. It really was a big thing for me for ten years and I read a lot of stuff. *Fat is a Feminist Issue*, that came at the very end. But things like that helped me understand. I blamed myself for feeling not right all the time. I can still remember, I thought that the reason I was unhappy was because I was too fat. I remember a lot of that crap. That women were inadequate. Men can't really use that argument any more but it wasn't so long ago that they could, and with great authority, and no one would be bucking it.

My generation wasn't actively discouraged from autonomy but you weren't encouraged to have any. But the one after me you were encouraged. The one before me you were actively discouraged. Punitive things were done to keep you in your place. So I am in the middle. There was nothing to encourage you to feel confidence and a sense of your own self and if you actually were going to get that together there would be really obvious things pushing you down again. And less obvious things like feeling uncomfortable being the only woman.

In my early days in computers I'd go for a drink with the boys and someone would always end up pouncing on me if I stayed there long enough. I don't think I have suffered a lot, it's mainly been feeling ill-at-ease and not being quite right which I've taken out on myself. But I don't think I've had anything really devastating done to me.

When I was at Burroughs I used to always feel incredibly visible and self conscious and that is probably where gender and tech hit me in the eye because I was usually the only female. I used to try and dress as unsexy and as unattractive as I could and try and look corporate, but it didn't matter, I might as well have been in a slinky night dress. I'd enter a room and I'd feel the whole vibe change.

I didn't understand why I used to scare people but I think it is a combination of young woman and sharp mind. I didn't understand why that was frightening.

There are all different kinds of difficult men. I would try and bypass the different ones; I don't want to waste my time trying to bring them round to emotional health.

I had a little problem with a difficult programmer recently. He just thought he was too interesting to be interested in my task. So I just bypassed him, I programmed it myself. I wouldn't waste any time trying to convert him and I will never be doing him any little favours in the future.

I'm not very good at confronting. I'd have to be convinced that there was something to gain from it. I just go on to a new situation, that's my life. I have a long pattern, it's a little bit of a cop out for me.

I don't truly think I've had many things where they have said you can't do that because you're a woman. I just missed that period where it was that black and white. When I came in it was more like 'You can do it but you'll have to make sure that you're confident and can do it'. I was always in a new field where they had to take me, they had no choice and that was a lovely feeling. In computers and computer animation I've always been a pioneer. Not now, I've let multimedia get really happening before I joined it and I am just succeeding now.

I think possibly being a woman has been a help at times because men are always happy to see a feminine face around the place in a male dominated area. So although you feel you can't blend in I think there are advantages as well. In America, in contrast, there were quite a few women animators.

You have to have a certain confidence in yourself to work with computers because you are solving problems and you have got to have the confidence that you can solve it and that you can pull cables around and it's okay.

You need to have confidence that the computer is something that you can understand. You know that terror you feel when you see a big audio mixing desk and you think 'Oh God I'll never get this'. You really need to have a certain confidence to say 'It looks kind of awful but I am sure I can do it'.

Confidence isn't something that was given to me at all. I had to develop that. I guess I used Barbie. She was the role model that I was given. I bought my first Barbie doll in the States and I saw her as a model of femininity that I had been offered. It is an impossible feminine daintiness that you could never truly be. When I got my booklet about menstruation at 12, the girl on the cover was a dead ringer for Barbie.

The Barbie theme was a really big one for me. I had her doing heaps of confident things. I made a video called *Computers are Fun* where she is at the computer and raising questions like relationship between body and technology. I also made clothes for Barbie, lab coats and Dr Barbie. I was really interested in the tension between female upbringing and the confidence that you need to have to work with equipment. I don't think it was great art but it was interesting.

I've been really lucky. The only thing holding me back has been my own lack of confidence, not standing up for myself, getting into situations where its not really a gender issue but more a confidence issue. Also I haven't had any kids. If I had it would be quite a different story.

Deciding where I am going in the future has taken a sort of confidence. I've had to develop: number one, that what I am feeling and interested in is valid rather than just fuzzy and to be ignored, number two, that I can solve technical things – that it is within my capability – and, number three, that I can lead things. None of those are in my training. My training was to be a good little girl.

You have to get the confidence to lead. That's what I'm working towards now. I am just about to start getting more people in my team. I'm trying to work out a whole different kind of process, getting money together, talking to business people, that sort of stuff, so I am always learning. You have to feel that your ideas are okay, and that doesn't come with a conventional female upbringing.

If you have been trained to be a classic girl you have been trained to go and get a man when something is not working – like when I bought a car I thought 'Well there should be a man here doing this for me. Why do I have to do it myself?'.

I didn't have a vision. I've never had a vision. I have always wanted to get out of the discomfort of today. I was really just so unhappy. I bumbled and fumbled my way over the years to find out what it is that would stop me from being so unhappy, and part of it was integrating the technical abstract part of me with the creative part of me.

Lack of women in 3D animation

I haven't been back to 3D as an expressive form since my student film. The States was commercial 3D animation but I haven't done any 3D art other than my student film. Doing 2D flat images was more my art. I was a natural 2D person it was just that it wasn't available to me when I was getting started. I came back to it with PCs.

There have been psychological tests on 3D spatial ability where you have to imagine a 3D diagram rotating to a position, and women have performed less well than men. See, for example, *Alice Through the Microscope* [1980] for one of the few tests that women do worse than men.

I would have definitely failed them before I was a 3D animator but now I can succeed because I have just got so used to manipulating space shapes. I think that can be learnt – I am living proof.

Zoe Soufoulis says in *Whose 2nd Self* [1993] that girls aren't repelled by computers because they don't want to be rational, it's that they don't want to be irrational. They don't want to have emotional relationships with computers. They don't want to use them as substitutes for intimacy etc. and I think there is a lot to that point of view. So it's not really what's wrong with girls, it's what's wrong with computers.

Everyone will tell you that to be any good at computers you have to be willing to become obsessed and spend a lot of time in front of them. Girls seem to be repelled by things that are very abstract, very dry and very cut off from interaction. Interactionally challenged men and men with really weird relationships with their bodies are over-represented in the technical area. If you go to a room of computer boys you'll see a lot of guys who are right out of touch with their bodies.

Sexual harassment

It's a very hard thing to quantify. Nothing overt. There is a certain kind of man who I threaten and that is a man who actually feels inadequate himself and he is hiding it and he is afraid that I will reveal it. I've had that experience once or twice and we get into this very ugly dance but I don't know that you could call it sexual harassment.

A man who feels inadequate and is hiding it by blustering usually finds me very threatening because I am a bit of 'a spade calling a spade' person. He will be very uncooperative. I've been really lucky I think gender has been a plus for me. The only negative is my own lack of confidence in myself and my abilities and that has been a major thing.

ADVICE

Believe you can be a 3D animator. Find out what is required and find out the skills that you are going to need and get them.

Keep both sides, art and science, going even if in your particular environment there's disbelief that it can be combined – believe that it can. Because time is on your side. Look what's happening. We are undergoing a great amount of change and who can predict the form of art in the future. I do think it will change a lot. I don't think it will just be making a perfect thing that everyone looks at and says 'That's nice'. I think you'll be making things that embody a kind of intelligence or interactivity that people will use to make other stuff. Understand that it is all changing so fast that you might hear things that aren't true. So go out there and find out for yourself. There are plenty of opportunities to get information now.

Programming never goes astray. It's a really good idea to have a basic idea of what computers are, rather than seeing them as scary plastic boxes. Get skills, anything to do with spatial skills, manipulating things in space. Use every simulator you can get your hands on, flight simulators, make things in space, do tech drawing, push yourself to do things that maybe aren't calling you but come together to be useful sets of skills. If 3D interests you, you are going to have to develop an appreciation of lighting. Start looking at lighting, how it is used. Start looking at surfaces. Look for spatial experiences and make shapes.

You would have to consult the industries and see what they are looking for these days. Generally the industries aren't expecting that people will get their training at universities, because universities don't have the facilities, so they will be looking for someone who shows they can understand the technical and the artistic and has got stickability. If you want to do 2D, get your mitts on a home computer and start. You can also do 3D on a home computer if you have the patience, you have just got to wait all night while it renders.

You can study 3D at a few different places. I'd find out where they are, get experience and then go out and make your own opportunities. Don't wait for someone to knock at the door because they will never do that.

Believe that it is possible to get skills and don't believe that bullshit crap that women don't understand stuff.

Take initiative. Find out as much as you can about what is going on and then take initiative. I've stuck my neck out heaps and made things happen. Many times I've been aware that if I just sat back nothing would happen. Like my job in America – I was terrified talking to that guy at the conference, but without it, it never would have happened. Likewise with *Postcard from Tunis.* I came back from Cannes in February and I thought if I just sit back on the couch and do nothing it will never go anywhere, it will stay on my hard disk and it will never be anything more than that. I've worked my butt off to make sure that it gets known.

Don't let yourself be trivialised, have confidence in yourself, what you think, what you feel, what seems right, what doesn't seem right, what interests you, what doesn't interest you. You can work out what's out there and how you want and how you might engage with it. Believe that you can do it, that there is no innate thing in you that makes it any more difficult for you.

Take responsibility for yourself, which is something I was never trained to do.

CAROLYN REID

Carolyn grew up in Sydney and has an older brother and sister. Her father was a tradesman who had been interested in painting as a young man. Her mother did not have a career. She was the bright one of the family and her parents encouraged her to go to university. At school Carolyn loved science and was one of the only girls to do technical drawing and industrial arts. 'I've always liked to know why a piece of equipment does something so that I can find out why it won't do something I want it to.' At eighteen she did a panelbeating course at night and as a hobby she restores old cars. In her garage she has an award-winning sleek midnight blue 1968 Fiat 850 sports coupe which she rebuilt from a $300 unregistered wreck.

At the end of Year 11 she decided she was going to be an artist but her parents would not allow her to leave school unless she had a job with a future. So in the summer holidays she went through the Yellow Pages and spent six weeks knocking on 78 doors of agencies and art studios with a portfolio of drawings she had done at school. Finally one of them said they were impressed with the initiative that she had taken, and offered her a trainee position as a finish artist. She stayed there for two years and then decided she wanted to work in television.

Carolyn wrote off for any job in television and in her holidays she did work experience at Channel 10. Channel 7 finally rang and said they had an opening for a junior in the News Graphics Department, which she took. She was eighteen and the most junior in the five-person department but within a relatively short space of time she was doing graphics for the weekend news and carrying the same load as the senior designers, although she was still classed as the junior.

That was before computer graphics. 'We did it with colour bromide, Letraset, and airbrushing. Things that now take seconds on the Paintbox would take half an hour. I'm not that old but when I tell young people it sounds as though I was born in BC.'

In 1984 Channel 7 bought a Chyron MGM character generator which had multi-graphics mode. It was the year of the Los Angeles Olympics and she did all the graphics on the Chyron. 'I thought computer graphics was the way to go. I went to my boss and got all the records from the accountants on how much we were spending on consumable materials and made a case to show that if we bought a Paintbox, in two years it would pay for itself and be much faster. But Seven's attitude at the time was that it was just a passing phase.'

In 1985 Carolyn left Seven to do graphics for *Beyond 2000* which was just starting up after the ABC had axed *Towards 2000*. She got thrown in the deep end on an Image Artist, a cheap computer graphics system the ABC had bought – the only one in the country apart from the demonstration model.

> **I guess I am bold enough not to give a damn about whether it is acceptable for my gender to get involved with things. If I can do the job, whether it is spraying a car or whether it is making a commercial, or doing special effects, or running a department, I go in there, I know my job and I insist that I get treated properly.**

In the fifteen months she was at *Beyond* she averaged around 80 hours a week because she also became the demonstrator of the Image Artist in Australia. In July 1986 the British manufacturers came out to Australia with a new prototype. The general manager was so impressed with what Carolyn was doing with their 8-bit machine that they arranged for her to go to London to show others how to use it. 'They hadn't seen anyone push this thing that hard before so they said I had to come and work for them.'

She took her holidays from *Beyond 2000* and went to London, all expenses paid, to do demonstrations and teach and was offered a job. She came back home, left *Beyond,* packed up everything, but a week before she was due to leave they rang to say they had not organised the resident permit and it would take some weeks.

While she was waiting for her visa in late 1986 Channel 7 employed her to develop the graphics package for the Americas Cup and design the new package for the motor racing. Seven had ordered a Paintbox and the head of promotions approached her to reorganise the News Graphics Department and put it into the central technical area in order to make the resources available to the whole station.

Seven offered her a job as head of graphics which tripled her wages from eighteen months before when she had been a junior in News Graphics. She was now 22 and started working in the department but the formal announcement of her position and the restructuring was not forthcoming. 'There was a lot of backstabbing going on so I thought "Damn, if I am going to do this job I've got to get into it now. If I am not then I'm wasting my time here".' She went into the general manager's office and said 'You guys made me an offer, but nothing has been finalised. Either you want me or you don't. If you don't I'll go to London. If you want me let's make it official and get on with the job.' That afternoon a memo came out that clearly stated that she was now in control.

Her contract came up soon after Christopher Skase bought the Seven Network in 1988. The ATN heads of departments became network heads and she put a proposal to Channel 7 for integrating the network's graphics. 'They weren't interested so I decided to move on.'

In May 1989 she moved to Auckland New Zealand as head of graphics for the new TV3 network. The news director had worked with her at Channel 7. She had to design and set up a graphics department, find the people, hire them, train them and liaise with the building and engineering departments as well as designing the on air look of the station.

TV3 went into receivership so Carolyn worked on New Zealand's only Quantel Harry at Electric Pencil before coming back to Australia in mid-1990 to launch Harriet in Australia. As stations bought the machine she trained the people. 'I really had a very good lifestyle. I worked two to three days a week doing a vast variety of work. I met lots of people. I worked on a range of equipment – Harriet, HAL, Harry and Editbox. I was always given the latest toys, new software, I was out there to show it off and I had a very good income. I got to see the world on other people's money. It was great. Then I got convinced that I should settle down.'

After five years freelance in Australia, New Zealand and South East Asia she decided to buy her own equipment, and in 1994 she converted underneath her house into a suite and invested almost $300,000 in a Harriet and Betacam SP equipment. 'I realised it was going to be two to three years of real hard slog because it is a massive expenditure and it was all down to me to make it happen. There was the paperwork angle of running a company as well as actually getting the work and doing it. I knew it was going to be hard but I never realised it was going to be as hard as it has been. The price I have paid has been dearer than I ever imagined in terms of my time and my lifestyle.'

She got on the phone and rang six or seven hundred people in the Yellow Pages, the *Encore Directory* and *Production Book* and sent out hundreds of showreels. Since then her business has just grown through word of mouth and she has got corporate, commercial and broadcast clients. In 1997 she invested another $60,000 in two significant upgrades for Harriet-Express and Contour but she was not satisfied with the reliability of the system once the upgrades were fitted, returned them and had her money refunded in 1998. She then purchased another Harriet and in a week she had the money arranged, the machine installed at the rear of the main suite and linked it up to the SP gear and Harriet 1.

interview

HIGHLIGHTS

The day Harriet arrived in September '94 was a big highlight. It was a crazy four weeks between making the decision to buy a Harriet, paying the deposit, organising finance and getting quotes from builders to develop under the house. There was excavation and piers to be taken out, the whole place was just a normal under-your-house mess with a dirt floor and fibro walls. In three weeks the husband, the neighbours, father-in-law, all sorts of family members just pitched in so that Harriet had a home when it arrived three weeks later.

Landing the Head of Graphics position at Channel 7 because a 22 year old being given a position like that just blew me away. It was a big leap of faith. That position and the money and stuff was a direct result of the slog I had put in at *Beyond 2000* where I really gave up everything. But when Channel 7 recognised what I'd done and gave me such an awesome position it meant that all that hard work had been worth it and that was just so satisfying.

I was that brash. I look at it now and go 'how could I do that'. The politics were pretty nasty for quite some time. Because of my no-nonsense approach the general manager put me on an artificially high management level answerable only to him and the assistant general manager of the station which by-passed both middle and senior management. But I put in a lot of hours. The first three months after the announcement was made I think I took three days off in three months. It was a beautiful department, one of the best in the country. We had around five or six people, including me, and I'd do my shifts like everyone else and run the department. Like everything else, when I make a decision, I have a mission, I just forget everything and go for it. That's what is needed if you're going to get out in front of everyone else, it's what I did at *Beyond*, it's why I got the job at Seven.

I suppose flying to London was pretty exciting, too, my first overseas trip that was all paid for.

I've won various awards but at *Beyond* I won a certificate of special recognition for 'sustained effort under continual pressure of production'. That seems to sum up my whole career.

ISSUES FOR WOMEN

I had problems at Channel 7 but that was management. It would have been different if I had been a man. I was young, short, blond, female, and in 1987 there were no other women on senior management. I would hope the environment has changed by now. At that time it had always been Fairfax, the same old boys' network, and it was widely accepted that the political climate was not conducive to women in any position of authority.

There was backstabbing, very vehement objections and obstructions to what I was trying to do. I am sure if I had been a guy doing exactly the same thing you would get the old boys standing there in the executive washroom saying 'You see so and so, he's up and coming, he's direct, to the point, that kid is going places'. With me I am sure it was 'See that bitch upstart! What does that bimbo think she knows?'

I must admit I was politically inexperienced. Today, twelve years later, if I was placed in the same position with the same perceptions, I would probably be able to handle or manipulate the system and the situation more to my advantage. Certainly it became quite clear at the end that there were a lot of hidden agendas.

The problem was that the old boys network is more involved in playing games and fighting their little power struggles than making television, but I only realised that afterwards. I wasn't doing any of it for my own power and glory or to try and dominate other departments or get them under my control. I was just trying to get my job done and that's not the way you survive, particularly with my gender.

I am fairly blunt and to the point and when I think someone is an idiot and they are in my way and I have a job to do, even if I try to be fairly diplomatic about what I say, it seems to still come across that I think they are an idiot. I know my subject and if I knew what they were suggesting wouldn't work I'd tell them straight out. They didn't like the fact that I knew answers that they didn't. Had I been a man I am sure I would have been a network head.

I guess, also, that I haven't gone into 3D because of problems I had being a woman. I was doing a lot of freelance work with a guy who had a Harriet and he was fantastic but he was sharing an office with an architect who had a Silicon Graphics machine with Alias software. I'd been keen on trying 3D for quite some time and this guy had 3D for his architectural practice. I just thought 3D must be great because the only limit is your imagination.

I started training with him and learning a bit about it but then he stepped way, way, way out of line. It was an after hours incident, I probably should have called the police. I don't want to go into it but he was basically a slimy character. And it continued. I'd sit next to him at the machine and he'd rub up against me. If he wanted to show me something he'd grab my hand and use it to model with. Just constantly touching, sitting way too close. I told him to sit back and pushed him off but finally I couldn't even be in the same room as him because he just persisted. I guess that sort of soured the whole concept of 3D for me.

Lack of women in 3D animation

Guys are always encouraged to do more mathematical, mechanical things throughout their whole up-bringing and women aren't. It never worried me. I am not afraid of mechanical stuff, not afraid of computer stuff and I guess I am probably a bit fortunate that I've got the creative side as well as the technical and I like to use both.

General upbringing tells girls that when you get to 3D you're building models, you're building structures, it's not physically sawing bits of timber or welding metal, but you are constructing precise mechanical models. You have to do it with numbers and dimensions in your head, you have to build this shaped component which will then lead to that shaped component. It is very engineering based. In training men and women the guys tend to want to know the 'why' more than the women do.

I don't believe, apart from the sleaze bag, that I would have had a problem with 3D because I do work on real mechanical things and have a good understanding of perspective. I am looking to upgrade and if there are other areas where Harriet has application and 3D could be a supplement, then it could be added to the range of services that I offer. I haven't completely given up on it. I just got quite seriously turned off.

Sexist remarks

I think I tend to exude a 'don't mess with me' attitude. I have a strong level of self confidence so I've never projected myself as little girlie. I know my stuff and I expect to be treated accordingly. So whether it's clients trying to take advantage of the situation or bosses I think on the whole I put out this message that I'm not to be messed with.

Outside of my work I build cars and that is a place for a lot more sexism. I've taken on male dominated interests, not for any feminist reasons, but I just love cars and learnt how to fix them. You walk into a room and there are 35 guys and me to do panel beating and welding and you learn to deal with sexism. By the end of the year most of the guys had dropped out and I was still there and had good marks and I could panel beat and weld as well as any of them. The ones that remained just treated me like everyone else. But it was really daunting at first. That could be why I project myself as an equal. If a guy tries to mess with me, I have had the experience of being in a very male dominated field.

Guys like to test you. They would heckle when I was demonstrating. They will say 'Make it do this, can it do that, that and that'. I pride myself on not just knowing how to drive the gear but knowing it inside out. I would just do it quickly and put them back in their place because I know the boxes so well.

I guess I am bold enough not to give a damn about whether it is acceptable for my gender to get involved with things. If I can do the job, whether it is spraying a car or whether it is making a commercial, or doing special effects, or running a department, I go in there, I know my job and I insist that I get treated properly. I don't go in and say 'Oh it's a bit scary'.

Feeling vulnerable

I rarely feel vulnerable. Only when I am not 100 percent sure of the equipment. If I don't know that piece of equipment that's the only thing that shakes my level of confidence.

You always get difficult clients who want you to change the colour on layer one when you've dumped twenty layers on top. You learn to say 'Oh well they are paying for it' and get the job done.

Crying

Occasionally I cry with the stress of the job or not meeting a deadline. Sometimes after I have been working literally all night and several days, I'm pretty shaky about everything. I push myself very hard. Most weeks I do an all nighter. If something goes wrong, or I've made a mistake because I am just so overtired it can get to me.

THE FUTURE

I need to move the company to the next level so I am currently planning where I want to go and what I want to do for the next three to five years. Nothing remains the same for long in these high tech areas so you have got to be flexible when planning the future.

I doubt I will venture much more capital into equipment in the short term. I'd prefer to minimise the financial burden so that I can focus on the creative aspects of some of the new possibilities such as 3D and the internet. Harriet 2 came with Picture Port which enables me to take the graphics I've created on Paintbox and digitally convert and transfer them through my PC to the outside world. This has changed my approach even to TV work because I can email mockups to a client in full colour for approval and get immediate feedback and that speeds up the design process.

I am also harnessing the power of the Paintbox via Picture Port to build web sites. I really enjoy this relatively new field because it combines the creative with the technical and is a whole new challenge to come to grips with. It also makes good sense to maximise my existing equipment and get a foothold in the new media.

I'm also very keen to expand into other areas of production

including directing or producing. For me the challenge is in exploring these new areas, building on my previous experience, adding new skills and diversifying.

ADVICE

It doesn't hurt doing a graphic design course but I don't place a great deal of importance on that. I am more interested if you can do the job. I suppose I am walking proof that you don't need that bit of paper.

Beyond was probably my best training ground. It has been the basis for everything I've done since then. I had to teach myself the Image Artist because there was no-one else to show me and *Beyond* was expecting Paintbox quality. I had to work it really hard and to learn how it thinks and trick it into doing things that it normally would not do and the manufacturers said it wouldn't do.

I would suggest you get whatever computer graphics experience you can, even if that's a Mac or PC running Photoshop, which is probably all you can afford, but at least it shows that you can take a computer and do creative things on it. Although I wouldn't give anyone a job just based on work on this level of experience.

I've got to say the whole industry is sadly crying out for a better training structure for Paintbox. Some years ago when I was involved in training, Randwick Tech was the only teaching institution in Australia that had a Paintbox. And yet if you go anywhere, to any TV station or production house, you'll find a Quantel. You may also come across PCs or Macs and some Silicon Graphics, but the day-to-day bread and butter work in most places is on Quantel gear.

Young people approach me and ask how they can get experience and I have rung up Randwick Tech and tried to find out the courses that they teach the Paintbox in and they just say 'Oh, Paintbox. It's just there if students want to use it'. They've been given my name by Quantel as a guest lecturer but they have never followed it up.

You have to find ways of getting onto a Paintbox and learn everything you can and you'll get a job. There are just not enough trained people out there.

You could get any sort of video tape ops job and then suss out the graphics and play with the equipment. Whether you end up on Paintbox or not, general production knowledge is never wasted.

The lady who is now running Channel 7 graphics was a character generator operator in the newsroom. She had no design experience at all and no formal training but she had a good eye. Most people come in as designers and teach themselves the gear. This girl learnt the gear and we taught her the design and she is still there, twelve years later, running the department.

You have to be interested in the technical side and that is something that the girls don't manage awfully well. I've taken traditional TV designers and tried to teach them Paintbox or Harriet and the technical implications and some of them just never fully understand why rules exist. A lot of women don't. I think the reason I was able to get above all that is that I have a bit of a passion for the technical side. I'll read through manuals and technical papers and even if I don't understand everything I like investigating that side.

KIT DEVINE

Kit was the second eldest of four children (boy, girl, boy, girl). She grew up in England and her parents were equally encouraging of all their children. Her father is a businessman, her mother an historian and her godmother an artist. She initially wanted to be a pilot and concentrated on science subjects at school but she was shortsighted and therefore could not pursue it. She thought about aeronautical engineering but decided on something completely different.

She had always drawn and painted in her spare time so decided to go to art college instead. She discovered during the last year of her BA Hons in graphic design at London's Raversbourne College of Art and Design that the following year would be the first to use computers. 'I felt a bit like the dinosaur watching the asteroid hurtle towards me.'

In 1985 she did an MSc in Computer Science at Hatfield Polytechnic just outside London. The course was the first and supposed to be an introduction to computing for people from non-science backgrounds. 'It was far more technical than it needed to be – you don't need a degree in advanced engineering to drive a car.'

She visited Australia in 1986, liked it, and emigrated. Despite having degrees in graphic design and computer science she had no work experience but on the first day she looked in the paper there was an ad for a graphic designer with computer skills. She got the job and went to work as an interface designer for a company building a transputer-based machine which was to consist of a 2D paint package, a 3D animation and rendering system and a video editing system all in the one box. After a year she realised that the project was over-ambitious and unlikely to succeed and left. She went to several headhunters and told them 'Find me a job anywhere in computing' and one of them came back with an interview at XYZap for the position of trainee animator. Although initially unsure she decided to accept on a three-month trial and has never looked back.

XYZap had in-house software which did everything. The only other large 3D company in Sydney at the time was The Video Paintbrush Company which used Wavefront software.

After three years at XYZap she returned to the UK to work at Rushes for two years, a large post production facility in Soho. There she used SoftImage software. In 1992 she returned to Sydney and worked at Animal Logic for two years, again using SoftImage. Since 1994 she has been at Garner MacLennan and has switched to Alias software.

interview

HIGHLIGHTS

It's all just been one big highlight. The two years in London was pretty good for name-dropping sort of stuff. I worked at a very good company, Rushes, I did a shoot for Mick Jagger – one of his pop promos – and I was sent to LA for three weeks to work on the movie with Supermario Brothers to do morphing. You get a car, they fly you there and back first class, it's all that kind of stuff.

There are a couple of jobs I've done which I think are really nice. I particularly enjoyed working on the Sub Zero ad I did about four years ago. It looks beautiful. The look of it was more a piece of art really. You do an awful lot of ads for washing-up liquid and Protein B Plus sinking into hair roots and stuff like that.

I often compare it to being a pilot. When you learn to be a pilot you get your wings and you work your way up to captain and then you fly a plane for the next twenty years and you get more and more experience as captain. In twenty years time you will still just be a captain but you will be incredibly experienced. Getting to be captain is not considered reaching the pinnacle of a career, you have just started.

I have spoken to animators who feel that after twenty years of animation they are just getting to feel that they are quite good at it.

▸ You're constantly learning stuff, software is constantly being updated, you are constantly getting new releases. Every job is different. It is like being a carpenter. One day someone wants a beautiful boardroom table and the next day someone wants shelves in their kitchen or a little bedside table or a beautiful inlaid cabinet'.

After ten years I feel I am just beginning to get a handle on things. I feel that I am just going to go on amassing experience. Every year the programs get new releases and each new release has all these added features. I have been using Alias for nearly three years now and I probably know half the package well and half I can get my way round.

You're constantly learning stuff. Every job is different. It is like being a carpenter. One day someone wants a beautiful boardroom table and the next day someone wants shelves in their kitchen or a little bedside table or a beautiful inlaid cabinet.

In one week I might be working with five people on something and then the next week I might be working by myself doing a logo flip and then the week after that I might be working with one other person doing a morph. It changes. I might be supervising one week, I might not the next week.

Everything we do isn't ground-breaking. Every job you do isn't cutting edge, it is bread and butter work. Normally you sit down with a director and a producer and go through the storyboard and then you work out how long you think it is going to take. Then you quote on that basis. Again it varies from job to job. Sometimes you make a model before the job starts. With the Dr Peppers job where the Statue of Liberty walks into Sydney Harbour we had two or three weeks lead time where we got the model, put the skeleton in it, walked it around, put a bit of texture on it then the live action came in and we had three weeks to do all the animation with the live action.

Projects don't tend to go more than about eight weeks, or less than four to five days. Here we tend to do the high-end jobs, the eight week jobs – Dr Peppers, Nutrigrain, Reeboks. For Reeboks we had two skeletons playing basketball. We had to animate the skeletons and match them to the live action. That was huge.

I like variety. If I've been doing Vita Brits for three weeks, after three weeks I hate them, if I've been doing animating for three weeks then I'm looking forward to working on something else. I'm a jack of all trades. We all are. But some people particularly enjoy lighting, some people enjoy animating, others are particularly good at modelling. Jobs are allocated on availability and strengths and weaknesses.

I'd hate to get stuck doing one thing. Working in the US on a movie they have these huge big production houses and you are either a model maker or an animator or doing lighting and that's all you do. There is much more of a production line. A lot of people have this dream of Hollywood but I think a lot of it could be like an inbetweener in Disney. It is fairly soul destroying work. There were horror stories on *Dantes Peak*. There was one animator who had to do a lava flow and he ended up spending thirteen weeks animating it before the director was happy. So every day he'd sit down and he'd do the same lava flow but slightly differently and every day the director would walk in and say 'No, that's not quite right'. At least when I do a commercial six weeks later it is gone. I just can't imagine what it would be like to animate the same thing over and over again.

LACK OF WOMEN IN 3D ANIMATION

There are a lot more women Paintbox operators than there are 3D operators because if you have messed around with art you have always painted. So to go from painting in real life to a paint package is very easy for anyone. Not many people do major sculpture. There are maybe five thousand jobs in Sydney for Paintbox style programs and there's maybe thirty people doing 3D animation. So most people don't have access to the equipment and to the programs. There wouldn't be much gender difference if people did have access to the equipment.

Obviously when it is an emerging field very few people get into it so it is just those who happen to fall into situations. Because of the technical side, it has tended to be more male dominated. There just happens to be more men working in that area.

I had an arts background and a science background which is very unusual in anyone, male or female. So they figured I was a better bet to train up than someone with just an arts background or just a science background. Particularly at that stage, because the equipment was fairly technical. But not anymore. It's user-friendly compared to what I've worked with in the past.

I used to write programs so that if you wanted to make a chair leg you'd write a program that would make a square and then you'd push it to give you a chair leg. If you wanted something typed you would have to digitalise it. Now there are type libraries that you just pull in and you can alter them and it is very easy.

When I was first working at Zap we had one set of programs we'd use to model with and then we would go over to another machine to do the choreography and then you'd go to a third machine to render it out and then you have to record it onto film before you could see it. Now we have one package which does it all.

I would call myself a second or third generation animator, second in Australia, third in the US. Each generation is every three or four years. The industry got started in the US in the late '70s or early '80s.

In the early days you were a bit tied to your software package but once you've got a good enough show reel you can get a job somewhere else. I got a job here not knowing Alias and they trained me up.

I think that one of the things which may keep women out of the field a lot is the demands of the industry. Maybe 80 percent of the time you are working 9-5 but every so often because of deadlines and stuff, you have to work ten, twelve, sixteen hour days to finish a job. It is not very conducive to people who are married with children. Most women in this industry are single.

ISSUES FOR WOMEN

I've worked in Australia and overseas and wherever I go I have never had a problem. I think there is discrimination but I have never come across it and I've worked at a few different places. I am out and gay and that has not been a problem either.

I think it is a personality thing. I think that some people who have had problems think that it is because they are women but I think that it is because they have a personality clash with the people they are working with.

ADVICE

Get a good showreel. Go to art school and do graphic design. Go to the AFTRS or somewhere where they do have equipment, use it, make a short film and take it around and if you're any good someone will give you a job.

There are several good 3D animation packages – Alias, Waveform, SoftImage, Houdini, Lightwave, 3D Studio Max – and some of those work on PCs. 3D Studio Max and Lightwave are PC packages. They are not all that expensive and a lot of people have 3D Studio Max on their PCs.

Someone who wants to be a racing driver doesn't just go out and become a Formula One driver, you work your way up. You learn to drive a car and then you start driving cars at the lower end of the racing cars and then when you've proved you're a good driver you get a fast machine.

Access to the equipment is just as hard for the boys. The big difference now is that you can get lots of packages that sit on home computers and girls increasingly have just as much access to home computers as boys do. So if you are interested you sit down there and you do it.

I think you can make broad generalisations. You can say generally boys tend to go for the more technical things and girls don't but it doesn't mean that all boys are interested in technical things and all girls aren't. Boys tend to sit down and make space ships and girls don't. But girls are sitting down and making Barbie clothes, now that's 3D.

I think it is an advantage to have physics and some maths. There is an awful lot of stuff that you might be doing, real world phenomena, things like snow and clouds and water, and I've found a physics background is really useful.

Anatomy would be good. That's where my art school training has really helped. I also did martial arts for five years and that's about how bodies work and how bones and muscles work, which has been useful.

But an awful lot of people who go into animation come from a music background. None of the people I work with did computer design at college because there weren't college courses. They got into it the same way I did, stumbled along and ended up there and they have come from all sorts of varied backgrounds.

LYNNE CARTWRIGHT

Lynne did a degree in visual communication at Sydney College of the Arts, now the University of Technology Sydney (UTS). It was the very first year of the college in the early '80s. Lynne is an only child who was brought up to have a profession. Her mother has a PhD in pharmacy and has worked all her life but Lynne followed in her father's footsteps; he was a technical director in television.

Her first job was at the ABC as a graphic designer, where she worked with paint and paper and did cell animation. She stayed for seven years. While she was at the ABC they installed a Paintbox which she learnt and then went to the production house Video Paintbox. There she worked on a Harry and Paintbox as a graphic designer. At Video Paintbox she was also an animation supervisor and did storyboarding for 3D. She went freelance and was doing a lot of work as animation supervisor for Bobdog Inc and they said 'Why don't you learn it yourself'. So she worked out a deal where they put her on a retainer while she was training and in return she did work for them. Two years later she was involved in the formation of Animal Logic.

Now she comes and goes at Animal Logic. She has worked overseas, taught at the AFTRS and freelanced at the ABC. She wants to concentrate on 3D film work and that means she could go anywhere for long periods of time, from three months to two years.

She worked in New Zealand on a Hollywood funded film with 35 other people who were all working on computers. She was brought in specifically to do character animation.

interview

CAREER GOALS

Working in films doing visual effects supervising or animation supervising, which is what I have been doing on commercials for some time. I've been moving back into film which is where I wanted to go right from the very beginning. I got side-tracked into commercials but they have been a great way to gain experience.

The attraction of 3D is that I can animate, make things move, which is what I like to do. Paintbox and Harry are more about compositing and it is a very different way of making things move. In 3D I can do character animation.

I found some aspects were very easy. I just couldn't believe how quickly I picked some things up and how difficult other things were. I found the skills I had as a graphic designer and an animator were very valuable in doing 3D. I use SoftImage these days. I have tried doing a bit of everything but it doesn't really work.

I'm a character animator and do modelling and animation. I can also texture and light. On big overseas jobs I just do modelling and animation and work with someone else who does the lighting and texturing. On small jobs in Australia you do a bit of everything.

My big dilemma at the moment is whether I make the big move overseas or not. I am still trying to work out whether it is worth sticking out here to see what happens in film. I've put off the decision for years and I think I am going to have to make it now.

The film work is in the US. The Australian film industry hasn't had the budgets but it's beginning to change.

We are getting work here shot in the US. Not the whole film. Most films are sent out to more than one shop, they send out different effects to different people. It's a global village these days. We send stuff across the net for approvals and it's not such a big deal for a director to get something in the US and do a conference call and talk about it. When video conferencing starts in Australia it will be even easier. I hope there will be more digital effects in Australia.

LACK OF WOMEN IN 3D ANIMATION

I really have no idea why there's so few. I guess they're just not as exposed to it. It's a very new industry. I was the first person that I am aware of in Australia who didn't come from a programming background, who made the switch from a creative background. Prior to that the technology had been inaccessible to creatives, it didn't matter what sex.

SoftImage was the program that actually started to become user friendly and accessible to creatives. It enabled animators in Australia to work on the computers. In America traditional animators had already started working in 3D but they had been working with programmers and had special programs written. SoftImage is probably twelve years old here now.

I guess it has a computer nerd image about it and that is male. I was always interested in all the things that were associated with being a 'computer nerd', like computer games and science. Men come from programming and from art. You can't generalise but the ones who come from a computer programming background may be more into the texturing and lighting and the ones who come from design or art school get more into animation and modelling. But I can also think of half a dozen exceptions.

ADVICE

You have to have a sense of humour and be interested in films or videos or commercials or the area you want to work in.

I think art school is useful no

▶▶ **We are getting work here shot in the US. Not the whole film. Most films are sent out to more than one shop, they send out different effects to different people. It's a global village these days. We send stuff across the net for approvals and it's not such a big deal for a director to get something in the US and do a conference call and talk about it.**

matter what area you get into. I think you have to have a course behind you these days. The days when you could just get in and get a job are pretty much over. Some people have done different sorts of courses and done things on their home computer.

It is more important to have the design degree or the animation experience because you can teach anyone a piece of equipment. The harder part is getting the production skills, working in a team, all that sort of thing.

The problem with courses is that there are so few that have the expensive equipment. There was a course out at the film school [AFTRS] but that was only three months and I am not convinced that three months is really worthwhile when you consider that in Europe they have courses that go for years. Also how do you access the equipment after the course?

I still think that the apprentice system is the best way to work if you can get yourself attached to a company as a trainee. I don't mean straight out of school, I mean someone who has already got some skills. Animal Logic trains people but the industry is not all that big. It is such expensive equipment that you really have to be under the umbrella of a company to be able to hone your skills.

[In 1998 the AFTRS commenced a twelve month MA with the opportunity to extend another twelve months to an MA Hons.]

DIRECTING

The job of director is seen as a glamour creative job. It does not involve handling equipment but as director you are finally responsible for what the audience sees and the job of the crew is to help you achieve your vision. It is a very powerful position.

Between the '30s and the late '70s in Australia there were no women directors. Since the renaissance of the Australian film industry in the '70s and the establishment of formal training, in particular the AFTRS and the Film and Television Department at Swinburne – now the Victoria College of the Arts (VCA) – this has begun to change. Women have been given the freedom and found the confidence to experiment – and to make mistakes – in less threatening environments. The institutions have also been made acutely aware over the years of the need to encourage women applicants and, as a result, Australia leads the world in the number and quality of its women film directors.

Young women who now aspire to a directing career have inspiring role models – Gillian Armstrong, who led the way in the '70s; Jane Campion, Di Drew, Nadia Tass, Jackie McKimmie, Ann Turner, who got their opportunities in the '80s; Jocelyn Moorhouse, Kathy Mueller, Pauline Chan, Shirley Barrett, Samantha Lang, Emma Kate Croghan, Ana Kokkinos, Rachel Perkins, who have come forward in the '90s.

Between 1990 and 1997, seventeen percent of Australian feature films were directed by women. Given that it was 1978 when Gillian Armstrong emerged as the first woman feature director in 50 years, this is significant progress.

FEATURE FILMS

Directing a feature film is the pinnacle of most directors'

ambitions. It has the glamour and it is the most responsible of directing jobs because it is dealing with big budget productions. A film is the director's vision. It is the director who translates the script onto the screen. A producer has usually persuaded investors to put money into a film because the script is good, the lead actors are known and they have confidence that the director will translate this potential into a film which will meet their artistic and commercial expectations. The investors will therefore want to know who the director is before they invest.

Some women complain that men with far less experience than they have are given opportunities to direct features. There are stories of investors threatening to pull out if the film is to be directed by a woman. In one instance, Mandy Smith had already directed a feature and many television dramas yet she was told that two financiers knocked her out of a miniseries because they would not trust 'a girl' (p320).

The director works with the producer and production manager in pre-production – casting the actors, choosing the heads of departments (design, camera, sound, and editing) and deciding on locations. During production she is responsible for what images and sounds go onto the film. She works with the first assistant director who is responsible for keeping to the production schedule so that the budget does not blow out, and ensuring that the actors and the crew are ready. She works with the heads of departments and particularly with the director of photography (DOP), to ensure that the look of the film is her vision. In post production she works with the picture editor, the composer and the sound editor and directs any post recording dialogue with the actors and also the final sound mix. She then delivers, with the producer, the final film which should look and sound like the script that the investors put their money into.

It is a very demanding and often stressful job. In the production phase the director will be working with the actors and the crew which could be anything from fifteen to over fifty, mainly men. Apart from the film craft positions, men work on set-building, transport, lights, special effects and stunts – all traditionally male jobs. Everyone assembles on a daily basis according to the production schedule specifically to film the shots the director requires. Her immediate colleagues are the first assistant director (1st AD) and the DOP.

The shoot may be anything from six to ten weeks or more and in different locations where everyone works, eats and lives together. Each decision that the director makes throughout the day affects the way the shoot progresses. A production crew on location is like a small army with all the attendant problems of feeding, moving, accommodation, the unreliability of the weather and the potential for personality clashes and strife if things go wrong.

Some male feature film directors come from jobs where they operate equipment – such as camera and editing – often via directing for television. Others, however, come from jobs that do not require the operation of equipment, such as 1st ADs, producers, and production managers and occasionally writers and actors. Because the 1st AD is the person responsible for giving the director's orders to the predominantly male crew there are very few female 1st ADs. Women who are producers, production managers, writers and actors, and who aspire to direct, have generally not been given the same opportunities on the job as men, with the result that there are many fewer women feature film directors.

Whenever one makes this statement the names of the high profile women directors are put forward to refute it. The point is, however, that these women have been successful despite the narrower career options open to them: most of these women learnt to direct at a film school which is where they got the experience and confidence that the men could get on the job in crew positions. Also many of them have written their own films and used that as leverage to get a directing job.

ROLE MODELS

I have selected two women representing two different career paths.

Gillian Armstrong is a true pioneer and a legend for women directors. She was the first woman for over 50 years to direct a feature film, *My Brilliant Career* (1978), which won seven AFI awards including best director and best film. It also started Judy Davis's career.

She has gone on to make her mark with films about unusual women facing gruelling tests of one kind or another. *Mrs Soffel* (1984), her first Hollywood film, *High Tide* (1987) which won the best film award from the Houston Film Festival and the Grand Prix from the International de Creteil, *The Last Days of Chez Nous* (1992) which was nominated for eleven AFI awards including best film and best director, and *Little Women* (1994), which had both critical and box office success and garnered Oscar nominations for best actress (Winona Ryder), best costume design, best original score.

Gillian has also produced a series of documentaries on teenage girls coming of age in Adelaide. The latest, *Not Fourteen Again* (1996), won the AFI best documentary award.

Gillian's most recent film is *Oscar and Lucinda* (1997), an adaptation by Laura Jones of Peter Carey's Booker Prize-winning novel.

Gillian is regarded in both Hollywood and Australia as a trail-blazer for women. She has been awarded an AM for services to the Australian film industry and the Hollywood Crystal Award for women in film.

Her reputation is that of a director with artistic instincts and vision. Kevin Thomas of the *Los Angeles Times* said in his review of *Little Women* that the film says 'a great deal about Gillian Armstrong's own character and integrity as an artist. As she has proceeded from one distinctive accomplishment to the next, alternating between America and her homeland, Armstrong has remained uncompromised'.

Jackie McKimmie works from Brisbane and came to directing through writing. She is one of the few feature directors who has managed to maintain a career not living in Sydney or Melbourne. She did not go to a film school but mainly writes her own material and used that as leverage to direct her first feature film. She wrote and directed *Stations* (1983) which won the Greater Union best short film award at the Sydney Film Festival in 1983 and went on to win best short film in festivals in the UK and Italy. She wrote and directed *Australian Dream* (1987) which was screened at festivals in Berlin, Italy and Spain and *Waiting* (1990) which got a commendation at the Edinburgh Film Festival and won an AFI best supporting actress award and best actress award at the San Sebastian Film Festival. She directed *Breaking Through* (1990) which won the best documentary award by the Human Rights Commission in 1990 and produced and directed *No Problems* (1989) which won the Dendy award for best documentary in 1990. She has written *Hair Like a Film Star* which she plans to direct in 1999.

Jackie is also a theatre director in Brisbane and has directed several of Nick Enright's plays and a circus theatre fusion. As well, she script edits SBS and ABC productions.

Both women have managed to have children and maintain a directing career.

GILLIAN ARMSTRONG

Gillian has an older sister and younger brother, and went to Vermont High School in Melbourne. Her parents were very supportive, considering their daughters' careers to be as important as their son's.

Drama and literature were her main interests and she thought she might like to be a set and costume designer. In 1968 she enrolled in Swinburne Art School to study design and was attracted to making films.

When she had completed the Swinburne course, Gillian moved to Sydney and eventually began work as an assistant editor in a production house specialising in commercials and documentaries. A year later, in 1972, she decided to apply for the first full-time course run by the newly established Australian Film and Television School (AFTS – now AFTRS). She was one of two women among the first twelve students accepted to study directing.

At the AFTS she made three short films: *Gretel, Satdee Night* and *One Hundred a Day*, the latter winning three AFI awards. Following graduation, Gillian worked as art director on *Promised Woman* (1974) and as props assistant for Margaret Fink, who produced *The Removalist* (1974). Margaret Fink had liked *One Hundred a Day* and she gave Gillian a copy of the Miles Franklin book *My Brilliant Career*.

In 1974 Gillian and Phillip Noyce, who had studied with her at the AFTS, were invited to take a package of their final student films to a festival in France. It was her first overseas trip and, while travelling, she realised how lucky Australian filmmakers were, having access to government investment funds. On her return to

Australia she applied to the Experimental Film Fund and received a grant to direct *The Singer and the Dancer* (1975), which won the Greater Union award for best fiction film.

At this stage, Penny Chapman invited Gillian to join the Women's Film Unit at the South Australian Film Commission. She was assigned to direct *Smokes and Lollies* (1975). 'The whole idea was to give a lot of women a break and they chose me to do the one about what it was like to be fourteen. I think they thought that I looked so young I would blend in with the fourteen-year-olds'. This project later developed into a series, with sequels in 1980 (*Fourteen's Good, Eighteen's Better*), 1988 (*Bingo, Braces and Bridesmaids*) and 1996 (*Not Fourteen Again*).

Gillian then worked with Errol Sullivan developing *Cathy's Child* and with Margaret Fink and Eleanor Whitcombe developing *My Brilliant Career*, which took four years to be funded. She had to choose between the two and finally decided on *My Brilliant Career*. This was Gillian's first feature and it won seven AFI awards and was selected for competition at the Cannes Film Festival.

Following this success, Gillian was invited to Hollywood to develop feature films but chose to return to Australia where, in 1982, she directed *Starstruck*.

In 1984 she directed *Mrs Soffel*, produced by Edgar Scherick and starring Diane Keaton and Mel Gibson. Gillian worked with screenwriter Ron Nyswaner for over a year before agreeing to direct *Mrs Soffel*, her first Hollywood feature. Working with her on the film were DOP Russell Boyd, who had shot *Starstruck*, editor Nick Beauman and designer Lucia Arrighi, both of whom Gillian had worked with on *Starstruck* and *My Brilliant Career*.

In 1985, the year in which she had her first child, Gillian planned to take a year's break but nevertheless made a community service announcement for the Decade of Women. In 1986 she directed a Home Box Office special on Bob Dylan, *Hard to Handle*.

High Tide followed, in 1987, and between 1989 and 1991, following the birth of her second daughter, Gillian made *Fires Within* and *Last Days of Chez Nous*.

In 1994 Gillian went back to Hollywood to make *Little Women*, with producer Denise di Novi. She took with her three of the crew from *The Last Days of Chez Nous*: Mark Turnbull, 1st AD, Nick Beauman, editor, and Geoff Simpson, DOP. In 1997 Gillian directed *Oscar and Lucinda* again using the same three key crew members. This time Robin Dalton and Timothy White were the producers.

interview

GETTING STARTED

I had a very supportive family and was encouraged at home to excel in what I was good at, and was applauded when I got into art school in Melbourne. I also think that it was very lucky that I chose an art school for my tertiary education because you were pushed as an individual to find yourself, your art and your creativity. The teachers were more broad-minded and there was much less sexism, I think, than there was in other sorts of courses at the same time. The girls and boys were never treated any differently.

I loved theatre and literature and I also liked to draw. I thought maybe I could design sets or costumes, so I went into the film course as a total innocent because that was the only place I could do production design. I started to learn about film in a nurturing environment. It wasn't until third year, when the course was trying to be more professional, so brought in a some real filmmakers as lecturers, that the girls first came up against some sexism, and it was sort of puzzling.

There were all these boys who immediately got the hang of how to use the cameras and so on. The other two girls – there were only three of us among the 30 students – started talking to each other and said 'Let's do our projects on our own... let's get a camera out on our own because we won't feel embarrassed about asking stupid questions'. We took the cameras home ourselves and worked out how to use them.

It's interesting, because later the Sydney Women's Film Group was set up and women were encouraged to work on all-female crews to gain self-confidence in technical areas. We did that naturally. We realised that the boys were taking over, they were more technically competent and we were embarrassed at showing how stupid we were at picking up the technical side of things.

The point is that I was slow to be technically competent, but I was lucky that I was in an artistic environment and I learnt about film where it was thought of as a means of creative expression and storytelling. It took me a long time to finally get the hang of it. But studying photography was a great help and ultimately it is your ideas that matter.

I didn't leave Swinburne wanting to be a director. I just thought if I could get a job in ABC Drama just holding a script, and be with actors, that would just be fabulous. I could earn a living and then somehow I could make little films that were mine.

The ABC, Film Australia and Crawfords were the only places to get a job. I didn't write to Crawfords because I was a bit of a snob, I was hoping to work with more serious drama. I did write, as the boys did, to the ABC and Film Australia. The ABC wrote back and asked for my typing speeds. I suppose I could have gone out and done a typing course and got in but I did have a certain pride. I had made a short film and I was hurt at that reaction when all the boys got interviews for floor managing, camera assistants, sound editing and so on. I didn't hear at all from Film Australia,

> ▸ **Denise di Novi [producer, *Little Women*] says that the women directors she's worked with are always the most organised and professional. Because for women to succeed in a male-dominated industry you have to try to be better. You have to be more prepared, more aware of everything and more focused and in control. Especially if it's your first film.**

which was then the Commonwealth Film Unit.

I finally decided that I would move to Sydney. Swinburne had a bad reputation in Melbourne because everyone thought 'Oh, these over educated arty young people are full of themselves and they don't want to do menial tasks' which was only partly true.

I got an interview at *Spyforce* with Tim Read and I went up to Narrabeen to try out for continuity. They put me on for half a day to train with the staff continuity person who didn't really want another young woman in the industry. I asked one question and she bit my head off. However, I mentioned to Tim that I had made *The Roof Needs Mowing* at Swinburne and he suggested that they screen it at lunchtime for the editors – amongst them were Sara Bennett and Lindsay Frazer. No-one was making short films at this time and there were no film students and so I was really quite a novelty. Someone said 'Don't go into continuity, you've got creative talent, go into editing'. In retrospect, this was the best advice anyone could have given me because there has traditionally been a block about script assistants going on to directing. Which is stupid because, when you think about it, it's a great place to really learn about directing, on the floor.

Now I was focused and I was asking for assistant editing work. It took me five months to get a job and I wrote hundreds of letters. I was a waitress and I thought 'I've got no qualifications'. I didn't type and hadn't ever even answered a phone system. By this time all my high principles about never working in advertising had gone. I was happy to do anything at all.

I went for one interview in a film production house to be on the desk and help out in the editing room but they decided that I didn't look sophisticated enough to go on the desk. A very kind lady pulled me aside and told me to put my hair up for my next interview!

I got really desperate because no-one was answering letters. So I started writing funny letters and I wrote them on brown paper which, at that time, nobody did. I cut up brown paper and said 'Save me from the dim sim shop'. Nick Beauman, who has ended up as my main film editor, wrote back and said that at Spectrum

Post Production they would often hear of work and I should ring him and 'PS I love the paper'.

I did ring him every two weeks and then one day I got home to my little flat and there was a guy outside – I probably didn't have the phone on – saying 'We are looking for an assistant editor and Nick Beauman recommended you. Can you start tomorrow?' That was at Kingcroft Productions.

They thought that I'd worked with Nick, when I had only ever rung him. But I could quite honestly say that I'd worked for Fred Schepisi because I did, straight after I graduated. I made tea and coffee on his film *Libido*.

I confided to the lady at the 729 Club where I was waitressing, hoping to be close to show business, that I had been offered a job and she said to me, 'Well don't tell them you haven't done it before'. So that was the next thing I learnt.

When I got there I thought, 'Oh my God, a Moviola. I've never worked one in my life'. Luckily the projectionist used to come in and watch me edit and he taught me how to lace it up. They made commercials and documentaries and they were encouraging. Bill Stacey, the editor, was a born teacher. He loved to teach. I was very lucky because that first job is so important. I had friends who went into production companies where mean games were played on them.

The year that I was in Sydney working in the 'real world' was a great awakening. I suddenly realised that there are many people who are working in film as a job who are actually not interested in film and many who rarely have a chance to work on something they really care about or are committed to and it made me really think. Also, I found that I was unhappy to be inside in the dark all the time, so I decided that I didn't want to be in an editing room all my life and that I really wanted to get into drama. That is when I saw the ad for the new film school.

By now I regretted the time that I had wasted at Swinburne. I realised how lucky we had been to have that creative time. It was the great awakening of experience in the real working world.

I went to the interview for the film school knowing that I wanted to learn about working with actors, and I wanted to be the prime creator. I wanted it to be my film. It was a wonderful year. When I finished at the film school I was making short films and working on other people's features, and then I made my first longer film, *The Singer and the Dancer*, which was put together with Steve Wallace's film *Love Letters from Taralba Road* and got a successful small release. Despite the success of both films I realised that you can't really make a living from short films.

I was trying to do art department jobs in between making the films I wanted to make, and I realised that I had to find a way to make the films I want to make and make it my living. So I am going to have to make features. I didn't have this burning ambition. Coming from an art school background it took me a long while to move from the concept of filmmaker to film director.

There is a fallacy that has grown up that I only got my break with a woman producer, but actually I almost did *Cathy's Child* for Errol Sullivan as my first film. Finally I had to decide between the two and decided that a woman had to direct *My Brilliant Career* because the men who read it never understood Sybylla, the main character. There was always a male vision: she was unhappy because she couldn't get a man, or because she was ugly. I thought I can never let that happen. A woman should direct it and I am the only one around at the moment.

I was never really a documentary filmmaker. *Smokes and Lollies* was my first job as a paid director and I was thrilled to get it – and then it became a personal quest to follow the same people over time. I think documentary filmmaking is very, very hard. It doesn't completely suit my personality. I like to control my film visually and you don't have that control in documentary; you are in the hands of whoever is shooting. It is also morally tough for me invading real people's lives.

I actually think it is easier for me to recreate through fiction than to try to capture reality and to tell a true story. My interest has always been in storytelling and the power of the image. I love to create a world and bring the characters alive. That's a real buzz for me, and that's fiction filmmaking.

As a director, I always did my homework and prepared. I knew about the script, the locations, and had worked closely with the DOP and first assistant before shooting. I would recommend that to anybody going out to do their first film. You'll be in a situation with people asking a million questions and I always found that my safety blanket was to really think something out – have a structure in your head even if you change it on the day. Denise di Novi [producer, *Little Women*] says that the women directors she's worked with are always the most organised and professional. Because for women to succeed in a male-dominated industry you have to try to be better. You have to be more prepared, more aware of everything and more focused and in control. Especially if it's your first film.

What I really learnt on *My Brilliant Career* is that you mustn't worry about failing. I had Don McAlpine [DOP] say, driving out to the set, 'Do you know that this is the highest budget for a first-time filmmaker in Australia?'. The key thing was not to worry because I could have totally freaked out. I just had to do my best every day and hopefully make a good film. I knew that I was being watched and if the film failed it might have been quite a few more years before another woman got a break, because there was this whole thing of 'can a woman do it?'.

People were sticking their heads around the cutting room door saying to Nick Beauman, 'Does it cut together', like I was a total fool or something. Or Margaret Fink and I must be on together – we had to be lesbians for women to work together. What I learnt was that I had to block it out and get on with it.

Another lesson I learned was on *One Hundred a Day*. I was trying to explain to the cinematographer what I wanted and he wasn't quite understanding. I was about to say 'It doesn't matter, I'll just shoot a wide shot' and Adrienne Read, who was my script assistant, pulled me aside and said 'You know what you want. Get what you want'. She had seen my shots. I thought, 'Yes, she's right; I should try and see how my shots cut together and if they fail, they fail. At least I'll learn'.

On *My Brilliant Career* the focus puller tried to pull a joke on me when I was setting up my shots, saying I had to name the lens and mark a cross where the camera had to be. But actually my photographic training meant that I had learnt about the effect of the frame and about various lenses. I was always able to visualise how I wanted things. I was never in a position on set where I didn't really know what I wanted to do, even if I didn't always have the exact lens size.

In those days I had a theory about men over 40. I felt that they were just so entrenched in their sexism and how they treat women that they were best to be avoided. But then my producer Edgar Scherick was in his 60s when we did *Mrs Soffel* and I had to confess to him, 'Edgar, I'm very worried about having you as a producer because I have an in-built rule that I shouldn't work with men over 40. He disproved my theory. He was just fantastic. He is now in his 70s and still laughs about how Gill said she wouldn't work with a man over 40. But he was a very special exception.

I do think you see mediocre male directors go on and on, but it is much harder for a woman to continue if her second film fails.

HAVING CHILDREN

I had never thought about having children. I'd never really been interested in them. But Margaret Fink was very influential. She was a very close friend of Germaine Greer and I remember her patting my hand and saying, 'You are going to have children, aren't you? You are not going to end up like Germaine who has fretted all her life'. Germaine's *The Female Eunuch* had been a pivotal thing in my growth and it was a big shock to actually hear that.

So when I was in Canada making *Mrs Soffel* I was in my early 30s and your biological clock starts ticking. I thought, 'Well, if I'm going to have children I should do this now'. So I did.

I thought I'd take a year off with my first baby and try and plan a film to do in Australia and see how it went. So I developed the script of *High Tide* with Laura Jones and Sandra Levy, who was the producer. When we were on location I took a nanny. I put that in the deal, which is something that women have to do if they've got children. It was Fred Schepisi who told me to ask for a nanny. He had already done that as a male foreign director in America.

The women producers I worked with after I had children [*High Tide* with Sandra Levy, *The Last Days of Chez Nous* with Jan Chapman and, in America, Denise di Novi on *Little Women*] have all been very supportive. During pre-production on *Little Women* my younger daughter was starting school. I was casting in America but Denise let me fly home and be away for three days so I could take my daughter to school on her first day. She said 'I want you to tell everyone only a woman producer would allow this!'.

I've been very fortunate that I can afford to have a nanny. That means she can do things like bring my child to the set to lunch with me, or if I have to leave on an overseas job the family can travel later and join me.

I do try not to shoot six-day weeks unless we are on a really unique location which can only be shot on a Saturday. Otherwise you don't see the family at all, you're sleeping in on Sunday and doing your homework. It's a treadmill.

But also it's for my physical well-being. I don't think I'll do a good job if I'm too tired.

I certainly learned early on if you are going to be a working mother and you are in a position of power you have to be very strict about wasted time. You want to be home as quickly as possible. That worked wonderfully at Merimbula on *High Tide*. I could actually wrap, go home and read stories to my baby and put her to bed and then go to the rushes. On the last three productions in Australia I have had the production offices as close as possible to my house so that I can be home as quickly as possible. You do everything possible to save those precious minutes for your family.

One of the advantages for me is that on a bigger budget film they can give you more of a family lifestyle. I've been flown with nanny and baby to script conferences in America when I was breastfeeding my second child. When I'm shooting, the children have to come with me. They went to school in Canada for *Little Women* and when they were very small, two and five, I did a film in America and we lived there because it was ridiculous to try and go back and forth on a plane.

I've also been very lucky that I've had a partner who has really made the sacrifice. He has taken leave of absence to come with me and be the house husband because we felt that at least one partner ought to be around. It is thanks to his generosity that I've achieved the balances.

I've worked with many great men and they are sensitive family men and we have had kids together and they are just as involved with their children. On *High Tide*, Mark Turnbull – who has been my 1st AD on seven films and associate producer on the last three – had a baby so he and his wife were actually in the house opposite us. They and my nanny and baby spent time together.

Little Women had so many children. Denise di Novi had a room set up next to her office with playthings in it. Susan Sarandon had her kids around all the time. But it is really a situation best left for lunch break.

I'm always asked by journalists, 'How can you be a film director and a mother?'. But in a lot of ways our life is privileged compared to many women, such as lawyers or anaesthetists, who are on call every week. You can take time off. The shoot which takes ten to twelve weeks is the time that is most critical.

I don't know how women do it who have had children earlier in their career before they have actually got any financial security.

My advice is to try and get yourself established before you have a child, otherwise you are going to have a child in day care who you never see because it is so expensive to have a nanny. It's hard. And you have got to have a supportive partner.

There have been scripts that I have read and I have thought 'Well that wouldn't be a location that would be great to take children, or for family life'.

I was once asked by an American journalist, 'We love your films but why don't you make more? Why has it been so long?'. I had to say, 'Well, I am a mother as well'. I try to take time off between my films and spend time with the kids, so perhaps I am not as prolific as a male director.

EMPLOYING WOMEN

When I first started out I felt the most important thing for women was that my films actually succeeded. I had seen people, men and women, employ their friends as crew and seen them fail and feel really let down. On *My Brilliant Career*, Margaret came to me and said this person is the best at that, and that person's the best. She used to find out who was the best at everything. I was very much encouraged by that. I felt that I should not risk the success of my film, when it was being judged on whether or not a woman could direct, by putting on a woman who was not the best at her job. So I just employ people who are the best at their job and there is a mix of male and female.

It was a very different situation in America in the late 1970s because there were so few women. It was a whole different world, a much more conservative world that never existed here in the young industry that I started out in. There I was considered an absolute freak. They really were worried in America about raising money on a woman director. I don't know what they thought I was going to do, faint or get blown away or collapse.

The strange thing is that when I first started some of the toughest times I had were actually from some of the women in the industry. The most sexist articles that have been written about me were written by women journalists – can she do it? She looks so small and young surrounded by all these big men. That surprised me.

There were those women who loved their power in a male-dominated industry, loved being the only woman on the set and didn't know how to operate with a woman boss. They thought they had a whole thing going with their male God director, who they were secretly in love with. There were some actresses a little like that as well. But all that should have changed by now.

WORKING IN AMERICA

It's completely different. It is big business, it is corporate and more conservative. Also, back then most of the men who were heads of production at the studios, who were actually in charge of the money, were in their 60s and they really could not cope with women in power, young women responsible for all those millions.

There is a very big difference to starting out in Australia in the

'70s, because the Australian industry is arts-based. The people who were choosing films for government investment were all arts bureaucrats, and the women's movement actually had been very, very strong in Australia. It really had an effect on many of the young men here. The Australian men were actually, surprise, surprise, so much more liberated than the men in America.

Here it is still a much more open environment. If you show talent you can get somewhere. My short films won awards at the film festivals and that is what gave me my break. That's what got me out of the cutting room. People just started sending me scripts left right and centre because they liked my short films. *My Brilliant Career* probably also really helped women filmmakers everywhere because it had an appearance of a big film, a 'real' movie. It broke that perception that women do little dramas, 'kitchen sink dramas'. I didn't realise it at the time.

People think of Hollywood as one mogul making a decision. That's a fantasy. Basically, you're working in a bureaucracy. For me, and most Australians who work there, it's a shock to see how many levels there are before anyone can make a decision.

When I went there, there were no women directing, no women production managers or producers, but here we have a long history of wonderful women who production manage and produce. When I did *Mrs Soffel* in 1984 only two other women, both ex-actors, had directed in recent years in the USA.

AUSTRALIAN WOMEN DIRECTORS

I'm continually asked why are there so many wonderful women film directors with a personal vision coming out of Australia, compared with America. They're not just good, competent directors, they actually have their own personal stamp on films, and I think it has to be due to the film schools here. I needed film school as a place to play around and learn. I wouldn't have been strong enough or had enough confidence if I had started at the bottom in that male-dominated industry. In the '70s it was good to be in a nurturing place to work out what I wanted to do and to finally get the confidence to do it.

Here there are now so many women directing that no-one thinks twice. Percentage of population, I would say Australia has more women feature directors and producers than anywhere in the world. It is still hard for anyone, male or female, to get their foot in the door but if you make a short film that shows talent, and you have the ability to work with a team, you generally progress. I think Australia should be proud of the number of wonderfully talented and unique women directors we have.

Yet there are still hardly any commercial directors, which amazes me, and there are still areas like sound and cinematography where there is male dominance.

JACKIE McKIMMIE

Jackie wanted to be a writer. She grew up in Sydney and started at the University of Sydney then left because she followed her husband, Chris, to Perth.

In 1970 she started an associateship at WAIT (the West Australian Institute of Technology) which ended up being a BA oriented towards writing. 'I thought I'd found heaven. It was theatre, literature, poetry, I was very interested in poetry, I saw myself as a poet I suppose.'

She used to act in an experimental theatre company, wrote a Super 8 film, wrote plays, edited the student newspaper and had her first child while she was a student. 'It was all quite intense. I used to go to the movies all the time but I always thought to make films you required such magic skills and I never thought I would do it.'

In 1973 she had her second child and went to Sydney and started teaching in the art department at Kogarah Tech. She taught communications and made films with the students using a student's 16mm camera.

She then went to Brisbane with her husband and two sons in 1976 and got a job at the Brisbane Independent School as a librarian. She applied for an innovation grant to set up a darkroom to do photography and got some Super 8 equipment. Within six months she was taking students on filmmaking camps, and working in the darkroom with them.

'It was hardly a course, it was like, "What do you want to make a film about? All right write a script". They always had multiple murders, naked girls tied to trees being whipped, and smoking cigarettes – it was an alternative school. We were winning all these prizes for kids' films and we became sort of famous. It's probably because no-one could believe the subject matter.'

By 1980 the filmmaking course was funding itself and Jackie was hitting 30 and thinking about what she wanted to do because it was all too easy. She had written a couple of plays which had been produced in Brisbane and various other places around the country. She had started to write her third play but it was not working so she decided she had to make it as a film. She resigned from the school and gave herself two years.

interview

FIRST FILM

At the beginning of 1981, I'd been down to the Playwrights Conference with the last play I'd written. I'd been feeling optimistic and I started writing this film. I wrote a treatment, went to the AFC with it, got knocked back at an interview in Brisbane, but I felt they were very positive about knocking me back. I felt that it was really close.

This must have been about May, and in the paper that Sunday my stars said, 'Push yourself, today you're going to meet a man that's going to change your life'. I don't believe this stuff, but it said it, 'Push yourself'. I went down to get takeaways and I ran into the producer, Jan Murray, and he said 'how did you go with the AFC?'. And I said 'Oh they didn't give me the money but they really like it', pushing myself 'and they thought it was really good, and I just need to do a bit more work on it'. And he said, 'Oh we're looking for scripts, why don't you throw it towards us'. It was when 10BA had just started. So I went home and instantly got it out, and was there 6 o'clock the next morning dropping it off. I didn't hear from them until well into July. And I thought that's it, I'd have to go back to teaching. There was no-one in Brisbane making films, I didn't know who else to go to with it and I thought 'Well that's the end of that'.

I was literally saying to Chris, 'This is it, I'm going to ring up and see if they'll take me back because this script is not going to work out'. As I was saying this to him, it was unbelievable, the phone rang, it was Jan Murray saying would I take $9,000 for this film. I would have given it to them. It was only a treatment, it wasn't even a script.

So that started me. They called it *Madness of Two* [1981]. It became the most horrific experience of my life. This was in July, there was no script, he said they wanted to shoot it in October. I started writing like a maniac. I'd never seen what a script looked like.

> ▶ **The expectation, particularly if you're a writer–director, is not that you are telling people how to do their job, you're just telling them what you want them to do.**

It was based on a true story about this woman who killed her kids, I was deeply affected by the story so I was really passionate about it. I'd gone on a recce to Moreton Island with the Brisbane director and he hadn't read the script. So I said to the producers 'I'm sorry I don't think that he's serious, I don't want to work with a director who doesn't know the script when we're looking at places to shoot it'. It seemed to me that they were undervaluing or devaluing the whole process and I was starting to become assertive.

Anyway, they took me to Sydney to look for directors and I met Hugh Keays-Byrne, who became the director and Christina, his partner, who became the production manager. They opened my eyes to what real filmmaking was about. Passion and commitment and how you can do it. They're real collectivists in their collaborations. Hugh involved me in everything, he let me come to rehearsals, he was always talking to me about the script, we'd have all night sessions sitting up rewriting it. It was a truly a wonderful process for me.

But when we got into production it all changed. The film didn't get made the way it should have done. Near enough seemed good enough with a lot of the people and there was a lot of drugs. It was a real eye opener for me. I thought even though I don't know anything I've got to have more control over the next thing that I do.

DIRECTING

So I went to the QFC [Queensland Film Commission] with another feature on rock 'n' roll. I was going to produce because I thought the producer's the one with the power and a guy who had been an editor was going to direct. But the QFC was very patronising about my ability to deal with the musicians, although I had been living with Chris, who is a musician, for ten years. They said 'Go away and come back with something small'.

So I had this thing called *Stations,* a short story that I'd always wanted to make into a film, and wrote it in three days. I didn't go back to the QFC, because everyone said 'They won't give you money for that because it's a women's film'. So I thought 'Fuck them' and went to the AFC. They really loved it, and gave me some money to do a few test scenes because the director hadn't directed before.

By then I was starting to feel really itchy about him directing it, thinking maybe we could co-direct it. I'd got Noni Hazelhurst and Tim Burns and a few other people who had already been in the first film with me. I thought I'll deal with the actors and he can deal with the crew.

We did the test like that and it turned out all right. But I'm still feeling uneasy and thinking that I could deal with the crew too. It doesn't seem that hard. If they know what they're doing and you tell them what you want they'll know how to get it. So I said to the director 'I really feel that I've gotta do it', and he then became the 1st AD.

It was my first 'bitch' type action in Brisbane, and so before we started I had developed a reputation for sacking the director. It became an important issue with people and I had it thrown in my face for several years after that. Then I did say I didn't want him to edit it. I wanted to get this other editor from Sydney. I just started to see how it could really go further than he thought it would. I just had to do it.

Stations was a really interesting experience for me. It was fantastic and really hard. Chris was doing all the art direction on the smell of an oily rag. All the Sydney people who'd come up were living here, there were fifteen people living in the house. We had the rushes in the house with the silent projector – we couldn't afford a double head projection system – so every night we'd look at them lip reading what they were saying, and it just looked terrific.

I thought 'This is for me, I've gotta direct, if you're going to write it, you might as well go that one step further'. And so that's how it started.

The first film I directed that was someone else's was *Top Enders* [1987] for the Children's Television Foundation. That was all right because I'd extensively rewritten it with the writer, who was in England and didn't care. That was a very gruelling shoot with a crew I'd never worked with. I thought if this is what real filmmaking is about, commercial filmmaking, I'm not sure I'm suited to it. I thought that maybe I'll just be a writer. But then I thought I've got to go back to why I wanted to direct in the first place, and it was the idea of the image. So I made *No Problems* [1989].

I conceived this little film as a series of images, based on the sound of this woman's voice and what she was talking about. I just used images and evocative sounds because I knew I was good with actors speaking, but I didn't know whether I was good at anything else. That film recharged my batteries and I directed a script by Nick Enright, *Breaking Through*, which was a dramatised documentary about an abused woman which was a fantastic experience for me. Nick was wonderful, he just left me alone and said 'Now its yours, do what you have to do with it'. But he trusted me.

Then I did *Waiting* which I had written and that was fine. Then I did a script by some new writers. I should never have done it. I thought I could save it and fix it up but the writers didn't trust me. It was horrific.

Now I have made a vow that I have to take more control of what I do. I have recognised that film takes up so much of your life, a feature film takes two years minimum, so that if I'm going to stay in films I should be doing stuff that I would die if I didn't do. And that's stuff I've written myself. So that's the decision I've made.

PROBLEMS WITH LIVING OUTSIDE OF SYDNEY

When I'm in Brisbane I'm mainly writing, you can do that anywhere. The films that I've made up here I've produced myself, I was co-producer on *Stations*, and then co-produced *Australian Dream* and then produced *No Problems*. All the other films have been made somewhere else. I've never had to find a producer here. If I had had to when I was starting out, I would have been rooted. No-one up here would work on my film *Stations*, one woman DOP wouldn't do it, she was too nervous, other DOPs I asked didn't want to do it because it was a woman's film. So I finally got Andrew Lesnie from Sydney.

When I made *No Problems* in 1989, I was regarded as this sort of moron when I'd already done about five films. Again it was very very difficult to get someone to shoot it for me in Brisbane. I couldn't afford to bring anyone from down south. It might have been gender-related but none of the people who I approached in Brisbane had seen any of my films. I did get someone in the end and he wanted his wife to be the focus puller, she'd never done it before. That's how dismissive he was. He told me afterwards he did it for love rather than money, and yet he got about 15 percent of the budget. I spent more on him than all the other salaries combined.

I think it was not just that I was a woman, but that it was a short film. People don't understand that short films are little works of poetry. They thought that for someone to go back to making a short film after making long films there must be something wrong. I thought how could they complain that I don't work with people up here when every time I try to I can't get anyone.

Because of the success of *Stations*, I had producers flying me down to Sydney. I've always had a Sydney producer because there is no-one in Brisbane. If only there was someone fabulous up here that I felt good about I could go and see them face to face whenever I feel like rather than having to go to a flat in Sydney. But everyone is starting out here and you wouldn't trust your film with them.

We've often talked about whether or not we should go and live in Sydney but Chris doesn't want to and I've never pushed it because I've realised that now it doesn't matter where I live. I could be in Sydney and then I'd get asked to do something in Melbourne. Last year I got asked to do something in New Zealand for six months and the films that I've looked at that were possibilities for me in the last year were in Adelaide, Melbourne and Northern Queensland.

MANAGING CREWS

I expect people to be really nice to everyone. I try to have a great rapport with the continuity person. I talk a lot to her about what I'm doing, and I talk a lot to the 1st AD and the DOP and the sound recordist. I always include them in my planning and they deal with their departments.

Generally speaking I'm very low key, I'm very quiet on the set. I speak to actors personally rather than to the whole set. If someone has made a mistake I try to ask them to do it in a different way without revealing that they've made a mistake. Actors are really exposing themselves on the set, every time they get in front of a camera, and so I try to respect that. Even if they're bad, I'll just change the camera angles, I'll let them do it their way but then I'll suggest they do it another way. But I'm really very aware of there not ever being any hint of humiliation or lack of respect to the actors. It's really important to me.

With the crew, if anyone is giving me the shits I speak to the head of department. If I sense there is some problem from the crew, I'll speak to the 1st AD about it and get him to go and sort it out.

When I directed *Waiting* in 1990 at the ABC in Sydney we did a facilities deal and worked with their crew. I felt their attitude was that I'd only written it and I had no right to be there. But I was directing and I'd brought my own DOP in from outside.

That crew resented people coming in from outside. They'd all had their jobs for so long, they were there until they died basically, and they resented that I was a woman. The only woman director that they'd ever worked with was Jane Campion and they used to speak so disparagingly of her. You'd think working with someone as good as she is would have opened their eyes to a few things. I had fraught relations with almost all of them at one time or another, not all the time, not consistently, but they were all blokes.

The ABC focus puller got sacked at my insistence, because he wasn't doing his job. The ABC kept him on the shoot, they never sack anyone, but we brought in an outside focus puller which led to bad feelings from all the crew and I became known as the sacker.

When I get my back against the wall I become really withdrawn. It is respected if you shout but my knees go funny, my stomach goes in a knot, I'm just this woos. It's like I become frenzied and panic stricken. I rehearse what I'm going to say and it's awful. It's not that I can't be angry with people, but I can never respond angrily on the spur of the minute which is probably what I should do.

In *Waiting* I wanted a cake, there was this scene where the actor had to cut a slab of the cake, which he's not meant to eat. They should have had half a dozen cakes in the esky, but they had to go and ice another cake because I insisted that it was cut. They were griping so much about it and I felt like saying, 'It's my decision whether I want the cake cut or not and you should have it there'. Because I couldn't say anything like that, I just knew that they were griping and carrying on because they had to go and ice the bloody thing again. There was no question that I would back down, but I can't deal with it up front. So what I do is say to the boss [the producer Ross Mathews] 'Oh they're all carrying on about the cake', and he'd say 'Don't worry about it'. But I'd feel wounded that they'd had the hide to behave like that.

ISSUES FOR WOMEN

The way I came in through writing, it's irrelevant whether you're a man or a woman.

I'm not a technical wizard and I never will be, I find it really boring. I have listened to boys with their toys saying this is possible, or that isn't. I think that sometimes I've accepted advice which, if I knew more, I would not have done.

Although being interested in technical things is not a gender issue I do think that they might have talked to me differently if I was a man. It's not that I haven't had a lot of assistance, it's just that sometimes I've felt I might have got better advice.

Because I'm a writer-director people are mostly far more tolerant of any technical shortcomings I might have, and certainly less inclined to place me in a gender position. They wouldn't be there if it wasn't for me. I am the one who thought it all up in the first place and all the things that they're now doing started out as a little germ in my brain. I'm sure they never think that and I'm sure they think I'm a fool and an idiot half the time, but the bottom line is that this is my thing.

Domestic arrangements

Chris has always been there. When I was pregnant I was a full-time student, and so we started out saying you'll look after them when I'm at class and I'll look after them when you're at class. We hardly ever had to get babysitters because we always had the other person. When we first went back to Sydney from Perth Chris stayed home and wrote kids' books and I'd go out to work. No-one was doing it then and people thought that he was a poofter. It's just what we always did, and we hardly ever talked about it.

When I did that first film in 1981, Dylan would have been eleven, and Blake was about eight. It amazes me when I see all these young directors having babies and still directing, I truly don't know how they do it when their kids are little.

As far as money goes I'm really lucky in that I've earned big slabs of money periodically – enough money to keep me going for several years, if I spread it out. Chris has always been really good about keeping everything going, he earns a regular amount of money at Griffith University and when I'm not earning money it's not an issue with us. But I've put in my share.

Sexist remarks and sexual harassment

One film I did was a real boys crew, every second word was

cunt, cunt this cunt that, and they'd say, 'Oh what a fucking cunt that guy is'. They weren't trying to be offensive or anything but it jarred on me, every time. And so one day I said 'Look I don't care about your swearing, but why don't you just start calling them fucking prick instead of fucking cunt'. They stopped saying cunt.

Sexual harassment goes on but I'm always really picky about the crew. I try not to have people who I don't like. You can't help it when department heads employ who they want but I've never had any really arsehole heads of departments, other than women. Some women have spent so long in really shit jobs that when they finally get somewhere they can't forget it, and you come in and you're a writer-director and they think you haven't had to suffer.

But because I always have a say in who the heads of departments are going to be, and Ross was good at getting people who I'd get on really well with, I've never been aware of sexual harassment. It might happen and I don't know about it because I'm removed from quite a lot. But I wouldn't tolerate it. If I knew anything was going on they would actually be sacked.

I had one experience, it was one of those things when you're not sure whether it happened or not. I was sitting in a car with an actor, and one of the crew just stuck his dick in the windscreen at her – he used to wear shorts all the time. He sort of flashed it in and flashed it out. We spoke about it together and we didn't know whether we'd imagined it, but we were convinced it had happened.

Our way of dealing with that was to ignore him for the rest of the shoot. We decided we would ignore him completely. This was quite a few years ago, before anyone was talking about harassment or anything like that and we didn't say anything to anyone about it.

Feeling vulnerable

I feel really vulnerable at the time when the script is looking for money, and I feel really vulnerable just before you start shooting. When you're wondering if you've made all the right decisions so far. And then every night during the shoot, I have nightmares. In Sydney, I was in an eighth floor apartment and I used to lock the door in my bedroom which opened onto the balcony. I was terrified that I might get up in my sleep and jump over the balcony because I just wanted to get away from all the pressures. Not that I ever would.

I'm a real old workhorse, I've come to admire my stamina, I actually think I have more stamina than almost anyone I know. Physical and mental, I just keep going, I just think about that, keep putting that foot in front of the other foot and see the light at the end of the tunnel. It's why it's good not to make a film living at home. You've got to be able to live on four hours sleep a night and be totally tunnel-visioned, and somehow I can do it. I mean you break your heart every day, and every night when you go to sleep you wish you could keep going. I can see why people do drugs to keep going. The worst time of all, though, is when a film is about to come out. That is worse than all the others combined.

But during the shoot I feel proud when everything has come together in a way that goes beyond what you expected. It's just this marriage of every single force that is there at that moment, and you think 'Fuck, it's great'. It doesn't happen very often. I could count it on one hand.

Crying

I've felt close to tears on probably half a dozen occasions. I just walk away, I feel if a woman were to cry, it would be far worse than a man crying. On *Breaking Through* everyone was crying all the time because of the subject matter. I nearly cried in anger a few other times, but I've just had to walk somewhere else, or I'd go and sit in the AD's car and put the windows up and turn the music up really loud.

Coping with criticism

Criticism cripples me, absolutely cripples me. People better not criticise me. I cannot deal with it. I'm so used to people being really nice to me because I'm sort of nice to them. If someone were to criticise me to my face, I would feel shattered. It's terrible, I have no way of coping with it. People don't do it all that often. Sometimes it gets relayed to me and I'll mull over every nuance of the criticism and usually I'll take it to heart and I think they must be right. Unless I totally don't respect them at all.

ADVICE

If you're a writer you're in a better position and if you're a writer-director I'd say you're halfway there. To be a director without being a writer is going to be harder. Because everyone is interested in auteurs you get away with the lack of experience if you've got that other skill.

In terms of becoming a director, if you're not a writer, find a short film script, a ten-minute short film script from anywhere. I keep telling Film Queensland [now the Pacific Film and Television Commission] they should advertise a short film script competition and the prize is that the film gets made. It gets made by one of the young directors and one of the up and coming producers, because the scripts that they're coming up with aren't good enough. This way they all have a calling card.

To me, a young director has got to find a good script, a good ten-minute script, that's all it needs to be. Then she has to go to the Australian Film Commission first, then to Film Queensland, because they'll only put in $50,000 or $35,000. For a drama you probably need about $80,000 to do something really well on 16mm or 35mm.

Get the best possible crew you can, get people who know much more than you, that's always my motto – be the one who knows the least. Just be game to say it how you see it and be very clear about what you want out of the script. Don't worry about getting paid. The short film is a fantastic way to go and if the worst comes to the worst, scrape together a few thousand and do it on video. But have a fabulous script.

Find scripts by advertising in *Viewpoint*, the Writers' Guild newsletter. Say you want a ten-minute short script, ten-minute ideas are really not that hard to come up with. They are really like a little poem. Better than a 25-minute one. People get confused with what they're doing and they try to make a small television program. They're better off saying it is a little film, and if the area you want to move into is drama, then make sure you have scenes where people are talking and walking. There's not much point doing a really wonderful arty film with no-one talking or walking and then say 'Look, I'm really good with actors'.

I think going to the AFTRS in Sydney would give you confidence. I sometimes really regret that I didn't have any technical training. But you really don't have to know that much if you get people who know their jobs. People want to be stretched. The expectation, particularly if you're a writer-director, is not that you are telling people how to do their job, you're just telling them what you want them to do.

The biggest lesson I suppose I've learnt is that nothing is ever what it seems. It isn't. You had better start out feeling pretty good, because it never gets better, it only gets worse on any shoot. So the higher you are starting out the longer the good feelings will last.

YOUNGER WOMEN FILMMAKERS

The interviews with women in the film industry in this book are with role models who have successful careers. But what about the younger generation of women filmmakers who are not beginning to gain substantial achievements – has working in the film industry been easier for them as the role models suggest?

This section is based on in-depth interviews with nine of these women. They are:

▸ Carolyn Constantine (cinematographer, *Pent Up House*)
▸ Kathryn Milliss (cinematographer, *Thank God He Met Lizzie*)
▸ Linda Murdoch (sound editor, *At Sea, Fresh Air*)
▸ Cate Cahill (sound mixer/sound editor, *Piccolo Mondo, Water Rats, The Wiggles Movie*)
▸ Julie Pierce (AD recordist/sound engineer, *Portrait of a Lady, The Truman Show*)
▸ Reva Childs (editor, *Island Life, Somewhere Between Light and Reflection*)
▸ Karen Johnson (editor, *Following the Fence Line, Walking Through a Minefield, Wind, Tears*)
▸ Samantha Lang (director, *The Well*)
▸ Rachel Perkins (director, *Radiance*).

Eight of these women had gained tertiary qualifications and one – Julie Pierce – developed her skills through volunteer work. Samantha Lang studied at the Sydney College of the Arts, followed by a BA in directing at the AFTRS; Linda Murdoch completed a BA in New Zealand and a one-year sound course at the AFTRS; Reva Childs studied for a BA and a Bachelor of Commerce; Cate Cahill studied at the School of Music in Canberra, did a degree in electrical engineering, then a BA in sound at the AFTRS; Karen Johnson went to the University of New England, then moved to AFTRS for a one-year editing course; Kathryn Milliss studied at the

University of NSW, then the Victoria College of the Arts for a BA specialising in film; Carolyn Constantine studied part-time at North Sydney TAFE for four years; and Rachel Perkins did a one-year producing course at the AFTRS.

A major issue for many of the women was the conflict created between work and home life by the nature of filmmaking, which juxtaposes long, long days – often on location – with periods of no work at all. Carolyn Constantine commented that she 'did have a partner and I don't now. It was work that affected that relationship... you either have too much time or no time at all'.

Cate Cahill, the only mother in the group, admitted to being so overworked with the combination of job and children that 'sometimes you're just happy to take the easy road'.

Many found their greatest supporters were friends or partners. Several had partners working in the industry, and while this could mean coping with extensive periods apart, it also meant that there was an understanding of the constraints. 'It requires a huge amount of tolerance, a huge amount of trust', said Samantha Lang. 'You have to know when your relationship's a priority and when your work's a priority.' Bronwyn Murphy (pp29-39) referred to similar challenges in her interview and talked about strategies she and her partner had developed to deal with them.

SEXISM AND HARASSMENT

Interestingly (and depressingly), the experiences of the younger women concerning sexism and harrassment were similar to those of the role models interviewed, although attitudes varied widely, partly depending on the different roles of each of the younger group. Generally they emphasised that dealing with inappropriate male attitudes was not a feature of their working lives, nor a major concern. At the same time, there was a degree of sensitivity about relating their stories for fear of exposing the perpetrators, being considered a troublemaker, missing out on jobs or damaging their reputations.

Most remarked that the industry was changing in terms of gender balance, behaviour of men and in the number of female crew. There was still a strong sense that women are often obliged to fit in to the 'macho and blokey' environment, or to seek work in circles where women are respected.

A few who worked with predominantly male crews said that they had adopted masculine behaviour themselves in order to be accepted. Kathryn Milliss commented that 'when I was much younger I had the feeling that I should be, I probably pretended to be, a bloke a bit... as the years progressed I relaxed and allowed myself to be more girlie'.

Samantha Lang stressed that there was a greater degree of gender equity in Australia than in other countries. 'In Australia you're probably going to get the most equal treatment, on the surface, than anywhere else. But your sexuality always comes into it. In the end it comes down to common sense. If, say, a producer is flirting with you overtly and you find that offensive you can stop the meeting or say 'I don't like your behaviour', or you can continue politely and then never see him again. Maybe that's going to cut off an opportunity for you but why would you want to continue that opportunity if he was a jerk anyway?'

There was a feeling that sexist behaviour today is camouflaged and that practices that undermine women tended to be covert. 'Our generation of men is so bludgeoned with the notion of political correctness that discrimination is no longer overt', Samantha observed. 'The sexual harassment thing is a really difficult issue for me because it's not on the table, it's something you have to navigate your way through. Because we've had very strong female directors emerge... I think that men really have the perception it's not hard for women. It's so clearly male dominated in America and Europe, whereas in Australia, the men don't see it that way. One of the biggest problems is that they don't recognise that there is a problem any more. It's really not hip any more to complain.'

Like the older generation they all felt that sexist behaviour was more problematic earlier in their careers and they agreed that younger women trying to break into the industry could well be discouraged by the attitudes of some men.

The majority of the women had developed a degree of confidence in handling inappropriate behaviour, developing through experience the ability to avoid it.

SELF CONFIDENCE AND ROLE MODELS

Emphatic statements were made about women needing to be more confident, more ambitious, take more risks and demand rights in order to progress further in the industry. It was regularly stated that women undervalue themselves professionally and fail to put themselves forward for jobs as readily as men.

Carolyn Constantine said that 'women tend to undervalue their skills more than men. I see a lot of men out there who have done not very much but they're blowing their own trumpets very loudly... as a woman I know in my heart I've probably got more experience and am probably just as capable... you've got to keep reminding yourself about that'.

Those working with complex equipment spoke of having to repeatedly prove themselves as technically proficient before being taken seriously. 'I often wonder why men think that women can't be technologically capable. It's not a very hard thing to do', said Cate Cahill, '[but] every gig you've got to prove yourself.'

Everyone agreed that the situation for women had improved in recent years thanks to the efforts of the previous generation. Strong female role models were seen as a crucial impetus for change.

'When I started out', Kathryn Millis said, 'the industry was more male dominated than it is now... there were more and more women working as the years progressed and I think that actually had a very positive effect on the crews. It made them more balanced, more productive... it made the climate on set different, it improved. The old thing about women can't lift equipment was gone by the time I started. We were just expected to lug the lot and you got the muscles to do it by doing it. People like Jan Kenny [see pp11-25] and Erika Addis helped break those stereotypes in the first place. I think that they're the real vanguard, they are the people who had to really disprove those kinds of ideas'.

ADVICE

All the women interviewed promoted the advantages of a tertiary education and several emphasised that film school was an important starting point to get into the industry. Samantha Lang spoke about the important role of the two training institutions she attended (Sydney College of the Arts and AFTRS). She described the visual communication course at the former as 'seminal because it really taught me how to look at things'. Although she was not fully aware of the benefits of the course on completion, in retrospect she claims to have drawn upon a lot of what she learnt there. The course at AFTRS gave her 'the direction and the confidence' to make short films, which opened doors to further employment.

Linda Murdoch was particularly enthusiastic about her AFTRS experience. 'Go to film school where Annie Breslin is the head of the sound department and Annabelle Sheehan [see pp75-92] is the head of teaching. They are the two major inspirations in my life.'

The other main recommendation was to get hands-on experience of making films through whatever means, whether through work experience, as an unpaid attachment, by volunteering to work on student films, or spending time at facilities.

Carolyn Constantine said young women should 'just go out there and do it... Just look at the way the males are doing it, push yourself a bit faster. It is important even at the very early stage to just start shooting stuff, even though you might be clapper loading... the amount that you learn doing your own stuff, however bad, even if no-one sees it... It will probably be the most valuable thing you've done that week'.

A key theme and a strong message throughout the interviews was the need for younger women to display self confidence and determination.

Reva Childs said that the most important thing for her was needing to have confidence about her work and her ability and not to be intimidated by somebody else's opinion... 'To always keep talking it through until you are satisfied that you've got what you want or need. I think probably in my earlier days I may have looked at a man who seemed incredibly confident and thought, "Oh maybe they do know better", because they often exude a confidence, which in reality isn't always backed up by their knowledge or ability.

Cate Cahill reiterated the importance of having confidence in your ability, the need to take risks and to occasionally bluff. In applying for jobs many of the women had been reluctant to promote themselves and to ever suggest they could do something without being absolutely sure; men seemed far less hesitant about self-promotion. 'Perhaps the men who want to be mixers are going to be a lot more aggressive than some women are prepared to be. You've got to have a really thick skin, you've got to be able to get in there and push yourself and not worry what is said about you.'

According to Samantha Lang, 'As a director, it's not about how great your skills are in the beginning, it's about your ideas. To develop a point of view and a way of looking at the world is the most important thing... because everything else you can learn. It's also about assuming your own power...'

Rachel Perkins thinks that 'women have got to demand the opportunities and the right to do things and have got to really take control... make big leaps and pursue things with fierce energy and commitment. It's about taking risks and always challenging yourself and not accepting lesser positions, being ambitious, all of those things. When I became an executive producer I just pretended that I knew what I was doing. I had no idea but I learnt'.

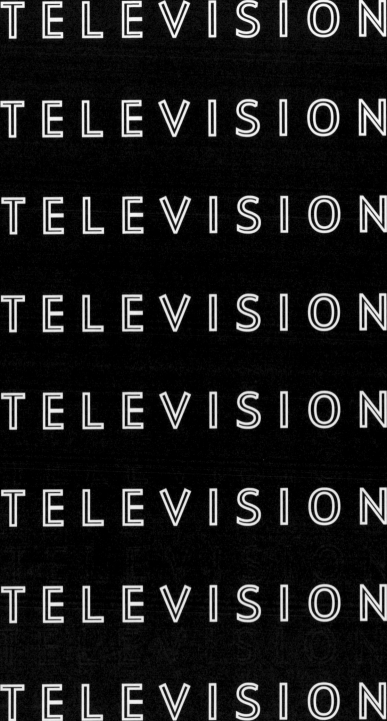

Working full-time in a television station is a very different experience from working freelance on a film crew. Television stations have an organisational culture that was set up in the 1950s and 1960s when a woman's place was regarded as being in the home, and there are some men in senior positions who have difficulty in thinking otherwise. There is still a very male culture and there are very few women in senior management positions or on the boards of the stations or networks.

Television trains its own staff, usually on the job. This has meant that most people come straight from school into stereotypically gendered jobs. There have been no career paths for women or points of entry for women trained elsewhere. Television has been very slow to recognise as a source of recruitment the multitude of media courses that have grown up since the 1970s. It has also been slow to work with the AFTRS to tailor courses for their needs. In contrast, the film industry was kick-started in the 1970s when the government set up the AFTRS, and was also influenced by the second wave of feminism that was just beginning at that time.

Traditionally, getting a job in either film or television has been a case of who you know. Because film is a freelance industry, with a high turnover of jobs, women have had more employment opportunities. They have been able to get training in non-traditional jobs and break in, whereas women wanting to work in non-traditional jobs in television have not only had to challenge the male stereotyping of the jobs but also had to break into the 'boys' network' to know when a job was available.

The ABC has had more formal employment processes than the commercial stations and so it has been easier to introduce affirmative action and equal opportunity initiatives. However, a number of both women and men got their first jobs on equipment in the ABC through personal contact, filling in when someone was away.

In the last few years, since I started interviewing for this book, there have been great changes in the management practices of commercial television.

The 'old boys' club' which many women identified as a barrier to getting jobs in television has started to break down due to a growing community awareness of discrimination, along with four specific factors: industrial legislation reforms which have forced commercial television managements into introducing modern management practices with formal selection processes; high-profile sexual harassment cases which have resulted in employers being liable for paying out compensation; the Affirmative Action Agency reporting requirements; and the introduction of Pay TV which has poached staff.

The three commercial networks have gradually changed their employment practices and introduced human resource departments to look after the training and career opportunities of their staff, although they vary in the way they are affecting women (see Appendix 1).

This section is divided into two parts: interviews with women managers in each mainland capital station (Hobart has been excluded because it does not have the population base to be treated by broadcasters as a major capital city station); and descriptions of the jobs using equipment in television and an outline of the experiences that the women who work in these jobs have had, along with their employers' views.

THE WOMEN MANAGERS

It was not possible to profile senior women working with equipment in television in the same way I was able to do in the film industry because there was only one, Camilla Rudd. She had come up through engineering and had then moved sideways into management. She has now left broadcasting.

Instead, I interviewed 22 of the most senior women – nominated by their managing directors – in the mainland capital city stations. They were two producers (ABC Adelaide, Melbourne); a consultant (BTQ-7 Brisbane); five publicity and promotions managers (ATN-7 Sydney; HSV-7 Melbourne; GTV-9 Melbourne; NWS-9 Adelaide; NEW-10 Perth) three managers of traffic (SAS-7 Adelaide; ADS-10 Adelaide; NEW-10 Perth) eight managers in human resources or administration (ABC Sydney; SBS Sydney; TCN-9 Sydney; ATV-10 Melbourne; TEN-10 Sydney; NWS-9 Adelaide; QTQ-9 Brisbane; STW-9 Perth), two program managers (TEN-10 Sydney; NEW-10 Perth) and one building services manager (ATN-7 Sydney).

This research was done over a period of four years and, in that time, managements, people and positions have changed and although there are now more senior women, they are still relatively few. I have profiled five women (one in each mainland state) in the hope that their experiences will serve as useful role models for other women in television.

Some of the managing directors did not immediately know who their most senior woman was. One identified her position and then had to call out to his secretary to ask her name. Most of the women were surprised when I told them that they had been identified as the most senior woman at the station, and would sometimes dispute it and identify someone else.

Most of the women who have management positions in

television, and have risen through the ranks, managed publicity. A more recent cohort of senior women has been recruited from business management or law straight into management positions or has been employed to set up human resource departments.

The senior women who came up through working in television to manage their own areas tended to be very focused on their own jobs and were locked into their own crisis management. Consequently they had little time to think about or question the broader issues of women in the workplace. On the whole they had succeeded in climbing the corporate ladder and, therefore, felt that they were proof that it could be done if women worked hard, kept their heads down and concentrated on doing their job well. A number were not prepared to be quoted. The general attitude was 'In this sausage factory, it has always been the one who works the hardest who will get where he [sic] is going. You can say to all newcomers "If you're good and don't tread on toes, you'll get where you're going. Each one makes his own rung up the ladder".' All senior women agreed that it was much easier for the younger women coming on, although perhaps not as vociferously as this program manager: 'Now that there is maternity leave; my God it is so easy, they've just got it made'.

Often these women had been expected by management to take on the extra duties of looking after women's issues in the station. Not surprisingly they did not have time to be very proactive about it. In addition several women were expected to combine two jobs when they were appointed to their management positions whereas, when the job had been done by a man, he was only doing one job.

In contrast, the women who had been appointed to human resource positions and were in the senior management structure could effect change if the other senior managers were prepared to back them. Probably the most powerful was Maureen Crowe, head of resources at SBS. She was responsible for all resources – finance, building and technical, as well as human. This gave her considerable clout on the management team. Appointing one woman into management who has her own demanding job and leaving it up to her to 'look after the women's issues and the affirmative action reports' can marginalise the woman and the issues. As Maureen Crowe said 'One of the burdens that senior women carry is that, unlike their male counterparts, they do have this sisterhood, this extra little road to walk down, which says as well as doing your own job please also do another job which is to help women'.

There is also the question of critical mass. If there is only one woman on the management team it can be very lonely and equal employment opportunity (EEO) issues can easily get marginalised or not brought up because of the put-downs from male managers. However, when there are two or more women there is back-up for EEO issues and the men are inclined to take greater notice. This bonus was commented on by the senior women who had been on the management team at the Ten Network.

The lack of management processes for promotion has bred a 'boys' club'. Sam Thomas, who was human resources manager and one of the most senior women at NWS-9 explained 'The problem is that in the past, in the industry as a whole, there has been a lot of on-the-job training but nothing's been structured. It's been 'the old boys' room. You could tap X on the shoulder, the next person in line, he's worked here for ten years so he must be able to do the job, and tell him that he is going to get the job. This has made it very difficult for women to get into what are perceived as male areas and to rise to positions of power'.

A number of senior women identified male mentors who helped them get their jobs. Some women, who had left to rear children, were brought back into the workforce through an employer contacting them to do a specific job (Dina Browne BTQ-7), and the employer was then prepared to adjust her work patterns (Glenys Gill NEW-10). Hector Crawford paid for a nanny for Susan Wood to encourage her back to work. She is now head of publicity in Melbourne at HSV-7.

Younger women I interviewed also identified managers who were particularly helpful in getting them started and looking after them. This fits with the image of 'one big happy family' that many managers like to portray of their department or station.

Some senior women, particularly those in charge of human resources, said that women had told them that they really appreciated that they could talk to a senior woman about their problems. Some women felt that the general attitude from their older generation supervisor was 'Bloody women having kids, they're never here. I don't care if you've got a sick child you've gotta do the job.' Whereas, they say, if it's the blokes who want to play golf there's no problem.

There were several stories of women in management not automatically getting the trappings of their position. One woman had to ask many times for a mobile phone when she was promoted, whereas her male predecessor had received one automatically. Robbie Rust, who had been promotions and presentations manager at ADS-10 Adelaide, said 'When I became traffic manager there was a car that went with the job but I never saw the car. I pursued that for four years until I got it. There were always excuses. If I'd been a man I'm sure I wouldn't have had the same trouble. Then they tried to take it away from me when I was promoted and was no longer responsible for traffic but I pointed out it was cheaper for them to let me have the car than pay me what it was worth in my salary package'.

Very few women had enjoyed clearly defined career paths. They had tended to take opportunities as they arose. Some of the women had families and most came to their management position after their children were older. Many of the younger women managers had delayed child-rearing and had not contemplated the problem of combining child-rearing with a high-powered job.

The women varied in their management styles. The ones who came up through television tended to manage all-female areas. They worked closely with their staff, attended management meetings to discuss issues which related to their areas, but were not involved in policy issues. Some made a point of chipping away about equal opportunity issues but tended to do this at a one-to-one level or as asides at meetings rather than initiating the issues as agenda items. On the whole they were happy to be involved in issues which related to women but did not have time to go and seek them out or initiate meetings with women. The human resource managers, on the other hand, had a much more proactive approach and set up meetings and made contact with women at all levels.

Most of the women had similar problems about feeling vulnerable when arguing a point with a roomful of men and felt angry when sexist remarks were made. While reluctant to show it they usually made a comment to indicate that the remark had not gone unnoticed. All had had to work out their own techniques for dealing with the male culture and the subtle put-downs. A number had grown so used to it that they didn't notice any more. Others said they didn't mind as it was part of working in television and you had to accept it or get out of the industry.

In the course of doing the interviews for this book, I was struck by how closely the experiences of women in television management parallel the experiences of women in management positions in other male-dominated industries. For a review of some of that research, see pp337-363.

CAMILLA RUDD

Camilla Rudd, ex ATN-7 Sydney building and services manager, was one of the very few women who had worked in the engineering department in a TV station, and the only woman who had come through the engineering department and reached a management position.

She is the second youngest of five girls. Her father was a carpenter and a builder. He had no sons. She was interested in mechanics, rebuilding engines and cars and panelbeating and was encouraged by her father. There are only a few women that she'd met who feel so comfortable doing these sorts of things, and 'it is important that you feel comfortable'.

She left school after completing her HSC in 1975 and worked at TCN-9 Sydney as a technical trainee. She was the first woman trainee they had ever had. While they were more interested in training her in operational aspects of production, handling the equipment, she was more interested in the engineering maintenance side. As part of the trainee scheme she did the four-year part-time Film and Television Operations course at what was then the Gore Hill Technical College. During her years as a trainee she was made a shift leader, but was still being paid as a trainee, and the hours meant that she couldn't continue with her studies.

In 1978 she took a technical position with TVW-7 Perth where she could do more maintenance on cameras and studio equipment. She says 'I remember the first day people just stared, they couldn't quite work out this woman who was walking up the corridor, who was going into the engineering field. They were fairly conservative, it was a time when the men had to wear ties, the women skirts or dresses – a memo went around saying the only woman who could wear slacks or jeans was Camilla because of the type of work she was doing.'

She continued her technical studies while in Perth, then came back to Sydney where ATN-7 offered her a job. After a while she felt that she wasn't really getting anywhere, so she did a degree in engineering at the New South Wales Institute of Technology (now the University of Technology, Sydney). She missed out on getting the job as deputy engineer in 1992 although she had been doing a lot of the administrative work for the position. When she asked why they said that she was immature in terms of management – although she suspects that the director of engineering at the time was more concerned about the 'old' management's attitude if she had to deputise for him. They advertised for someone to fill the position from outside.

She left having children till late 'so that I could get a bit further ahead with my career'. In 1994 she took maternity leave and returned to the position of building and services manager to juggle a new job, a new baby, being a member of management, and the chair of the affirmative action committee. She said that the odds were that she wouldn't have got that position if it hadn't been for Chris Chapman, managing director of ATN, and her old boss, Roger Barrett.

In 1995 she left ATN-7. She was hoping to work on the Olympics while at Seven, but the opportunities were not there. When she did resign she was six months pregnant with her second child. After a year at home, in 1997 she joined SOCOG (Sydney Organising Committee for the Olympic Games) as venue technology manager. She said that at SOCOG there are more women in senior and technical positions and the organisation is not caught up in the old traditional male cultural situations that she experienced in the broadcasting field. 'There is an appreciation by management that women have a lot to offer.'

Camilla says that it is an advantage to come from a science stream at school to get into engineering. Women in broadcast engineering have to be committed to the many engineering aspects of their careers – certainly glamour is not one of those aspects. You never get your name on the credits, you never get a good pat on the back. 'I think there are so few women in broadcast engineering because they think of television as a glamorous business, not one that incorporates a career in engineering.'

'When it comes to any aspect of engineering you've got to go in feeling "I know what I'm doing – I feel confident" but if you don't know, you've got to be prepared to say "I don't know but I'll learn".' Camilla says that if you go in thinking, 'Oh this environment's scary, I'm the only woman here' then it is difficult. 'You're just one of the guys, not that you have to *be* one of the guys, but you just don't make yourself any different.'

SUSAN WOOD

Susan Wood, former HSV-7 Melbourne publicity director, had a department of six people and was responsible for the publicity for her own station as well as sharing, with Lindy Anderson, head of publicity at ATN-7 Sydney, responsibility for the network's publicity. The Seven Network was the only network to operate this way.

Susan grew up in the bush and went to an all-girls' boarding school in Melbourne: 'There was lots of pressure on the girls to achieve things'. She didn't want to go to university and was interested only in television. She left school early and went to Lee Murray's radio school. From there she got her first job in 1969 at Channel 6 in Shepparton, when the television station came to Murray looking for staff. 'They weren't looking for women of course, but to his credit, Lee said you must see Susan with the others and after the interview they gave me the job.'

At Shepparton she presented sport, produced and presented the kids' show, and wrote and reported the news. From there she went to Mildura for a couple of years where she redesigned and presented the kids' show, operated a camera for the football show and operated the audio at night. She was also given an hour on Wednesday in which she could do anything and that became the *Women's Magazine Program*. The television station was owned by the local newspaper so she also supplied copy for the television page. 'I learned so much from that news editor subbing my copy', she says. She left Mildura in 1971 when she was 21, exhausted.

She had a rest at home and then went to Melbourne where she

rang HSV-7 out of the blue. They interviewed her and offered her the job of continuity writer in presentation. She was there for six months and then went into publicity in 1972. 'In those days it was like the bush, you did more than just publicity. I'd do that from 9 to 5, and then go into the newsroom and be director's assistant on the news, sport, *The Margaret Whitlam Show*, *Meet the Press*. Anything that was there, I grabbed.'

She did that until 1979 when she started a family and was home for six years child-rearing. She had no intention of returning to work until Hector Crawford rang her and offered her part-time work and to pay for a nanny for her two sons. She worked at Crawfords for eight years and then went back to HSV-7 to head up publicity in 1992.

At HSV she had to face the problem of child-rearing and school holidays. At one stage the HSV management discussed childcare facilities for their staff but it didn't come to anything.

She believes that the biggest problem for a woman with children is fitting the kids in amongst the time commitments. 'Hector Crawford was so wise when he offered me a nanny, because that's what I needed to get back into the workforce and be able to do the job properly. So I make sure now, whenever we need someone to really do a good job, that we give them an environment in which they can do that job. If that means picking up something like a parking spot, like a nanny, like a gym course, we've all got different needs – well we do it.'

Susan was the only woman on the management team. 'We do look at women's jobs and have trained a couple of girls as news camera operators. On our floor crew we have a couple of young girls doing cable pulling. We're actually looking to see if there is another way to become a camera operator that is not via the floor.'

'Peter Gibson, who's second in charge in engineering, went off to speak to the engineering students at both RMIT and Melbourne University one year and he didn't get one woman. We're promoting the idea of sharing jobs from state to state and, within our own workplace, exchanging skills so that we can have an exchange program working, Sydney-Melbourne, Brisbane-Sydney-Melbourne, take in Adelaide and occasionally take in Perth with exchanges.'

Susan said that she does feel responsible for women in the workplace but she is not in favour of affirmative action. 'If we are to ever achieve real impact, and real balance and real satisfaction, I think we've got to get in there all together. I've felt we were sending out the wrong message by saying that the equity committee had to be a women-only group.'

She advises women who want to get into television to jump in. 'Wherever, whatever, take any job. Go to the bush. There are traineeships, there are part-time jobs, there is so much available in any television station. In my view one of the best jobs to start with is answering the phone because you learn everybody's manner, you learn who they are, where they are. Often this will lead to on-the-job training in another area of interest to you and the employer. And have patience.'

DINA BROWNE

Dina Browne, BTQ-7 Brisbane consultant and ex director of network children's programs, trained as a teacher in South Africa, specialising in speech and drama because she had always wanted to be an actress. She taught in Swaziland and then in 1968 travelled to Europe and Australia where she discovered television. She did a variety of jobs in Sydney trying to get into television, but found that it was a closed door.

She moved to Brisbane for personal reasons, did an audition for BTQ-7 and was offered the job of producing and presenting the local preschool program, *Dina and Percy,* which later also went to Sydney and Melbourne. She did that for five years as well as a whole range of other things. She was one of the first female journalists working in the newsroom, where she was confined to baby shows and church fetes. The only time she had an opportunity to do a hard news story was in 1971 when there was a gas explosion and she and a male journalist were the only two people at the station. However, when they got there the police would only allow the male journalist on the site.

When her children's program finished in 1975 she went to the Education Department as a producer of preschool education resource materials. During that period she had a child and was out of the workforce for two years.

In 1979, Channel 7 asked her to be a reporter on their new current affairs show, *Hayden Sargent's Brisbane,* and then asked her to produce the children's program *Wombat.* She returned part-time and had her son with her when necessary in school holidays.

'I could justify having children around because I was working in children's television and BTQ has always been a very easy station to work in.'

Wombat started as a local Brisbane program and went to the network in 1980. She became network director of children's programs in 1989. In 1993 the network dropped that position and she was kept on part-time as a consultant. She said that she was not surprised to be regarded as the most senior woman 'because I have been here for a long time, so I'm seen as the most consistently visible woman, but I don't think that I'm necessarily the most powerful. I don't carry as much power as some of the younger women who are in promotions, for example, but I certainly have a kind of venerability.'

BTQ had a management committee which consisted of heads of departments. Now that Dina is no longer on full-time staff, there are two women, the heads of publicity and promotions, on the committee.

The major career problems that Dina had as a woman was that she was married and had to stay in Brisbane. 'It would have been much better to do the job in Sydney or Melbourne because it would have given me the opportunity to know the executives who made the decisions. If people know you personally, particularly if you're a woman and you work well with them, they get to understand you and don't pigeonhole you. There is a double whammy being a woman and flying in for the odd meeting.'

Dina said that when she first started in television Ian Duncan was a cameraman and then director of the preschool program, and Kel Geddes was a floor manager. 'We were all starting our careers and were all on the studio floor. We are about the same age but they kept leaping ahead. They didn't have the academic qualifications that I had, a university degree and teaching experience, but they have certainly enjoyed a great deal more power and status. Ian went on to become program director at HSV-7 Melbourne and Kel became program director of every station, then head of TVNZ.'

Dina has seen a lot of changes in attitude from the men. One general manager used to call me 'girlie'. 'I was constantly saying to him that no women were represented in positions of power on the station and that they should have women in the exec meetings. He would say "come on, girlie, why do you want to be with a bunch of men?" His reason was that it would impede discussion if there were women in the exec meetings, because the men wouldn't have the freedom of expression that they enjoyed.'

She believed that social change in Australia and affirmative action had made people conscious. 'People at the top are beginning to realise that if you start encouraging girls in school and recruit them from the start they will come through the ranks and then you will get women in significant numbers at the top, instead of having to advertise and only getting one woman applicant.'

MARGOT PHILLIPSON

Margot Phillipson, ABC executive producer, television, and acting manager, TV programs, graduated with a science degree and a diploma in education. She is the third of four children and her parents supported her in whatever she wanted to do. Her father was a bank manager so that she moved around the country every three years which she believes made her very independent.

She was a tutor at Flinders University and then taught science, maths and photography in a disadvantaged school in Adelaide. In 1974 she got a specialist traineeship in the ABC Education Department in Adelaide. Her qualifications in education provided the pathway to directing, one of the few avenues for a woman in the 1970s.

Within two weeks Margot had made her first three radio programs. She then went to Sydney for a four-week intensive television directors training course and came back to Adelaide to produce educational programs.

By 1978 she felt it was time to move on so she took two years off when she got a research development grant to do a Master in Education specialising in children's television. She became pregnant during that time. She went back to the ABC after two years and applied for the senior producer's job when children's and educational programs were amalgamated. 'I knew I'd come back to work because I loved work. I thought you could just have a child and carry on. But when it came I knew my child was more important than my job so I looked around for what I considered the best childcare and got a full-time nanny. I put out a lot of money but it gave me great peace of mind. I found someone who I thought had the same sort of moral background and I didn't have to worry about holidays or sickness.'

Two years later she took a year off to have a second child and came back to another reorganisation – TV and radio were split – and got the job of executive producer in children's television.

During that time she produced children's drama programs and the ten-part serial *Finders Keepers*. Then the ABC stopped funding dramas and went outside to co-producers. Margot was pushed up into management. 'I had been doing some active management work under duress; I didn't particularly want to do it but there was a very big push for women to be involved in management and I was virtually told "You'll do this or else you'll not progress any further".'

'That was the hardest thing for me, to move from being a hands-on person to being a manager,' However, in 1992 she combined managing with production work and took on all local productions, which included a lot of sport. She organises co-productions and stands in for the state manager, television, when he is seconded elsewhere. 'I've been lucky because I've always had someone to go to. I've had a lot of support and I haven't thought of myself as a female particularly. It's only when I got into management that I became much more aware that I'm female and that the senior people see me as a female.'

She had been the only woman on fifteen-member management committees in Sydney and had found that difficult at times. 'I think there are some senior men who just don't really see women in management positions. One guy said three or four times at a meeting "Isn't it great to have a female". I don't actually go to meetings as a female, so I spoke to him afterwards and said "Look don't say it again". He was shocked and went away and couldn't talk to me for half an hour. Finally he came back and said "I didn't mean to put you down". He had no concept of what he was implying by referring to me as a female. So as long as you don't publicly humiliate men I think you can slowly educate them.'

She also had to deal with the very male world of sport and with footballers. 'They were great guys but they would make sexist comments and wouldn't even know what they had said. For six months I don't think they ever looked at me at meetings. If they could ignore me they would. But now they look me in the eye and listen to what I say. They've changed. They just didn't have the culture. Now they have learnt to respect me and they realise that I actually work the same way as everyone else. They had to learn that a female could be on the same level as they are.'

Margot has had to make compromises. 'But that is about being married. When you're single you can go anywhere. Once I committed myself to a partnership I realised that it had to work both ways. I did it with my eyes open and I married someone who had reasons to stay in Adelaide. So I've stayed in Adelaide, which can be difficult in a national organisation.'

She has been supportive of women and tried to create courses to provide career opportunities and ensure that there were an equal number of men and women in the courses. She said that the ABC had been a great supporter of women and when David Hill was managing director it came from the top. 'Basically if there is a male and a female and they're exactly the same, you can't choose between them, you choose the woman. But the problem is that if you're a male and you don't want a female then they're not exactly the same. But there have been women's management courses and encouragement all along the line and we actively encourage women in the technical areas for work placement.'

'There have been some backlashes. I think there are some men who say "she only got the job because she is female". They will throw it up in your face and I think women have to suffer that. It means that females have to perform. I would always be the first and last in the office. I'll always be the super-whatever because then I will feel that they can't come back at me. That happens to women a lot.'

Margot believes that you have to understand that as a woman you are going to have to fight harder. 'But you have got to be aware that if you come on really hard you're not going to win. Men can bulldoze in and possibly get what they want but you have to work out a way of dealing with it that you feel comfortable with and that gets the results you want.'

She was worried about a women's club to counteract the men's club. 'I don't want to be part of a men's club or a women's club but you do need to seek support. I've been very lucky I have had very good support from my male supervisors.'

She advised women who want to get into television to look at where they want to be and get the qualifications outside instead of working their way up because jobs don't come up very often in the ABC. 'You also have to push like mad and have ideas. Come selling ideas. Everyone wants ideas and if you come selling ideas people will remember you. When there's a job they think of you and you can get a foot in the door.'

GLENYS GILL

Glenys Gill, NEW-10 Perth program manager, loved television and movies and in 1969 answered an advertisement for a secretary in the program department at TVW-7. She was nineteen when she got the job. In addition to her secretarial work she answered viewers' letters, kept program records and arranged for the delivery of movies and series to the station. 'The more I did, the more I enjoyed it.'

She left in 1974 to have her first child and was only gone a few months when TVW rang to ask her to do part-time work one day a week. She worked through her second pregnancy and came back for one or two days a week until the children were kindergarten and school age. Bill McKenzie, the general manager at TVW, asked her to return full-time as his secretary but agreed to her working 9 to 3 to fit her family commitments. 'In that job I started to learn about program contracts and other program negotiations. I was often asked to take minutes for board meetings and my knowledge of television became broader and broader.' When Bill McKenzie left to become general manager at ATV-10 Melbourne, Glenys asked to go back to the programming department to utilise her skills and experience. Glenys remained at TVW-7 until 1984 when she left to spend more time with her family.

In 1986 Network Ten was looking to set up an office in Fremantle to cover the America's Cup. Glenys was approached and through Bob Kemp was employed to become office manager. Rupert Murdoch owned Network Ten and News Ltd at that time, so a decision was made to set up a joint office for both arms of his media interests. 'Gradually crews, journalists and producers came over to Perth. I managed the office and organised anything they wanted. That lasted for six months, it was one of the most interesting jobs I've ever had. There was lots of hard work, long hours, but lots of fun. I met new people, dealt with print journalists and did whatever they needed. I also had the opportunity to become involved in the production side of television because they needed a director's assistant. So each morning I'd spend time with the print journalists who were filing stories for *The Australian* and then in the afternoon I'd be a director's assistant helping with the television coverage.'

At the conclusion of the America's Cup Glenys had a break from television. In 1987 Bill McKenzie telephoned to explain that Rupert Murdoch was selling Network Ten to Northern Star Holdings and that he had negotiated with the new owners to return to Perth to take up the role of managing director of the NEW-10 licence. He had been given the responsibility of getting the new station to air in a very short space of time and asked Glenys if she would be interested in a position.

'I had no hesitation in saying I would and he immediately asked "When can you come to see me in Melbourne?" I said "I can come over at any time". The children were now much older so I headed east. In the bottom drawer of his desk was a box of paperwork and he said "This is all I know, I'm trying to find out what product we own and what the network can give us. This is the start of the station". He gave me a great amount of paper and said "Take this home, read through the memos and tell me what you can find out".'

'The program manager at ATV-10 was flying to Sydney the next day and said "That's where all network contracts are held – why don't you fly up with me". I spent the next two days in Sydney, photocopying, talking to financial people and having a look at their program contracts to find out whether NEW-10 in Perth could access the product.'

Glenys had been given this responsibility because she knew about contracts, network and Australian rights and programming generally. She was employed from August 1987 and worked at home for two months going through the paperwork and compiling product listings for the new station. In October an office was set up in St George's Terrace and she worked from that office until May 1988 when she moved to the new station at Dianella Heights where she has been working ever since as program manager.

'The turning point for me was when Bill McKenzie said he would be extremely happy for me to work as his secretary but felt I had more to contribute. He said "I think you and I between us can handle the programming of the station". I felt confident. I had received a very good grounding in programming contracts and programming strategies and I knew I could do it. When he reaffirmed that to me by offering me the job of program manager, I thought it was great. That was my opportunity. Bit by bit we sorted through the problems and I became close to other Network Ten programmers interstate. They were all men, very few women worked in top positions at that time. But everyone had faith in me.'

JOBS IN TELEVISION

I interviewed over sixty women who do jobs using equipment in the mainland capital city television stations and the operations managers, all male, who employ them. None of the women wanted their interviews sourced to them but they were happy for me to use their stories to build a generic picture of what it is like to be a woman working in a job in the operations area.

All the women except two, who were about to leave the industry, were full of enthusiasm for their jobs. While nearly all of them had difficult experiences with the male culture, they all emphasised that these were rare and that most of the men they worked with were 'terrific'.

Writing this section on television I find I am caught in the middle of a feminist dilemma – should I only tell the positive side, which shows that working in television is much easier for women than it used to be, or should I write it as I see it, pointing out how it is still not equal for women, and risk the accusation of being an old fashioned feminist with a victim mentality?

Kathy Bail says in *DIY Feminism* (1996), young women today believe that they can do anything, they do not want to be associated with a feminist culture of complaint. They don't want to be identified with something that shows them to be at a disadvantage or be seen as victims.

There is also a question of responsibility. If there is still a difference in the numbers of women and men in different jobs, and women want to get into those jobs, then there are legitimate questions: why are women not there and what can management do to encourage them and keep them? Hopefully some of these stories will not only help women but raise issues with managements.

Mandy Smith (see p311) said that she is disappointed that not as many women have come up behind her to direct as she would have liked. She identifies that as partly due to the economic tightening of the industry but says that women she has talked to are having to do it all again and that it's not got any easier. 'You have to prove yourself, they are not going to meet you halfway, so you actually have to leap through higher hoops.' But she does go on to say, 'I still think it's coming from the women themselves. Women are still very much brought up not to put themselves forward with a great lot of confidence, they're not as well equipped as they should be to work in an industry that is largely male dominated and where the attitudes are entrenched. I don't believe they are on the floor, on the crew level, but I believe they are still in middle management, still in areas of finance, where the money is coming from'.

Thinking through these issues I have a feeling of deja vu. I entered the television industry 40 years ago with a belief that I could do anything – thanks to an affirming mother and a progressive co-educational school in London. I identified with the experiences and attitudes that Kathy Bail, who was born nearly thirty years later, described 'I grew up surrounded by women... somehow I just took the notion of equal opportunity in my stride in my teens and never felt I should be in any way disadvantaged as a woman' (1996, p11).

I trained as an actor where there is no discrimination (except the lack of lead parts for women). I managed to carve a career in television in accepted female roles of actor, researcher and writer and was in the right place at the right time to get a job as a television director in independent television in Britain in 1962. I did not identify as a feminist. I believed that if women had the will they could succeed.

It wasn't until International Women's Year (IWY) in 1975 that I became sensitised to women's issues. I was head of research at AFTRS and took over the women in the media initiatives for IWY which had been started by Jerzy Toeplitz, the founding director. I then recognised that I had had problems that my male colleagues had not – that I had not had the same choices; that I should not have had to put up with sexist behaviour; that problems were not always my fault; and that my inability to cope with the humiliation I was put through by an all male interviewing panel for a job at Gore Hill Technical College (as it was then) was not because of my inadequacies but a power game at my expense. I had had role models and a male mentor but that did not help me cope at the day-to-day personal level (see Appendix 3).

Today there is still the question, why is it harder for women than men? And if, as a male member of television management, you become defensive when reading these stories then ask yourself 'What can I do to encourage more women to get work and feel comfortable and stay in the non-traditional areas in the organisation'.

So here are some of the stories of how women get on in non-traditional jobs in television. Hopefully more women will be encouraged to apply for them and managements will support them.

OPERATIONS

Television stations have two main functions. The core business is to keep a service running 24 hours a day broadcasting programs and, if it is a commercial station, put commercials to air. This is the responsibility of the operations and engineering departments and they employ people to work on equipment in jobs which have no parallel in the film industry.

The second function is to produce programs. The jobs in television production are similar to those in film production, except that they use video equipment which requires different skills. The jobs in departments which use equipment, such as camera, audio, editing (videotape and switching) and graphic design, are usually full-time and also come under the operations department. The director and director's assistant (DA) are also often full-time employees and can come under the operations department.

The producers and writers who provide the content for programs are usually employed on a contract for specific programs, except in the newsroom where the journalists and news producers are full-time employees.

The operations department is divided into sections, with supervisors heading the sections and answerable to the manager. The managers and supervisors are usually the most experienced staff and therefore the most senior. They are responsible for employing the people who work on the equipment. Because operations managers have come up through the jobs using equipment there are no women managers and very few women supervisors.

Traditionally, therefore, operations departments have been male preserves. Women were usually employed in the stereotypically female jobs of receptionist and secretary. Secretaries could get promoted to DA, vision switchers and producers, or they could work up to more senior positions in other departments such as sales, promotions or publicity.

However, as a result of equal opportunity programs, media training courses and the success of women in the film industry, television stations now employ women in operations departments. Women who had trained as graphic designers began to get jobs in videographics, where they have become heads of departments. Gradually women from media courses were employed in junior positions operating videotape machines and moved into jobs as editors and, sometimes, as news camera assistants and occasionally as news camera operators. But they have not been so successful in getting jobs as studio camera operators or working in the audio departments.

THE CULTURE

Television is seen as a glamorous place to work and, while people who work in it know this is not the case, it does give them a status. 'We consciously create stars and big egos which you have to keep nurturing, and this rubs off down the line so that you get caught up in your own publicity.'

Television works to very strict deadlines. Everyone works to get programs to air on the second, and mistakes in the operations area are usually very public. This means that operations departments are in a state of constant crisis management and there is a culture of 'the show must go on regardless' which can be used as an excuse not to worry about the way people behave. After the crisis all is forgiven and forgotten so that any post mortems are about what went wrong and how it was put right, not what was said or not said in the heat of the moment.

As one woman working in the videotape area explained, 'We are the engine room, we are the ones who turn out the product, we expect to work long hours and do extraneous things. If someone falls down you jump in and do his job. We're on air, there is not time for "sorry we can't do it now".'

There is no doubt that the television industry is different from most other industries. There is a very high level of dedication and, as a survey of Nine Network staff found (see Appendix 1), there is very high job satisfaction.

One woman said, 'No-one is ever bored – absolutely the opposite. We never look at our watches; wouldn't know whether it's day or night. You can get up at 3.30, be in here by 4.30 in the morning, everyone is buzzing, you're not tired, and at 11 at night you walk out and you think, "God it's dark; what was it like when I came in? I can't even remember". You're dead after a year, you've gotta have a holiday because you're mentally and physically drained, but here you know that you work for the best, you're working with the people who get the ratings. And everyone gives up salary for job satisfaction.'

People identify with their jobs. They have a very strong commitment to the stations they work in and want to do better and better work. The staff work as a team and share the highs and lows of panic situations, often on a daily basis. 'It is not a job where you can lay down rules. Often you need to employ people at very short notice on short term contacts and then the program works and they have got a job for years. Or, alternatively, it flops and you have to lay people off. Employment decisions are often made very quickly.'

What has surprised some people who have come to management from other industries is the great loyalty staff have for their station in spite of working conditions which are below acceptable standards in the industries they have come from.

One operations manager explained 'Historically this company has basically sat back and employed people, told them what to do and if they didn't do it properly they were sacked. You end up with a whole lot of people who know what they have to do but with no career path or direction and that's why not one of our senior managers, apart from finance, has any form of qualification in management.'

Another (male) manager suggested that there are two types of people who work in the operations area. 'One is a craft person who is good at his or her craft and has therefore become a senior person. They are often prejudiced against women. Then there are the more senior people who are far less focused on a particular craft and they don't think that way at all but they don't address the problem because there are other more pressing issues.' He said he was committed to a balanced workforce 'because it would create better harmony and be seen as a fair and good place to work which would mean that productivity would go up'.

Another said that he had woken up to the fact that the technical operations area does not require technical left brain people but rather people who can look more broadly and think laterally about relationships and he started to look for women to train.

Without exception, all operations managers said that any woman wanting to get into television had to be persistent and never take no for an answer. They were divided about the usefulness of courses. On balance they all agreed that the most important thing was to get your first job in television and once you were working in the station you were in a much better position to work out what you wanted to do.

One supervisor illustrated what he meant by persistence. 'I've got a girl who every morning for the last four weeks has rung me from London at her own expense. 9am the phone is gonna ring, it's going to be Amanda, she's just got home, it's 11 at night. She is coming out next month for a holiday because she is so determined to break into Australian television. She's got some skills, she is working at Sky in London as a vision switcher, but we would probably have to retrain her. I can't give her a job, because she's probably only got a one to two year visa, I can't limit myself to even two years, I've gotta say five. She knows this, so I have given her a chance to get into the freelance market in Sydney, and if she can find somewhere to live, and drive a car, and get herself organised, well I'll see what I can do. But that's the kind of interest that I really want. Someone who knows what it's like and had people yell at her, but it's gotta be that kind of a committed person.'

CAMERA

Programs made in television stations are shot on electronic video cameras and recorded onto videotape. The cameras and skills required to operate them are different from those needed for mechanical film cameras. The video camera operator, unlike a film camera operator, is not expected to strip down a video camera in order to clean it. This would be done by electronic engineers and maintenance people who are employed by the television station or by the manufacturer's servicing department.

When television first started, video cameras were large and heavy and it was not possible to edit videotape. Studio and outside broadcast (OB) programs were produced live, switching between a number of cameras, while news items were shot on 16mm film. Today, television cameras used in the studio and on OBs are much smaller. Programs that switch between cameras as they go to air or are recorded are called multicamera (or multicam) productions to distinguish them from single video camera productions which are used for news coverage and location drama.

Television stations employ a number of news and studio camera operators on staff but there is little interchange between the multicam operators and the single camera operators who shoot the news. Both types of camera operator are employed on a roster system to cover the regular programs that are produced. In capital cities freelance camera operators are sometimes employed to supplement the station's crew for a particular program or for the run of the program.

Unlike film, the camera department working on multicam shoots is not responsible for lighting or adjusting their cameras for 'exposure', that is done by a separate vision department.

NEWS CAMERA OPERATORS

All television stations have a number of news crews, each of which consists of a news camera operator and an assistant, who helps the operator carry the equipment and is responsible for recording the sound.

The news crew is rostered on shifts, shooting whatever stories come up during the day for the late afternoon bulletin. A journalist is usually assigned to each story and is responsible for the content of the news item. The camera operator drives the camera car and once they get to the location she has to make quick judgments about the best way to shoot the story and, if necessary, quickly light the scene or person.

A news camera operator spends a lot of her time waiting in the camera car for stories to break, or scurrying from one story to the next across the city. No day is the same and there is a lot of equipment handling in and out of the camera car.

While there are still very few women working on television news camera crews, there are an increasing number of women journalists on the road with the camera crews. This means that a female camera assistant or operator can often have another woman in the camera car. However, she is often the only woman when the the camera crews from all the stations are setting up and vying for good positions or hanging around waiting for press conferences.

ISSUES FOR WOMEN

All the women I interviewed agreed that the job of news camera operator or assistant was fantastic. It provides interesting challenges, you meet interesting people, no two days are the same and you can go to places where you would never normally go.

However, being a news camera operator is probably one of the hardest jobs for women in television because it is still a novelty, both within the stations and in the community.

It requires loading the camera in and out of cars and carrying it to different locations and often shooting with it on your shoulder.

Traditionally, television stations have felt that the job was too hard for women. Some news editors would not allow women journalists to cover certain jobs, let alone have a woman camera operator.

There are still a few male camera operators who do not think that it is a job for women and they can make life difficult.

One woman identified the problem this way: 'For a lot of the guys in the commercial stations, the news camera is the pinnacle of their career and a lot of the reasons why they go into camera work is because it's an expression of them as men. When they see women doing it, it's like a challenge to something that they consider very male and personifying their maleness.'

A female journalist described these types of men more crudely: 'It's as if the camera is an extension of their dicks, they think they can poke it in anywhere'.

Most male camera operators deplore this attitude and are very supportive of women. Many will go out of their way to give advice and share their knowledge with their women assistants and give them opportunities to operate the camera.

Traditionally you start as a camera assistant although with one person crews there are fewer camera assistants being employed. As a camera assistant, you have to spend a lot of time with your male camera operator in the news camera car killing time. Everyone says that it is important for women to realise that if you are unlucky enough to be paired with someone who has a bad attitude you should not take it personally, it is he who has the problem not you.

One woman said that as a 20-year-old assistant she didn't know how to cope with the sexist remarks she was getting. She talked to some of the senior cameramen she worked with and they made her see that the guy was hostile towards women generally and that it wasn't her personally. One of them suggested she write down all the things he said and confront him with it. She did this and explained to him that she was going home after work upset because of the things he was saying. He was taken aback and said he didn't realise that he was having that effect on her. The behaviour stopped and she felt empowered by dealing with it in that way.

Most women camera operators have amusing stories about how

the police and the public usually assume that their male camera assistant is the person in charge.

All women agreed that there needed to be more women news camera operators because then people would get used to the idea that it is a job for women too. However, operations managers complain that women do not apply for the jobs.

Women camera operators disagreed about whether a quota system to raise the number of women employed would work. Some thought that women who got their jobs through quotas were given a particularly hard time because the men considered it unfair. Others thought that it would be the only way to begin to even up the numbers and make managements conscious of the problems.

When there has been more than one woman in the news camera department the women have enjoyed the novelty. There was one example where two women had been rostered together because the management had hoped they would compete with each other and become rivals. In fact they helped each other, took it in turns to shoot, had a good time and the journalists enjoyed working with them. Other women who have worked together talked about a more relaxed atmosphere and a lot of laughter.

Many women news camera operators see it as a good way to go on to produce or direct documentaries or do more challenging work on camera.

GETTING STARTED

News camera operators have generally started as an assistant. The camera operator gradually allows them to shoot scenes and, over time, they move on to become a camera operator.

In some commercial television stations, with the introduction of lighter equipment, there is a growing tendency to drop the assistant and have the journalist hold the microphone. However, if it is likely to be a difficult story then an assistant is used. This reduction in assistant positions on news crews is creating problems for training news camera operators.

In the ABC in Sydney and Melbourne, traditionally sound and camera are two different departments, so that a sound assistant does the job that a camera assistant does in commercial television. But this practice is changing and ABC news crews are becoming more like the commercial crews, where the camera assistant looks after the sound and aspires to be a camera operator.

As a generalisation, women working in the ABC have either entered through an ABC trainee scheme, which no longer exist, or have done a university arts degree specialising in visual arts, photography or production.

In Sydney during the 1970s and '80s there was a film and television production course at Gore Hill TAFE which had a reputation for providing entry into the ABC. A number of women who are still working in the ABC in technical areas came through that two-year diploma course, although many did not complete it.

Women in commercial television usually come straight from school. However, in Adelaide there is the media and professional skills course (MAPS), which is a one-year fee-paying course at Hamilton Senior Campus, effectively a Year 13 practical advanced certificate course for people who want to work in television and film. Women are given equal opportunities on the equipment and the Adelaide commercial television stations all recruit from this course for the jobs where equipment is used.

None of the women news camera operators appeared to have gone to the AFTRS in order to get a job in television, generally because they did not want to do more study, or they thought it would be too hard to get in. However, one assistant operator took a year without pay to do an AFTRS one-year extension course in order to try and enhance her chances of being promoted at the ABC. She was successful.

ADVICE

To get a job as a news camera operator you have to be persistent.

Make contact with the person responsible for employing the news camera crew by writing, visiting, and then continually following up with phone calls.

Offer to do work experience; come in at weekends as unpaid labour and go out with the camera crew so you get known. In this way you should know when a job comes up.

Work as a volunteer on low budget films in order to work with the experienced camera operator who is employed on the shoot; work on student films and get jobs through meeting camera operators socially.

Stand up for yourself. It is physically challenging and the hardest part is maintaining your confidence when you are establishing yourself.

To start with you will probably have to prove yourself every day but talk to other women on the station working on equipment and you'll find that they have usually had the same experiences.

Don't be too defensive by taking things personally when they aren't meant personally. Realise that often people feel threatened by you because you're a woman doing what they think is a man's job.

MULTICAMERA OPERATORS

The skills required for a multicam operator are quite different from those required for news. The television studio and OB cameras are larger than the news camera and are not loaded with videotape. Multicam is used mainly for live productions and for programs that will be recorded as if they are live. Each camera has an operator who will be responsible for certain shots in the program. A switcher or vision mixer (who may be the director) will switch to whichever shot she wants from the variety of shots the cameras are offering. The lighting of the studio or location will be the responsibility of the technical director who will be in the control room.

STUDIO CAMERA OPERATOR

The studio camera operator works as part of the camera team with the rest of the studio crew, which consists of the floor manager, sound, lighting and staging. All the camera operators will take direction from the director in the control room. The production will either go live to air, such as the news, or be recorded onto tape with a few breaks, such as quiz programs. The skill is to change position and shots quickly and be ready when the director wants to take the shot on your camera.

Regular programs in the week's schedule, such as the news, current affairs, game shows, and some commercials, are produced in the studio during the week. The crew is rostered on for a shift and individuals may have different programs to work on during each shift depending on the demands of the production schedule. The work on any one shift is much the same each week unless there is a new show.

OB CAMERA OPERATOR

Sport is the main type of program to use OB cameras. Outside broadcasts are produced in a similar way to studio programs, with a control room in the OB van. The cameras have to be taken to the site and positioned to capture the action. The camera operator offers up shots in a predetermined pattern and the shots are switched, as they are in a studio, to go out live and/or be recorded onto videotape.

The jobs of studio and OB multicam operator are similar enough to be interchangeable. However, multicam operators sometimes use single camera if there is location work associated with studio programs, so that the old divisions between studio multicam operators and location single camera operators are breaking down, except in the case of news camera operators, who remain separate.

ISSUES FOR WOMEN

The working environment for a multicam operator is quite different from a news camera operator. You work with other camera operators on a crew, either in a studio or on location. Together with the other camera operators you provide shots in a pre-planned sequence for the director's approval. The skill is to anticipate the shot the director wants.

The job can vary depending on the production. The standard format programs, like the news, are not very demanding for the camera crew and there can be a lot of waiting around while other production problems are sorted out in the control room. But complicated live-to-air productions and OBs, where the camera operator has to follow the action as it happens, can demand physical and quick creative skills.

Women enjoy this work because it uses visual and operational skills and is rostered, which means that you know what you are doing each day. It is also the job that has traditionally led to directing, although that is now changing.

There are still very few women multicam operators because they have traditionally been recruited from staging – which involves shifting scenery – and women have seldom been employed in this area. Therefore women multicam operators usually have to work on all-male camera crews which vary in size depending on the number of cameras required for the production. Very often the whole studio crew is male and this can be an interesting challenge.

Some women said they have had to get used to being the only woman in the blokey male culture and several said that there is a very difficult line that women have to draw, working permanently with the same men on all male crews. 'You have to negotiate to be accepted at one level but not lose your self respect at another... Over time you get to know their different ways and most of them are fine once you have proved yourself.'

OBs often provide more challenging camera work but they are also much harder physically because the equipment has to be set up and taken down. Women working on OBs have to work out the extent to which they will let the men help them lift equipment. 'It's not that we want to be one of the boys but we don't want to be mollycoddled either', one female OB camera operator explained.

As with the job of news camera operator, more women would make a difference to attitudes and to the culture within a crew and a station. The few women camera operators are providing important role models for other women at each station and are showing managements that women can do the job.

Because programs are rostered in advance it is possible to organise commitments around the schedule and, like jobs in video graphics and video operations, it is probably possible to work part-time or job share around child-rearing. However, there are so few women working on cameras that this possibility has not come up.

GETTING STARTED

The studio camera operators in city stations have traditionally come through staging. There seems to be no training reason for this except that one of the staging tasks is to pull the camera cables around and look after the props on the studio floor, which provides an opportunity to observe what happens. Very few women apply for staging jobs. However with the introduction of task analysis (see pp354-6) this traditional job progression is changing.

Stations that do employ women camera operators have usually made a conscious effort to try and employ them, or they have come from a regional station where the studio crews are smaller and also do single camera work.

Most women camera operators have got the job through sheer persistence. One woman in a country town had to wait two years until the facilities manager, who would not employ women, moved on.

ADVICE

Find out who employs the camera operators at the station and hound them, keep writing, keep ringing and try and see them so that they can see what kind of a person you are and remember your face.

Try getting a job in a regional station, but first find out what their attitude is to employing women in the area.

Don't be put off by the odd sexist joke among the members of the crew and work out how to handle it because you are going to have to continue to work with the same guys.

Seek out other women on the station and discuss problems with them.

AUDIO/SOUND

For television, the mechanics of recording sound through microphones and mixing the sound sources, either for live recording or onto tape, is similar to the techniques used for feature films. However, 'sound' is usually called 'audio' in commercial television – the ABC has a sound department – and the process is collapsed so that the production recording and the final sound mix happens at the same time on live-to-air or live-to-tape shows. The audio mixer on a multicam television program is responsible for the audio crew and sits at a mixing desk.

MULTICAM PRODUCTION

There is usually a minimum of two sound people on a production: an audio assistant on the studio floor or on location to look after the microphones, and an audio mixer in the control room.

The composition of the camera shots and the sequence of recording them determines where the microphones will be placed and therefore how the sound will be recorded. In a simple production, such as news or an interview where there are one or two static microphones, usually only one person is employed who sets up the microphones and then mixes the sound. If there are a number of microphones which have to be moved or changed in the course of a production, or a microphone has to be operated on a boom and moved to cover a number of people, then the function of operating and moving the microphone/s may require one or more people on the studio floor, or location, and an audio person in the control room who will mix the sound sources. The audio mixer will perform a similar role controlling the sound as the vision mixer does for the pictures (see p292). If the production is live, with a complicated range of sound sources, such as recorded music and effects, then there may be additional audio people in the control room who will assist the audio mixer. The audio mixer is responsible for mixing all the sources to support the pictures selected by the director and switched by the vision switcher.

On location there is usually at least two audio crew: one (the assistant) to look after the microphones, which are placed to pick up effects as well as commentary, and one to mix the sound in the OB control van.

On the studio floor the audio crew works closely with the camera crew, as the shots that the camera is taking will determine where the microphones are placed. If a boom is used the crew will also work with the lighting director, or technical director, to ensure that there is no boom shadow in shot.

The audio person's job is a mixture of technical knowledge, operational skills and sound design. She has to physically set up and rig the microphones, operate a boom, and mix all the sound sources with very little direction. A director seldom directs the audio. The audio mixer is expected to follow the script, direct the audio crew and mix the sound.

Most of the creative sound work in television is done by the picture editor and mixed in the post production suite when there is time to enhance the vision by sound effects and music. Audio mixers can specialise in post production work in some stations or get rostered between live studio work and post production work in others. The editor and the audio department in a television station work together full-time on a range of programs.

SINGLE CAMERA PRODUCTION

Most TV single camera productions are for news or current affairs programs. In commercial television, the news sound recordist is not a sound specialist, she is the camera assistant – a job which leads to being a camera operator. Traditionally in the ABC the news sound recordist is part of the sound department and this job is regarded as part of the overall training in the sound department. Although this is changing and ABC news crews, like the commercial stations (if they take assistants), tend to take camera assistants.

Post production sound editing is done by the picture editor. On simple television productions, such as news, any sound mixing which might be needed is usually done by the audio mixer when the program goes to air.

ISSUES FOR WOMEN

Working in audio in a television station provides an interesting mix of creative sound design skills and technical operational and maintenance skills. Unlike working in films, you are not pigeon-holed into production or post production. You can work on a wide range of sound jobs from recording and mixing for live and recorded studio and OB productions to working in post production adding sound to programs, including dramas. Television stations also provide a wide range of different types of sound equipment and there are the advantages of a full-time job. Also, working on a rostered crew can more easily lend itself to part-time work or job sharing.

However, it is difficult to get a job in an audio department without some knowledge of the equipment and this has created a technical barrier to entry for many women.

A male culture therefore still exists in some audio departments. One sound assistant said that you have got to get used to the idea that the sound studio is regarded as a boys' room. One woman who had been a trainee in commercial television but now works in films complained that technical one-upmanship was used to make her feel stupid. 'They were always asking me to get equipment by names I'd never heard of without explaining what the equipment was. This made me feel totally incompetent until one day I was asked to get the "fuck" box and then realised that they were making up the names and no-one from another station would have known what they were.'

The audio crew works as a team and women are therefore dependent on the men on the crew to explain what has to be done. This is different from working on a camera crew where each person is responsible to the director for the shots they get on their own camera.

Women working in commercial television tended to be thrown in the deep end. The ABC had a formal training scheme where there was an accepted responsibility in the various departments for the senior staff to train the trainees whether they were men or women. There were also training supervisors – usually men – with whom trainees could discuss problems.

All the women interviewed said that most of the men were very supportive but there were one or two who resented women being in sound and this could lead to difficult situations. These usually involved young women who found it difficult to confront older men who were taking a rise out of them.

Here are some examples of incidences and how women have coped:

'All the time stupid remarks like, "Where did you learn to mix? Cooking school?". I usually just freeze and give them a deadly glare.'

'When we were on location one of the technician's caravans had wall-to-wall nudes and I was expected to sit in there. I'd sit outside and then I'd be accused of being superior and arrogant.'

'When I was a sound assistant on current affairs I was constantly excluded from conversations with the journalist, the producer and the camera operator about the next shot. I used to try to butt in to get their attention but they would ignore me, then suddenly they would be setting up and I wouldn't know if it was a wide shot. I'd find I wasn't equipped and they would make derogatory remarks. Now I'm getting more forceful. I'll demand to know what they are doing.'

When asked about the gender balance in audio departments in commercial television, operations managers said that women do not have the technical expertise because they do not enrol in tertiary technical courses.

All women agreed that it can be a rewarding job and that more women need to get into television audio to break down the male culture and thereby change the perception that it is a male job.

GETTING STARTED

Do a TAFE course in sound.

Some women who have found a TAFE course too daunting in the first instance have learnt the technical side through more general courses and activities, such as film and video production, technical theatre or music recording for community radio. They then go to a TAFE course specialising in sound.

Try to get a job in sound transfer. While it is a fairly mundane operational job of copying sound tapes, it has been a starting place for some women in both the ABC and commercial television. Like the other jobs in television it is often a case of getting into any job and being persistent about what you want to do, spending spare time watching and asking questions of the sound guys and being seen to be eager, so that hopefully someone might take you under his wing.

One woman said 'I played instruments and liked putting stereos together, a band needed a sound engineer and showed me how to do it. I did some composing, it was used in a film. I went to the recording and got interested. I helped the lead technician and he taught me everything about making up leads, wiring up, and I ended up wiring a suite. I found someone to teach me.'

ADVICE

Learn the technical side, which means knowing how the equipment works and what it can do.

Find a course, even if it is for radio or the theatre. Develop your skills by working in community radio, on student productions and learning from others.

Pursue volunteer work on productions where you can use your skills and learn.

Contact women who are working in sound and ask their advice.

Talk to the heads of the audio departments at the television stations and find out the technical competence they require and make sure that they know you're interested in getting into sound. If they are negative about women in the sound department seek the advice of the equal opportunity officer at the station.

EDITING

The career path for an editor in a television station is usually through working as a videotape operator and from there progressing to post production editor or news editor. The vision switcher, although not regarded as an editor, does in fact make editing decisions with the director so that job has also been included in this section.

VIDEOTAPE OPERATOR

A videotape operator is the most junior job in the operational area. Videotape operators have taken over from telecine operators, whose job – generally seen as male – involved carting cans of film around and lacing up projectors. But today television stations accept that videotape operator is a job which can be done by women as well as men. Some managements go so far as to say that there is an advantage in having gender balance in the videotape area. It is the entry point for many women who want to work with equipment in television.

The videotape operator is part of the operational crew. The job involves operating the videotape machines for recording material from various sources, copying and assembling material for broadcast and playing programs to air. The crew works in shifts and there is usually a number of operators on any one shift. The work depends on the programs and production schedule. The videotape operator is responsible for assembling the day's programs and putting them to air, or she is assigned to a production and works with the technical director or director.

A videotape operator's work sometimes includes doing simple post production editing. This will usually be butt-editing to join sequences of a multicamera production. In smaller stations videotape operators can also learn to do more complicated post production work on commercials, promotional tapes and edited highlights.

The videotape machines are usually located in a central operations area, often in the bowels of the station with no daylight. The area is traditionally a male one because it deals with equipment and because in some stations seniority in the operations area depends on having a Broadcasting Certificate (Operations) qualification from TAFE. This is a theoretical course in basic electronic engineering which few women have pursued. However, most television managements now accept that women can be good videotape operators and that it does not need a theoretical knowledge of electronics.

ISSUES FOR WOMEN

A videotape operator is a great job for young women who have no qualifications, who like working with equipment and want to get into television. In most stations there are a number of women working in videotape, and in some almost half the videotape operators are women. This means that gradually the male culture in the operations area is being watered down, although there are still very few women in senior positions. (See Camilla Rudd, p246, who was an exception.)

Most women working in videotape are young and tend to accept the male culture, language and behaviour. They either let it brush over them and seek out female friends in other departments, or consciously become 'one of the boys'.

The main problems women have are those of discrimination. One woman summed it up this way: 'When I started here I had done computer editing which none of the guys had done but I went into "on air" which is probably the lowest area you can go. If I'd been a guy with my experience I would have gone straight into production. I had to work twice as hard as anyone else to get where I wanted to go. I have to be better than the males just to prove myself whereas a guy would slip into the position'.

A common complaint was that senior men had old-fashioned attitudes towards women working on equipment. This meant that the men were provided with opportunities to fill in on more senior jobs and given the more difficult work when someone was sick or on leave. As a result, women were disadvantaged by lack of experience when promotional opportunities arose. Others said that the discrimination was a manifestation of the 'boys' club': 'They all go out to the pub and mix socially so that when the jobs come up they go to their mates'.

However, these things are changing as managements reorganise their human resource areas (see Appendix 1) and implement proper selection and promotion processes. Most women said that there are not the same problems with younger managers.

One example of old-fashioned attitudes was a supervisor's reaction to a woman when she became a mother. 'Then he treated me as if I had become another person and kept asking me if I could manage the work – the same work I'd been doing for years.'

The videotape area also seems to provide more opportunity for sexist comments because operators are constantly looking at images on the screen. 'At Nine they used to get Skychannel and the guys would sit round and watch half-naked women writhing around. I'd say "Hey guys, that's enough... if you want to watch go down the other end and watch".'

The most common complaint, however, was about the assumption that because you are female you have no technical knowledge. There were stories similar to those that women news camera operators told about people always asking their male assistant for information. 'If there's a technical problem men from other departments will seek out a less experienced man. They'll go out of their way to ask someone else rather than a woman and they never make eye contact with you if there is another man in the room, even though I'm the senior.' Most women learn to become assertive and gently point out that they are the ones who have the answers.

GETTING STARTED

Many women have found that videotape operating is the easiest operational job for a woman to get in a television station. With the exception of stations in Sydney and Melbourne, and the ABC, women have become videotape operators straight from school, although most have had some media production experience while at school or, in Adelaide, through the MAPS course (see p273).

In commercial television in Sydney and Melbourne, and in the ABC, videotape operators are more likely to have had some tertiary training or they may have had experience in production houses or regional stations.

Most women videotape operators got the job because they hassled the operations manager. Even if they eventually want to get a job on camera or in sound they start in videotape because it is easier to get those jobs. One woman in Adelaide said, 'I tried for a long time... they got sick of my letters. I knew the operations manager and I used to hassle him. For five years I hassled him. Finally I was living in Alice Springs when the station rang me on a Friday and said "Can you get down by Monday for an interview?"...'

Some women have been so keen to work in the operational area that they have taken more traditional female jobs, such as secretary or receptionist, in order to get in and then applied for the job of videotape operator when it was advertised internally. Others have had friends working at the station who tell them when a job is available. Occasionally the job is advertised outside, particularly if the station is trying to improve its female profile, but usually there are so many people who have written to the operations manager, or who have friends in the station, that there is no need to advertise outside.

Videotape operators do not necessarily aspire to be editors when they start, but once working in television a number have become interested in editing. Some women see the position of videotape operator as a way to other jobs at the station, such as presentation coordinator, vision switcher, videographic designer or director. Others have married and see that it is a job they can do part-time, and so combine with having a family.

The speed with which videotape operators can move to other work depends very much on how the station is organised. Some are very hierarchical and have qualification barriers to more senior operational positions, others have a multi-skilling philosophy. A station's attitude usually depends on the amount of program production work that is done and the size of the station. If the station produces a variety of programs, not just simple commercials and promotional tapes, then there are a lot more videotape editing and post production opportunities.

One videotape operator/editor in a station which encourages multi-skilling said, 'If editing is what you want to do just do it. If you come across obstacles from the males be prepared for it and stand up for what you believe and if you want to go on and be on the production desk as a producer just do it'.

ADVICE

Understand what the job entails because 'there is a lot of sitting around doing nothing but there is also a lot of pressure'.

Do a course so that you know something about the operation of equipment and how to use a videotape machine.

If you are doing a course and you get a job opportunity take the job. 'There is no course that can teach you the pressure... You don't understand until you're standing down there and something goes wrong. There is black up on that screen and you've got to fix it because everyone is sitting at home watching that black.'

Be prepared to move and start in a regional station, because people move from the regional stations to the larger city stations. Be aware that some regional stations may not be as keen to have women working in videotape. The employment of women depends very much on the personal biases of the operations manager rather than on the senior management.

Get an attachment or get to know someone who works at the station and ask to sit in so that you know what the job is and you can make contacts.

Getting the first job is probably the hardest. 'Just keep knocking on doors and reminding the stations and the person who is responsible for employing videotape operators that you want a job and you're ready, waiting and eager.'

NEWS EDITORS

The news editor in a television station is usually part of the news room and works quite separately from the videotape operators and post production editors. She is responsible for cutting the news footage each day and works with journalists when the stories come in.

The news editor cuts the picture and sound together and there is no time for post production enhancement. Usually the story is entirely dependent on what the camera operator (and sound recordist if there is a camera assistant recording sound) brings in. The journalists will know the points they are trying to make and may have to record additional commentary but that will usually be the limit of any post production work. The news editor is usually working against the clock and her day revolves around the times that the news bulletins go to air. There is usually not much time for contemplative editing.

In some stations the news editor might double up as the news camera operator; in others the job of news editor is a way to become a news camera operator.

ISSUES FOR WOMEN

It is a challenging job and there are many women news editors. It is a good way to get experience in editing. You work on your own and, with journalists, are involved in the daily news and part of the news room hype that gets the news to air each night.

News editors usually come under the head of news and the working environment depends on the culture in the news room. Some still have a very male culture in spite of employing a lot of young female journalists. Other news rooms which employ younger male journalists are more supportive of women.

Women news editors have opportunities to educate their male

colleagues about what they see as acceptable coverage. A number of women said they had challenged journalists about particular shots in a story which they felt denigrated women and they had usually been successful in getting them taken out or cut shorter.

Sometimes there were sexist remarks from male journalists when they viewed shots in the cutting room. Women editors differed in their responses. Some let it go because they felt it wasn't worth the risk of then having to contend with derision. Others made a point of responding by saying 'God you're childish' or 'Hey guys, give me a break', which at least made the men aware of what they had said.

Some women complained about male put-downs. One woman said that a sports journalist would denigrate her when she made suggestions by saying 'Oh, you're a girl, you wouldn't know anything about sport'. She retaliated by ridiculing sport and refusing to cut his stories.

GETTING STARTED

News editors can come from videotape operations and might start in news transfer where they transfer stories in and out of the station and monitor the overnight international news.

The important thing is to be familiar with the editing machines and be able to work fast. One editor in a smaller station came straight from a media course after she had done some work experience where she sat with the news editors and learnt to use the machine when they were not using it.

Some news editors come from editing in production houses.

ADVICE

Start in a regional station because it is easier to get in.

Hang around the news room so you know what is expected.

Sit in with the editor and see what the job entails.

If that's what you want to do just do it, push yourself and don't let people push you down.

POST PRODUCTION EDITOR

In the commercial television stations in Sydney and Melbourne there is a lot of production. The job of editing can range from simple editing – putting together sections of pre-recorded multicamera productions, cutting down existing programs to fit a time slot, and making promotional spots – to the sophisticated editing of a single camera production or commercial.

The creative skills required depend on the complexity of the production and the technical skills depend on the editing equipment used. The post production editor uses similar equipment and therefore needs similar skills to editors of features and small budget films, commercials and corporate videos (see p118). A post production editor can, therefore, acquire skills which allow her to move between the film and television industries.

Some commercial television stations are affiliated with post production houses, where a lot of program and commercial editing is done. These usually employ their own staff independently of the television station.

ISSUES FOR WOMEN

Depending on the types of programs that are produced, and the size of the television station, post production editor can be a very creative job using artistic ability to put together sound and images, or it can be an extension of the more technical videotape operating jobs, one that you can aspire to by learning simple editing on the job as a videotape operator.

In smaller commercial stations where most of the post production editing is relatively simple, the job is seen as an extension of the technical operations area. This means that the number of women doing the job usually depends on the mix of men and women in the videotape operations area. At the ABC, on the other hand, and the larger stations where there is sophisticated single camera editing, post production editors have tended to be recruited specifically as editors.

The most common problem women found in commercial television was getting the opportunities to do the more interesting editing work while they were videotape operators, thus gaining experience to apply for editors' jobs when they came up. Some editors complained that there were still male directors who refused to work with women editors. 'It is not said in so many words but women editors are never rostered to work with them and this attitude can stop promotion opportunities for women.'

Education programs about discrimination and the implementation of job selection and promotion procedures by commercial television stations should counter this.

GETTING STARTED

It is possible to start as a videotape operator and work your way up to post production editing but these jobs are much sought after and women usually have to change stations or work in production houses in order to get promotion.

All editors agreed that if you wanted to start as an editor rather than as a videotape operator, then some sort of training was essential before you tried to get your first job. While it is possible to learn on the job in a small production house, a good practical tertiary course can help you to get a job as an assistant editor, or even an editor on a small independent production. If you have not been trained you have to start sweeping floors and work your way up.

Most editors who did not come from videotape operations, including those in the ABC, got their jobs by word-of-mouth, filling in for someone who was absent, or coming in on a contract for one job and staying.

The change to non-linear editing has provided opportunities, particularly within the ABC, for women from the independent sector, because they have had experience on the new machines and have helped train staff. The ABC, however, is now cutting down on its production staff.

ADVICE

Start as a videotape operator and work your way up.

Get a job in a production house and learn the basic skills.

Develop and maintain your skills with the latest equipment.

Hassle the operations manager for a job once you have those skills. One operations manager told the story of a woman in England who wanted a job as an editor and rang him from England every morning to see if there was a vacancy. He said 'that's the kind of interest I want' (see p268).

VISION SWITCHERS

Vision switchers, or vision mixers as they are usually called at the ABC, are the editors who select the shots offered by the cameras in multicam productions. The vision switcher sits in the control room with the director – although sometimes the director does their own switching. The job will vary in complexity depending on the demands of the production.

Vision switchers in some stations may be responsible for the character generator, which provides the titles and credits. In other stations this is done by the graphics department or by the director's assistant (DA). If a production such as news has a lot of graphics, titles, photos and films being inserted into the studio picture as it goes out live-to-air it can get very complicated for the switcher. Vision switchers at the ABC claim that their news productions are probably the most complex. They have no commercial breaks to provide set-up time for the next segment and they are live-to-air for an hour because they go straight into the *7.30 Report*.

Live sport can provide the switcher with different challenges, and in some sports the reactions have to be very quick to follow the play being covered on different cameras. The switcher's job is to cut from camera to camera to cover the action, and then feed in the replays, scores and interviews.

Different policies about the training of vision switchers have gender implications. In some stations switching is seen as an extension of the technical staff, the equivalent, for vision, of the sound mixer, and therefore part of the camera crew and traditionally a male job. In other stations it is seen as an extension of the DA's role, and therefore part of production and traditionally a female position.

The vision switcher works very closely with the director so, logically, it could provide a career path to becoming a director. This is beginning to happen as a result of job appraisals and skills audits, and women are getting promoted from switcher to director (see pp354-6). At Channel Ten in Sydney, when switchers became redundant and directors took on the role, a woman switcher was promoted to director.

Because of the history of television production and the evolution of the equipment, the vision switcher does not usually handle tape, so it has not traditionally been a path to post production editor. Skills audits and the convergence of technology, however, could mean that this will change.

ISSUES FOR WOMEN

Vision switching is a very responsible job, particularly when programs go out live-to-air. The switcher determines what picture the viewer sees and, when all hell is breaking out in the control room, they are the ones who must remain calm and keep the show on the road. Many switchers want to become directors and that is gradually happening.

The switcher is often the link between the technical staff and the production staff. Women in commercial television complained that male vision switchers were often paid more than women for doing the same job and that men were often rostered onto the more interesting programs. One complained officially and found that she was then being consistently rostered onto the unpopular shifts.

One woman said, 'I didn't have a pay rise from the day I started as a trainee to the day I left five years later when I was one of their senior vision switchers. Males were coming in... doing the same job and getting $15-16,000 more. I had directors going up for me, I had my bosses going up to this guy and I went up on several occasions. He just said to me "I hear the squeaky door and I know it needs oiling". When I rang him up to resign and said I had had enough he said "That's fine".' Hopefully this could not happen today and if it did you could expect some action from the head of human resources or the affirmative action committees.

There was an example of reverse discrimination. One vision switcher said that an American director had said to her, 'I much prefer working with females as vision switchers. I feel a little bit guilty yelling at a man sometimes when things go wrong, but I don't have any hesitation yelling at a female'.

GETTING STARTED

Vision switching is such a specific job to television that most vision switchers have come from other jobs within a station. As with editing, it is a case of knowing the equipment.

Some vision switchers came from videotape via coordinating in presentation. When the ABC had a training scheme, vision switching was one of the options that was offered along with camera and editing in the vision strand. More recently they had workshops to encourage women into these operational areas, and selected them from the workshops into on-the-job training schemes so that some women in traditional female roles, such as secretarial positions, had an opportunity to transfer to operational positions. A few went into switching.

There are different degrees of production complexity for vision switchers, so they are allotted to programs depending on their experience. News is seen as one of the most complex.

ADVICE

First of all make sure it is what you want to do. It's not 9 to 5, it mucks up your social life because of the shifts, and sometimes you work fourteen hours a day.

Get into television whatever way you can, using whatever skills you've got, and then work your way through the system by getting off your butt and sitting alongside a vision switcher in your own time.

Collect as much technical knowledge as you can.

Show that you're eager. Speak up and ask to try the job. Let people know that switching is the job you want.

VIDEOGRAPHICS

Computers have made graphic design a technical job and part of the operations department instead of the art department. The work used to be done by hand so that painting and drawing skills were as important as those of design. Today, design skills are still critical and drawing skills have their place but the computer does a lot of the work.

The computer was first introduced to television graphics in the form of the character generator. It replaced caption cards, which were printed by a hot press and put in front of the camera in the studio. Simple graphs and animation were made by moving cardboard parts in front of the camera.

The character generator was usually put in the control room so that captions could be made up quickly and changed as news and sports stories unfolded. Because the female DAs and/or the vision switchers had typing skills they operated the character generator, so titling became accepted as a female job. There were some stations, however, which put the character generator in the videotape area where it was used by videotape operators, who were mainly men.

In the early 1980s a user-friendly 2D graphics generator, Quantel Paintbox, was introduced. You could use it to paint, manipulate photographs and draw graphs and maps. It was a very expensive piece of equipment and the men in the graphics department were usually the first to teach themselves how to use it. However, as the demand for Paintbox work grew, more staff were trained, or taught themselves, and the Paintbox is now used by both men and women. In some stations where there is a lot of 3D animation the men have gone over to those programs and left the 2D to the women.

Television stations organise their graphics departments in

different ways. News and sports programs are the main users and the videographic designer builds up a library of images for a production which she creates in advance. They are kept in a stack or digital system library (DSL) which the vision switcher puts to air. In some stations it may be part of the graphic designer's job to operate the DSL on air. She is often altering graphs and diagrams as the program goes to air.

In some stations there are more women than men in videographics and women are sometimes head of the department, which generally makes them the only female department head in an operations area.

ISSUES FOR WOMEN

Supplying visuals to a visual medium is a fulfilling, creative, demanding job. You work on 'state of the art' equipment and you are in a department that has been described as the 'hub of the station' because it has input into every show. This immediacy and the ability to change your work quickly and be part of the production team when the programs go to air is what designers find stimulating.

It is generally accepted that this is a job in the operations area that women can do well. Like digital artists in the film industry (see pp159-198), people working in videographics find it challenging to use computer equipment to do creative design work. You get a brief from a director or producer and work by yourself and are judged on your finished work and your ability to produce it to deadlines.

Most designers have had art school training and are recruited on the basis of their portfolio and qualifications. In commercial television it is not uncommon to find that the designers and the engineers are the only departments that consistently employ people with tertiary qualifications. Sometimes the women who work in videographics are the only women at the station who have had tertiary training.

The working conditions in videographics depend on how the functions of captioning and creating visuals and the equipment are organised. In some stations the character generator, still-frame store, Paintbox and 3D computers are in one room and people are trained to operate all the equipment. In other stations there are specialists.

Designers may become part of the production crew when the graphics go to air but this depends on how the department is organised.

It's an area with great opportunities for women designers who are interested in high output, variety and working to deadlines. There is a growing number of part-time and freelance jobs in videographics so that it can be combined with family commitments.

Women did not identify many problems that were gender-specific to this job. The main issues that came up related to the male studio environment when working on productions, and these were very similar to the issues identified by women who worked in the camera and audio departments.

GETTING STARTED

An art school qualification which includes computer graphics is becoming a prerequisite. However there are examples of women who have done art at school, compiled a portfolio, and gone into a job straight from school (see Carolyn Reid p177). There are also examples of women who have moved sideways within commercial television and trained on the job, but this is not common.

One woman who was working as a pay clerk and who had done art at school enrolled in an evening design class and hassled within the station to get into the area. Another had started typing captions and then trained herself on Paintbox when it was not being used and is now head of design.

The women who have been to art school are ready with a portfolio of their computer graphic work and contact the graphics department. They hang around, get to know the head of department and organise an interview. Like most jobs in television, getting your first job is a case of being in the right place at the right time. The trick is to be there when someone goes on leave, is sick, or resigns.

It is experience on the station's software programs and equipment that counts and until recently only television stations were able to provide that. However, art colleges and a growing number of production houses are getting the equipment and programs. If you can get a job as a gopher in a production house, or persuade them to take you on for work experience, you can develop your skills on the equipment when it is not being used.

3D animation is where the major challenges are for women today. At the moment men appear to be dominating this area but there are many opportunities for women who want to get into this area (for role models see p165-198).

ADVICE

Find out who is in charge of the videographics department. Ring them up and send in a really good, thought-out resumé which shows your design skills. Follow up with a phone call. Visit and show your portfolio and see what goes on. Try and be around the department for a period of time so people get to know you.

Learn as much as you can about every aspect of television and approach people one-on-one.

Get to understand what the job entails. It doesn't suit everybody. The type of work depends on the station you're employed by and what programs they make.

ENGINEERING AND OTHER TECHNICAL JOBS

As well as producing programs, recording them on video or sending them out live, a television station also distributes the programs to a satellite or terrestrial transmitter, which beams them to people's homes. It also receives television programs from other stations and countries via satellite transmitters. There are a number of jobs specific to maintaining the equipment and distributing the electronic signal.

ENGINEERING

The engineering department in a television station is responsible for ensuring that all the technical equipment works, that the station receives broadcast signals, and that quality pictures and sound are recorded and broadcast. This means that the equipment has to be maintained on a regular basis and repaired when it breaks down.

Engineering is also responsible for installing new equipment. Repair and maintenance is carried out at a bench in a workshop or on the equipment around the station. Engineers provide broadcast links back to the station from OBs, so are rostered to work on all such productions.

There are very few women working in this area, probably less than ten in the whole industry. Engineering, unlike most other departments in a television station, requires recognised electronic engineering qualifications. Stations take on trainees and give them time off to do a TAFE certificate course in electronic engineering if they are not already qualified.

The AFTRS also runs a program for trainees, who are also given time off to do the TAFE course. It takes two engineering and two operations trainees each year but the (female) supervisor of the trainees says it is extremely difficult to recruit young women to the program. A prerequisite for the course is maths and physics. However, a minority of girls do maths and physics at school and not many of them are encouraged, either within the school system or by their peers or family, to do electronics. It is only the very exceptional girl who will defy these pressures to conform and be the only girl in a class at university or TAFE and then the only woman in the engineering department in a station.

Most women have come to engineering accidentally, doing bridging courses in maths or physics when they leave school in order to qualify for an electronics course. They have then started an engineering course at TAFE or university and answered a newspaper advertisement for a trainee with a television station while they were studying. A few have come from other countries with engineering qualifications and have been surprised at the lack of women engineers in Australia.

The Seven Network stations have the most women engineers, and Brisbane BTQ-7 employed two women trainees together, which helped the loneliness that individual women experience when working in all male environments.

The ABC has an affirmative action policy to get more women into engineering and has two traineeships and a scholarship scheme in several capital cities for engineering students to do internships – but there is no guaranteed job (see Appendix 1).

Most women engineers blame the school system and the vocational guidance staff for not perceiving electronic engineering as a suitable job for women. Clearly if there is going to be any gender balance in this area of television then a major job has to be done in the schools so that girls who are interested in science do physics rather than biology and boys understand that girls can be as good as they are in this field.

ISSUES FOR WOMEN

This is a career job and it is unlikely that you will ever be out of work. Women say that it is not difficult.

'I find it challenging. It's putting things together. I have the drawing and all the bits and pieces. It's like following a recipe and once you have done it a few times it becomes quite easy and is quite a soothing occupation. If you like craftwork, like embroidery or sewing where you need a lot of attention to detail, it comes quite easily.'

The women criticised the gender attitudes that start in primary school, where little boys are encouraged to pull things apart and fix them, and continue through to high school when peer pressure takes over.

One or two women decided to work in the area precisely because they were told that it was not an appropriate career for girls.

The biggest problem for women is being the only woman in an all-male department. 'It is lonely being with men all the time, as a group, and breaking into the little world of sports and beer.' One woman who has a seventeen-year-old son said that she manages to relate to the men who are parents. 'We have parenting in common rather than fast cars.'

Others said that some women might be put off by the messy work environment at the workbench but suggested that it doesn't have to be like that. All agreed that cabling under the floor can be dirty and that the trainees usually have to do that. 'It's not like mechanical engineering where you are up to your armpits in grease... but you do have to get your hands dirty.' One woman said, 'It's no more dirty than changing nappies'.

The women with family commitments said that one of the hardest things was the study because although they all got time off to attend lectures they didn't get it for homework. 'Homework has to be done in your own time. I go home and I have to cook the dinner. I can't go home and wait for someone else to cook it.'

All agreed that it would be good to have more women in the engineering department because they would not feel so isolated and 'it would tone down some of the male attitudes'.

GETTING STARTED

The most important thing is to make sure that you do maths and physics to Year 12, or do a bridging course when you leave school. One woman came to engineering in her forties and had not done any maths since Year 10. She had studied ancient history, Greek and Latin at university and been a teacher and a musician. Looking for a career change she was not having any luck getting work as a library technician and heard that the ABC was trying to employ women in engineering as part of an affirmative action campaign. She applied and is now earning more as a technical assistant grade 2 than a library technician and is studying part-time for her certificate which will enable her to be a broadcasting officer grade 1.

The women with qualification from overseas had got jobs very quickly after writing to all the stations. They were all amazed at the lack of women in the operational and engineering side of television in Australia compared to where they have come from – Poland, Germany, former Yugoslavia and Argentina. The European women had some arts training as well as engineering and resent the fact that this is not recognised or required as a part of an engineering course in Australia.

ADVICE

Go to TAFE or university and do it. Don't be put off at school by the prejudice against engineering for girls, and ask the vocational guidance adviser to get information for you.

Be prepared to get your hands dirty, and to do the shitty jobs because you'll get them at the start.

CENTRAL CONTROL

This is the nerve centre of a station where the switching takes place which directs the broadcast signals coming from various sources around the station to the transmitter, and also controls incoming signals. The controller is responsible for the smooth transition from programs to commercials and crosses to other program sources when required.

A job in central control can be a step up for a videotape operator and a few women have progressed to working in this area. The problems for women are similar to those identified by women working in videotape. It is a male culture.

VISION DEPARTMENT

The following positions are all located in the vision department:

TECHNICAL DIRECTOR

The technical director (often called lighting director at the ABC) has overall responsibility for all the technical equipment in the studio and associated control rooms and is usually responsible for all the crew apart from the producer and director, and for all the health and safety issues in the studio.

This means that the technical director (TD) has overall responsibility for the quality of the pictures and the sound coming from the studio. The TD works in the control room during rehearsals and is in communication with other key personnel: the director, vision switcher, audio mixer and camera operators. She is often directly responsible for the lighting and the lighting crew. On large productions there might also be a separate lighting director.

The technical director is usually the most senior technical person in the studio. Because a TD has usually come through the technical side of broadcast operations and often started in staging it is not perceived as a woman's job. In the last couple of years one or two women have come in to freelance.

Howard Crozier, assistant engineer at AFTRS, remembers that there had been two women technical directors at Channel 10 in Sydney twenty years ago. 'They had very difficult jobs as they were supervising an almost all male crew and were expected to troubleshoot technical problems. They were not well accepted at first, as it was unheard of to have female TDs at that time. They were not fully qualified in the engineering field but had much experience in the production side of the industry. Nevertheless, they gained acceptance and worked for a number of years in the role.'

The only woman technical director on staff in recent years had started as a base grade operations person and progressed to technical director as a man, which meant that she had no gender problems getting there. Following a sex change, she continued in her same job working with the same crews.

LIGHTING DIRECTOR

The lighting director plans all the lighting on the set and works closely with the designer and the director. She then works with the lighting crew on the floor and the technical director in the control room during production.

Lighting directors in Australia tend to come up from staging and can interchange with technical directors. There are very few women. In the US, the technical director is usually the vision switcher and male and the lighting director can be female, because the position is regarded as an artistic job rather than as a technical operations job. There are a number of women lighting directors in the theatre who started by lighting ballet, which is poorly paid, and moved into the theatre and then supplemented their income by lighting for television. They are usually freelance and move between the theatre and television. Tharon Musser is one of the best known Broadway musical lighting directors. She used to also work in television.

VISION CONTROLLER

The vision controller – also called the camera control unit (CCU) operator – is responsible for the picture leaving the cameras. She aligns the cameras at the beginning of the shift, and ensures that they are performing satisfactorily. The job has involved considerable technical expertise in the past, as aligning valve and later plumbicon tube-based cameras required considerable technical knowledge and skills. Modern CCU cameras require much less set-up time and are very stable.

In some stations this is a separate job and the vision controller works closely with the technical or lighting director to achieve the desired images. In others it is done by the technical director.

Just as there are few women technical directors so there are few women vision controllers. The ABC in Sydney has a woman who came from Poland and Germany where she was a producer and director and had a broader technical training than her Australian peers. She started as a switcher and moved to vision controller because she had had some technical training which got her the job – although she saw it as artistic rather than technical. Eventually she wants to work as a lighting director, which she also sees as a job requiring artistic as well as technical skills.

DIRECTING TELEVISION DRAMA

Television dramas are shot either single camera or multicamera (multicam), and sometimes a mixture of both. Most television dramas are either series, with a limited number of weekly episodes shot on single camera, or serials and soaps which are programmed more regularly and are shot in a multicam studio, although they may have some single or multicam location shooting. There are very few one-off television dramas.

The production crew and directors are employed on contract for a period of time or a number of episodes. Drama productions tend to have a six-day shooting schedule that is strictly adhered to in order to guarantee delivery. There are usually two crews and a number of directors, responsible for individual episodes. Television drama is mass production drama and a director will be judged on her ability to meet the schedule efficiently as much, if not more, than on her creative input.

Directing television drama can be the next step after directing documentaries and short films but women have often found it difficult to persuade production houses that they are as good as male directors. In the 1960s and '70s the only people producing drama regularly were the ABC and Crawfords in Melbourne, which produced drama for the three commercial networks. They produced single camera drama on 16mm film and multicam drama on videotape. Crawfords used their own film studios or studios in one of the commercial televisions stations. The ABC had a training scheme for directors but they only trained men. Women were expected to start as secretaries and could only progress into the traditional female jobs. Crawfords provided on-the-job training for men, who started in the mailroom, moved into transport and from there became assistant directors and floor managers or worked in props. While they progressed up the ladder, women were confined to the traditional female jobs of continuity, wardrobe and secretarial work in the production office.

From 1975, with the catalyst of International Women's Year, women started to push to get some of the traditional male jobs and the ABC provided training specifically for women. The AFTRS recruited women students to train in the traditional male craft jobs of camera, sound and editing, and women used those skills to start making single camera documentaries and short dramas, and to direct them. The AFTRS also developed specific short courses for women who worked in traditional female jobs. These courses gave women the confidence to go back to their organisations and ask to be considered for traditional male jobs, although not many made it through to directing.

SINGLE CAMERA

Directing a single camera television drama is not so different from directing a feature film, except that the budget is much smaller and therefore the shooting schedule is much faster, and it is usually shot on 16mm film or video, as opposed to 35mm film. The structure of the film crew is much the same although there are fewer people in each department and therefore the crew size is more manageable.

Since the 1970s women have been able to get funding for short dramas and documentary films and so get experience in directing single camera. With this experience they began to persuade the commercial television stations, the ABC and the production houses that they were able to direct drama. Film Australia also began to produce drama and ran a number of schemes to encourage women.

MULTICAM

When television first started there was no videotape, so all television programs, including drama, were produced live in the studio using three or four cameras and transmitted straight to air.

If a program was to be repeated it was recorded on film (kined) as it was being transmitted. Today, only the news, current affairs and sport are produced in this way, usually by staff directors.

Multicam drama was very restrictive but it was much cheaper and quicker than the alternative of film. In the 1990s videotape, smaller cameras and non-linear editing allowed drama to be produced on single camera video and move out of the studios. However, multicam is still the cheapest way to make drama because it is fast and requires less editing. Therefore, soaps and situation comedy, which need live audiences for the laughs and timing, are still made in the studio using multicam techniques. Some soaps are also produced on location using multicam.

Directing multicam is a different directing technique to single camera because the director plans the action in such a way that it can be shot by two or three cameras which cover the action as it happens. The camera shots are cut together by a vision switcher as they are recorded.

The director has to direct the cameras from the control room and tell the vision switcher when to cut from camera shot to camera shot. She is assisted by a director's assistant (DA) or producer's assistant (PA) in the control room and a floor manager in the studio. The audio mixer has a sound crew in the studio and follows the director's instructions. The entire production is recorded onto videotape by the videotape operator. Later, the edited sequences are put together and enhanced with graphics, sound effects and music.

Studio multicam programs are produced in a hierarchical controlled environment where the director is the centre of all the communication. Everyone has a role and there are relatively few crises. On the one hand this makes it easier for a woman because she does not have to negotiate different crises on location with large male crews awaiting her every decision. On the other hand the studio is a very entrenched male environment where men have been doing the same jobs for years and that can be very inhibiting.

The multicam drama director's skills are a mix of the single camera drama director working with the actors and plotting the moves and action and the technical skills of cutting between cameras to cover the action. Multicam drama directors usually come from television studio directing.

There are very few women multicam drama directors because it has been very difficult for them to train and get the experience working with a studio crew. Commercial television usually takes directors from the camera department, where there are very few women. The ABC has now stopped training. The AFTRS provides directing training for TV drama series as part of its directing course but does not run a specific multicam directing course.

ROLE MODELS

Mandy Smith and Helen Gaynor are both based in Melbourne and illustrate two different career paths typical of aspiring women directors in the 1970s and in the 1980s.

Mandy Smith trained as a director at Crawfords and then went to the ABC where she directed many of the quality miniseries that the ABC produced in Melbourne. She is now freelance and directs mainly single camera dramas and is developing her own projects. She won a Television Society award for workshopping and directing new talent for *In Between*, has been a board member of Film Victoria, has run directing workshops for the AFTRS, and works extensively for the AFC and Film Victoria as a film assessor.

Her most recent credits are *Sea Change, Heartbreak High* and *Good Guys Bad Guys*.

Helen, on the other hand, went to Swinburne (now the VCA) and, after some editing and continuity jobs, was the first woman outside the ABC to get into an ABC directors' course. She has taught multicam drama direction for the AFTRS, an Open Channel summer school, and various video workshops in Nicaragua. She has directed many series and serials for the ABC, TVNZ and commercial television, as well as directing and producing her own documentaries. Helen's most recent credits are *Neighbours, Australia's Most Wanted, High Flyers* and two documentaries *Auto*

Stories and *For the Defence.*

She had a baby in 1998 and has managed to carry on working.

Mandy and Helen are good, capable, experienced directors and both would like to direct a feature. However, they have earned a comfortable living as television directors and are loathe to give it up to develop projects in the independent film sector. Mandy has tried to get her own project funded and Helen has succeeded in getting funding to direct documentaries.

MANDY SMITH

Mandy Smith came from a very high achieving family. She and her two brothers were expected to be top of the class, to get top matriculation results and to have a tertiary education. Growing up she had quite a substantial exposure to theatre, art galleries, music and watching film on television.

She went to Monash and did the beginnings of an arts degree, where she discovered that she was interested in drama and theatre. She applied to the ABC and got a letter back saying that she needed 35 wpm typing. She borrowed a portable typewriter and tried to teach herself to type but gave it away and moved to Adelaide to go to Flinders which was one of the few universities in the country that did drama at a tertiary level. Directing in the theatre was her ambition but in her third year she worked on a couple of films. One was a student production with Scott Hicks (director of *Shine*) and she realised that she had found her vocation. 'It was quite remarkable, like the sky opening up – this is very exciting, this is the new technology, this is where you've got such a voice as a director, because you have so many elements in your control.'

In the summer she found three weeks paid work as a gopher on an Education Department documentary which was one of the first productions of the South Australian Film Corporation (SAFC). There were four on the crew and Mandy did a bit of booming, helped with the lights, organised the following day's schedule and bought the lunches. She decided not to go on and do honours at university.

She then worked with Anne Deveson doing some research and continuity on *Who Killed Jenny Langby* (1974), directed by

Donald Crombie, and as an assistant director on *Sunday Too Far Away* (1973). 'The people in the industry were terribly generous with their time, with telling you things, I remember the crews as being very supportive and very helpful.'

There were no trained people in Adelaide and the SAFC was flying everyone in, so she was trained in continuity by Sue Milliken. 'It was a marvellous tool because I had a real grounding in production detail.'

She found work as an assistant stage manager in the theatre and worked on a pilot for a children's series. Work dried up and, having been raised to believe you must have security of employment, she started panicking. She had applied to Crawfords a couple of times.

>> **I think it's very important that we stop talking about directors as being male. It happens everywhere, and it irritates me.**

'They took guys on through their mail room and they subsequently got to work as drivers and then onto a crew but women could only get into the organisation if they had a skill. You sent off letters and you get put into a file and they'd write back saying "We will let you know if we have anything".'

With no immediate job prospects Mandy decided to do a teaching diploma at Rusden CAE, where they had a strong film, television and theatre component. 'I had, in my mind, turned my back on a career in film. It just seemed that it was going to be too fraught with lack of employment and too daunting a job.'

But just before she was due to start she was offered six weeks work as standby wardrobe on *Picnic at Hanging Rock* (1975). 'They didn't ask whether I could sew, they didn't ask whether I had any experience. This was a big budget feature film so they employed a Sydney-based continuity person and they had to make up the quota of South Australians. They were basically shoving their one third quota in the lower crew positions. But it was the most fantastic experience. While we were shooting it we knew we were making this fantastic film that was going to be pivotal in the industry.'

'Peter [Weir] is very good at involving all his crew and his cast in the whole experience and the job as standby wardrobe on a period film is probably a little bit more important than if you are just giving out contemporary jeans and suits. You are also right up there. You are with the camera. It was not like being a gopher or stopping traffic or going to the airport with rushes – you are with the actors. I learnt so much from working with that crew, that team, that bunch of actors, being there all day every day watching every set up, seeing Peter work, the wonderful art department, the wonderful camera team.'

She struck up a very good working relationship with the costume designer, Judy Dorsman, and for the next three years she worked with Judy, who was Sydney based. Mandy was still based in Adelaide and she would join Judy wherever she was needed and worked in wardrobe on some of the really big budget and prestigious films.

After *Picnic at Hanging Rock* she received $2,000 creative development money from the Experimental Film Fund to make a fifteen-minute film. It was about New Circus that had started in Adelaide and was the forerunner of Circus Oz. This took all her spare time over eighteen months. 'I couldn't see myself going down that path which a lot of low budget filmmakers have. They have just struggled along, to support themselves, and have done other jobs that haven't been as taxing as working in the film industry.'

She did a lot of location shooting, in regional New South Wales, Victoria and South Australia. She did a bit of continuity, a bit of production assisting, and production managing on a couple of small things. Penny Chapman put together a package of four women's films that were made with all-women crews and Mandy was production manager on three of them. 'By now I very much knew that I wanted to be a director and I wasn't getting any closer.'

In 1977 she was given six weeks' work at Crawfords on *The Sullivans*. She had done costume research on a number of films that had military elements and was getting a reasonable reputation. She was brought in to send the boys to war. At the end of the six weeks, Crawfords asked her if she would like to stay on in the wardrobe department. 'I said yes I would but I want to be a director, and that is the reason that I am staying. The reaction was that it was not something that women did. We were very much slotted into production office jobs, continuity, script area, assistant film editing, maybe film editor if you could get up. They were the jobs for women, directing was not.'

Mandy gave herself a time limit and did a lot of lobbying and hanging around. It was her first experience of television. 'I remember walking into *The Sullivans* studio and not understanding. Where was the control room, Where was the director? It was totally different to what I was used to. So by getting involved, having this constant access, I started understanding the technology. It started being demystified. You could walk into any door and ask any question, you could watch for as long as you liked. I started feeling confident because I hadn't had any sort of technical background.'

She spent a lot of time in the control room watching the shoot in the evenings and would go to the assembly edit sessions at the weekend and ask to watch. She started lobbying quite heavily and after a while people like David Stevens and Bill Hughes, who were directors, allowed her to do some of the assembly editing. One day one of the directors got stuck in Sydney with a plane strike and rang her to send the assembly edit through. 'It was quite mechanical, but it was the foot in the door and it gave me confidence around the technology.'

After a year in wardrobe at Crawfords, she was moved into a job assisting the producer and was now officially involved in post production. She was doing forward planning, reading scripts, looking for locations, helping with breakdowns, wangling publicity. She gave herself a deadline, and once a month she would do the rounds of the senior executives and say 'This is what I would like to do, when will there be an opportunity?' Twelve months later, in 1979, a couple of staff directors left and Mandy became a trainee director.

interview

DIRECTING

It was very much a sink or swim situation. You walked around behind a director for four weeks, and it depended on the personality of who you were working with how much you were told along the way. Then the next four weeks they gave you a couple of scenes to do. I survived. A number of other trainee directors didn't. It was quite a stressful and traumatic thing to do.

There had been one other woman director in earlier years – Marie Trevor, who was one of the Crawford family. Crawfords had had this system where there were two directors, one spoke to the actors and the other one dealt with the buttons and technical stuff. Marie had been an actors director in that system. I still remember Hector Crawford asking me how would I talk to the male actors. He had this concept that the men wouldn't listen to me. He was right sometimes – they don't. But I basically crashed my way through.

I trained on a show called *Skyways* at Channel 7, using their crews. They were very helpful and very supportive. I did about four or five scenes and Ian Crawford saw what I was doing and two hours later I had an episode of *The Sullivans* to direct. It was two-thirds multicam studio and one-third single camera on location. Channel 9 parked their OB van outside the Crawfords studios, so it was fairly primitive compared to what we use now.

I look back and I don't know how I did it, I don't know how I had the courage. I think when you're younger you just go for it. I was on staff for two years at Crawfords and then I went freelance. Jim Davern was just starting *A Country Practice*. I had directed an episode of something he had written for Crawfords, he liked my work so he contacted me and asked me if I wanted to do *A Country Practice*. So I went to Sydney for three months and worked at the beginning of *A Country Practice* with Jim and then went back to Crawfords freelance on *Carsons Law* for twelve months.

Crawfords television had a very distinct house style and even though they were doing exciting television for the time it was fairly rigid. I got very locked into that. I was working very hard and found it difficult to break away. I was being paid and every good actor in Australia was turning up for those guest roles week in, week out, so I was working with some wonderful actors. Looking back I find some of the scripts that I had to work with a bit hard to stomach, but at the time everything was a challenge. Even some of the scripts that had a real lack of credibility it was a challenge to give them credibility, to put in some humanity, to put in some warmth, to create faithful or realistic characters as much as one could. I know that there was a whole group of ex-Flinders people who felt that I had sold out to mainstream television but it still seemed to me that I was just learning so much.

I'd had some development money from the AFC for an adaptation of a short story by Angela Carter that I was trying to write but I didn't go to the next stage. I couldn't wrap myself around it. That's where a film school is really valuable because of the nurturing you get to explore your own projects. By now I was very much on the path of working for other people.

In 1986 I directed a project called *In Between* which was an Open Channel co-production and that was a big sideways step into a different sort of work.

I have been interested in moving into writing and also very interested in getting a project of my own made. I had written a 30-minute two-hander that got very close to getting some creative development funding in 1984. Many years ago I'd read a book called *Haxby's Circus* and had tried over the years since about 1976 to get the rights and in the middle '80s I finally got them. I got AFC script development and Denise Morgan wrote the first draft and then I took over and wrote three subsequent drafts and tried very hard to raise the money. I think we came very close. I was now working with Ann Darrouzet, the producer, but then the bubble burst and there was no more money. It was just that bit too late in the '80s. All of a sudden the bigger films were not being made. That's still sitting in my drawer and still very much something that I would like to do. But that was a tremendous experience confronting the empty page.

I worked on *Fast Lane* with Andrew Knight and John Clarke in the middle '80s and that was terrific and expanding. I got enthralled by comedy and thought 'This is wonderful'.

A couple of years ago my goals got a little bit woolly because *Haxby's Circus* was quite exhausting. I worked for two years on trying to get this project up and then you fall in a heap and think have you got enough energy to keep going. I got into a round of children's projects but it's not the sort of directing I'm most interested in. I like using adult actors where you can work on the intellectual level as well.

Two projects at the ABC revitalised me, *The Damnation of Harvey McHugh* [1993] – even though it was very fraught with difficulties it was deeply challenging, partly because of those difficulties – and then *Janus* [1994], which was a tremendous experience. It was very fast but very challenging and for the first time I think television moved away from being something bland. What the *Phoenix/Janus* team did was they broke all the rules and threw television wide open. They brought the medium of television much closer to being a screen visual medium so that all of the tools you use in a film are there for you.

We had two cameras and sometimes three available to us at all times. No pre-mixing, we took everything into the edit suite. Non-linear editing is why television is coming back closer to film and the technology is actually freeing us up.

In the last couple of years I've done a whole series of projects that have been good: *Sea Change* – both series – and for five months I worked in Sydney on *Heartbreak High*.

HIGHLIGHTS

I think my main achievement, objectively, is becoming a director – being female in that environment and actually making people change their perceptions about directing being a job a female can do, and do well. Probably, subjectively, my main achievement has been writing the script and a few other more personal things, particular performances, they're things I'm very proud of. I feel very pleased about the work I did on *Janus*. I think that a lot of things about my abilities fell into place through the challenge of working on *Janus*. It's the marrying of all the elements of the trade, of the visual aspects as well as the script. I had quite a big script involvement in *Janus*. When you're a television director for hire you usually come in when the final draft is all but locked off, so being involved earlier was great.

I had never been interested in realistic drama, so that early on in *Janus* I had to wrestle with myself because I was thinking this is violent, this is ugly, these are horrible people. I needed to sort that out in my mind philosophically. This has been a dilemma artistically for me, because one bit of me loves doing comedy, and *Janus* didn't have a lot of that. A huge commitment was asked of me and it gets harder and harder to work on things that you are not totally committed to. I've turned stuff down and I've done things that I've regretted, which has been quite tough. You start feeling like the dog doing the tricks.

But I do think that in small ways in all of the work that I've done, I've made small attitudinal changes, by adding my personal and female perspective.

ISSUES FOR WOMEN

I think I've been politicised quite late in life which is an odd thing to say, but back in the '70s I didn't even do much reading of the feminist theory that was around. It obviously soaked in and it wasn't that I didn't join some groups, but I believed in just doing it, whereas now I don't. I value the theoretical, the discussion and the educational side and realise that we must talk about these things and actually change what people are thinking. It's not just about going and doing it, which is what I believed – that method has actually failed. I and a number of other women in Australia in both film and television have done it and it doesn't really change people's perceptions.

I have become involved in things like Film Victoria and organisations, boards, WIFT [Women in Film and Television], I've done the WIFT seminar for years 9 and 10 media students in schools, drama students, role modelling for women, that sort of stuff. I speak whenever I'm asked to, if I can get there.

Some men find it quite difficult to deal with women who are in power situations. I haven't had a successful relationship and I don't know how much that is a factor. I also think that I over-compensated earlier on and put up quite a tough outer shell to appear invincible, immovable, and all those sorts of things. It took me quite a while, some years, to be relaxed on set and to be myself. Early on I thought 'If I'm too friendly or jovial it will be misinterpreted'. People have all these preconceptions that you need to be super tough, so I think I did that early on and that was something I had to deal with.

I was very focused on all the career stuff, incredibly focused to do the one job and to succeed at it and you end up thinking, 'Here I am, I've got all these tapes sitting on the shelves, and that one's really good and that one's terrific, and, hey, I've got the cast and crew photo', and then you think 'What about the rest of my life?'. I certainly have observed over the years that the guys who do the job that I do tend to have a support system of the wife and the children. They get looked after by the wife, the wife sorts the bookings, and pays the bills, puts the rubbish bin out. That is over-simplifying because there are all the demands that family puts on people too – but I believe that it is very difficult for a single female if you don't have that sort of support.

I think my own energy forced me through and sometimes it's been quite tough. These days it's small attitude stuff rather than overt stuff and it's something you just let your antenna pick up: this person is not comfortable with me, this person is. My main regret is probably that I have not found a balance between career and the rest of my life.

I'm also disappointed that not as many women came up behind me as I would have liked. Part of that was the economic tightening of the industry. It just does seem that the women I've talked to are all having to do it all again and that it's not got any easier. You have to prove yourself, they are not going to meet you half way, so you actually have to leap through higher hoops and all those sorts of things.

The theory is that it should be easier, but it doesn't seem that it is. I think that much of it is probably still coming from the women themselves. Women are still very much brought up not to put themselves forward with a great lot of confidence. They're not as well equipped as they should be to work in an industry that is largely male dominated and where the attitudes are entrenched. I don't believe they are on the floor, on the crew level, but I believe they are still in middle management, still in areas of finance, where the money is coming from. I was told that I was knocked back by two financiers on a miniseries in the late '80s. I was the producer's nominated director, but they said 'No we don't want a girl, we won't trust a girl'.

I think it is very difficult for women working in most industries, but certainly in our industry, to do a job and be a mother at the same time. That is not something I have done. I didn't deal with all my feelings about all of that until it was probably too late. I kept on thinking 'Oh, one day I will have a partner and one day all of that will happen'. There are a number of women who are successfully doing the juggling act, but I don't know how they do it, and they're usually not working as directors, they're working in more flexible jobs – apart from people like Gillian Armstrong who's got the status to have the nannies.

The motherhood issue is a whole other thing. The energy that it has taken me to be as focused as I have has really meant that I have left out other areas of my life. Three years ago I moved to the country and I have got involved in things that are nothing to do with the film industry which has been really interesting. I've become more involved in the local community, in the regional arts festival.

Sexist issues

I have not personally experienced sexual harassment but I have certainly witnessed it, the milder form. It's akin to bullying, picking on people who are weaker and a bit more vulnerable and using the fact that they are female to pick away at them. Yes I've seen that. It was back in the days when it was acceptable behaviour and one put up with it. I look at it now and perceive it as harassment.

I've become quite rigorous about language, I think it's very important that we stop talking about directors as being male. It happens everywhere, and it irritates me. On the board of Film Victoria over the last few years there has been a 50/50 male/female representation, which was conscientiously done and I hope will be maintained. I would like to see that through all levels of government. I don't know what we do about television management. I think that that's probably our greatest problem in this country, the very narrow management area and lack of real competition and lack of what seems to me any genuine interest in Australian product from our commercial networks. I think pay television is only going to make it worse. I don't know how we change the attitude in the boardrooms. The funding bodies and the government bodies don't seem to be able to make anything other than very small changes. If we change that mentality then we will change what scripts are being bought and funded and produced and all the small attitudinal stuff.

Feeling vulnerable

There's an interesting psychology about putting yourself up to be judged. It is both terrifying and exhilarating. You're actually making a product that people are going to sit at home and watch on their television, millions of people, that's sort of very nerve-racking, it really is putting yourself out there.

Physically I still feel vulnerable, I'm very conscious of being safe. I'm not little, I'm 165cm and I think that has helped but if I'm going mooching around looking for locations by myself, or doing a bit of research for myself, or checking out a few things to plan in advance, I'm not as free as, say, a guy might be.

Coping with criticism

I am dreadful, shocking, I'm getting better but I've never been good. I'm very harsh on myself, probably overly harsh, I carry criticism like an albatross and stew over it, mull over it, and do a fair amount of recrimination but I'm getting better at balancing all that. Maybe this is something that women do.

Crying

Early on I did identify that women crying was not something that made people comfortable in a public situation and that was part of that early steeling myself. I was determined never to cry in public. I've done it twice I can think of, in both instances it was because of what I perceived as a gross unfairness and in situations where I believed I was being totally misunderstood, I hadn't been heard properly, I hadn't been given a chance to put my case.

ADVICE

It's different from when I got my foot in the door. When I started there were only 'girls jobs'. Jan Kenny, who came just after me, was the first woman in the country to touch a camera and Erika Addis was soon after that. I worked on Jan's first picture as standby wardrobe and saw the challenges they put her through. I didn't get those sort of challenges because I was there holding frocks with a tape measure. In a way I infiltrated my way in. I cannot load a camera – I suppose I could if I tried – but basically I have no technical background. I have all the second-hand theory that I need as a director.

It's about being tenacious. Go to a film school. The industry is very competitive, there is not that much money around. I think infiltration by getting any job is quite a good way to go as long as you don't get trapped. Sue Milliken [producer and former chair of the AFC] was continuity for a long time, but then there are other continuity people in Sydney I know of, who have been in the industry as long as I have and they haven't sprung themselves out, they do want to direct, they do want to produce, but they haven't been able to make that break. I don't know that there's an easy answer. I think, probably, you take whatever opportunity turns up, keep your eye on the end target and don't forget about living your life along the way if you've got time.

What keeps you going as a director is the goal, the vision that it is all possible, that we can get this day shot, that we can resolve these script problems, that you hang on to your central idea and believe in your own voice and skill, that you can get yourself over whatever hurdle is presenting itself.

HELEN GAYNOR

Helen grew up in a large Catholic patriarchal family. Her father was a solicitor and the sex lines were drawn fairly early. 'My brothers were always saying girls were stupid which made me feel inadequate and stupid.' She went to an upper class private Catholic girls school in Melbourne and had female role models. 'The nuns ran the school so that you were brought up in an environment where you could see a perfectly competent self contained group of women running their own affairs who obviously didn't need men around to exist.'

Her father expected the girls to be high achievers and go to university. She had done a lot of painting and photography at school and was good at humanities subjects so planned to do arts/law but then she heard about the film and TV course at Swinburne and was accepted in 1978.

Her first job after Swinburne was as an editor's assistant in a small production company that made commercials. Rodney Jay had rung Swinburne for someone to be the coffee maker/ receptionist /assistant film editor. 'We had some terrible arguments, I was only there for six weeks. I was just getting into my feminist stage and he was only three or four years older than me and very sexist. I didn't wear nice tailored suits, make-up, shave my legs, shave under my arms. I just couldn't be bothered putting my time and energy into assembling some of the ads. So I quit.'

She then got a job at Hawthorn Teachers' College putting together the audio visual component of a teacher training kit. While she was there Crawfords rang looking for female students to train for continuity. She went to Crawfords for two years doing continuity and was also trained as a director's assistant (DA) and a vision switcher.

She left because she was feeling frustrated. 'If I stuck there and really hassled I might have got to be a director in two or three years, because they had just started the first wave of women directors like Catherine Millar and Mandy Smith. But they both had an awfully hard time and I saw what they had to go through, the level of scrutiny of their work. Everyone was very suspicious of their ability, it was so much more intense than any male would ever have to go through.'

So she decided to develop her own material. She received money from the AFC to produce and direct a half-hour comedy called *The Trombonist* with Steve Kerney from Los Trios Ringbarkus, Tracey Harvey and Simon Thorpe. It was sold to the ABC and Village/Roadshow, blown up to 35mm and screened before some feature films. 'It was much easier to get money in those days, I didn't have to have a broadcaster, a pre-sale agreement, all the insurance components, the superannuation, etc.'

She went back to being a production assistant/continuity person and got a job at Grundys on a new show called *Starting Out* and then went to Sydney for three months on *Sons and Daughters* as a DA.

While she was there, the ABC advertised for people to apply to be trained as producer/directors. There were 800 applications from outside the ABC and she and Giampaolo Pertosi were chosen. All the rest of the course participants were within the ABC. 'There were four women out of ten and they all knew what a big break it was but I had no idea. I just wandered in and thought they are going to train and pay me for two months.' She did the training course in Melbourne in 1984 and was given a producer/director position in Tasmania.

She did news and current affairs in Tasmania for two months but she did not like living in such a small place. 'I started screaming and yelling and in the end threatened to resign if they didn't move me.' They moved her to Melbourne where she was the only female pool producer/director, and was assigned to different departments.

She started lobbying to get into the drama department and worked as a director on *House Rules* and then on the series *Inside Running*. In the six years she was there she did a huge variety of work but became concerned about getting stuck at the ABC. 'I liked the quality of programs, they are thoughtful and challenging and they were very formative years, but I was surrounded by people who were the same age as me who had been there for fifteen years and never worked anywhere else.' She freelanced as a director on *Neighbours* and *A Country Practice*.

In 1989 she sold everything and went to Nicaragua where she taught video and stayed for a year and a half. 'That was a big turning point for me. It was personally very challenging. There was no equipment there, no money, the electricity kept going off, it really made me understand the politics of poverty. I had to deal with loneliness, I was living with a family who didn't speak English. That was where I stopped being naive.'

> ▶▶ **The trouble with being a female director, and it still holds true – but much less today – is that you never know whether you are having problems because of your personality or because whoever you are talking to – and it's usually a male – can't cope with a woman authority figure.**

She bought Hi-8 camera equipment and went to Guatemala in 1992 and made a film with three other people about the whole issue of impunity. Then the producer of *Chances* tracked her down and persuaded her to come back. She was a freelance drama director, doing *Chances*, *Neighbours* and *A Country Practice* but had the footage from Guatemala. She did all the rounds of the funding bodies for about six months. 'They said "Oh gee, we don't like funding something after it's already been shot".' And I was saying, "Listen, we've got the script here, we've got the footage there, you can sit down and look at all the footage and compare it with the script and you will know whether you've got a good documentary or not. It's far more certain than going off on an idea. It's all there, you can see whether it's going to work or not." It was very stressful, probably the most stressful thing I'd ever done.'

She finally finished the documentary, *Impunidad*, and it went to air on SBS and won awards in the Columbus and Chicago Film and TV festivals.

She then went to live in India for four months and planned to marry but decided against it 'partly because it would have been very difficult to pursue my film career, and that's when I started taking myself seriously as a filmmaker.'

interview

Thirty-five was a huge turning point for me. I'd built up a commercial career and got these documentaries off the ground but I never took it seriously. There were all these conflicting things. I've got this tremendous drive to keep going overseas, I've put an enormous amount of time into my film and TV career, I've worked my arse off and friends have said 'Slow down, slow down'.

I don't want to wake up when I'm 60 and say 'I've only ever lived in Melbourne, Victoria, Australia'. There is a huge world out there and I want to see it. I don't want to just backpack through it, I want to live in it. I want to feel everything. I want to see everything, I want to put myself in dangerous situations, and contentious environments and be lonely and be upset and have to face myself, and have to go into the depths of despair, and up to the heights of ecstasy. I want to experience all that and I can't do it if I'm sitting in Melbourne.

It's partly about the industry – I like commercial TV directing because it's an aspect of being a program maker that I need to know about. But I'm constantly having to grapple with the politics of soapies and what it means, why am I doing it, why do people want to watch this stuff, and not be condescending to the audience. And it also pays me a fabulous amount of money and makes me feel reasonably successful. I'd rather be directing other stuff but by continuing not to take it seriously I'm not really dedicating myself to being a director.

HIGHLIGHTS

But my major achievements, I'd say, are the two documentaries I've made, they're filmmaker pieces. I can show them to people and say 'This is my work, and this represents me'. I did another one in South Africa in 1995. I directed, shot and produced the first one and I directed and associate produced and shot second unit on the second one. So it's my vision in both of those. The first one was terribly collaborative, so there is a lot of the vision of my two partners in it as well.

THE FUTURE

I really want to be a serious filmmaker and I really want to achieve the things I want to achieve, say the things I want to say, either via a feature film or drama. I have got to commit myself to a project for two or three years and it means not going off and doing other things I like to do. I am learning as I get older that I can't do everything all the time and I have to miss out on some things to achieve other things. It does upset me that I have to make those choices but I realise now that to do any sort of quality filmmaking I have to have that long-term commitment and internal discipline and focus.

It's a hard slog, and I think that was part of my resistance to taking myself seriously. If I really decide I want to direct a feature film I have to start looking for a script, I have to try and get script development, I have to get a producer interested and then we have to try and raise the finance, get a distributor. Then, also, I make myself a public figure, I put my ideas publicly on the screen and I am publicly scrutinised, my skills, my opinions, my personality and it's frightening.

As a director in the commercial world my ideas and my visions aren't exposed. They are not being called into question. My professionalism, in terms of being able to direct adequately for a program, are called upon – directing fast turnaround drama, or a show that I haven't produced, but my ideas and my personality don't enter into that contract. So you can hide a lot more. Only the producer and the production company knows what you've done.

I think my other ambivalence about going right down that road, is that I just don't want to be poor. I've always grappled with that, and commercial TV provides a good income. It's the secondary part of what I actually do, although it's my main money earner. When I'm working I give it 100 percent of my time and energy because I have to, because that's what people are employing me for, but I use it as a means to an end.

I am getting pressured quite a bit from various people, which is forcing me to make a choice about which path I am on. Am I a documentary director, am I a drama director. My agent was saying, 'The trouble is at the moment, Helen – producers think you are a documentary director who does *Neighbours* in between documentaries'. The documentary sector has been a lot more receptive. They do take me seriously and I love documentary, I'm very political and I love the personal. But with drama I love the script interpretation, the rehearsal process and I love working with actors, so it's that struggle of trying to keep both going at the same time.

But I feel proud about having got as far professionally as I have because I am a women and not that many women do it. I also feel proud that I have not fallen into the stereotype, and that I've continued living the way I live, going overseas to strange places and leading a fairly unorthodox life. It has been very uncomfortable for the last five years but I feel proud that I have actually done that even when I really doubted why I was doing it and I felt subjected to a lot of criticism and scrutiny.

Not living in Sydney

Melbourne has got a lot more power base than the other states but living outside of Sydney for any filmmaker is a problem. The decision-making bodies for the commercial TV sector, the ABC and SBS and the film sector are all in Sydney, so the power and the influence are all emanating from Sydney.

There is always this constant thing of trying to make sure the resources and the time and energy within the AFC, SBS and the ABC are put into Melbourne.

Everybody involved in the commercial drama production sector is used to having to go up and down, up and down all the time. It seems for two or three years everything is happening in Sydney, then for two or three years everything happens in Melbourne.

All the major film events happen in Sydney so as a program and filmmaker you are constantly having to try and get yourself up there because they're good networking places. Often you can't because you are working. So you feel it is more peripheral, more marginalised from the centre of power down here.

MANAGING PEOPLE

I try to develop a very collaborative atmosphere. With the actors I always have my own interpretation of where their performance should be at and why they are doing stuff but I tend to sit back and watch what they give me and then ask them questions if it doesn't fall into the same sort of ideas structure that I had envisioned. With established characters in soap it is quite different. The dynamic with that is not for me to come in and tell them how to do their character but to sit back and see what they are doing and suggest others things they may not have thought of before. That's what I mean about that collaborative approach. I say 'Look I feel this, what do you feel?' and they say, 'Well I feel this' and if they disagree with me we will work through it to find out why and what's going wrong for them. So I try not to railroad people.

And with the crew, I try and delegate because I think people like taking on responsibility and it makes them become more creative. I like to have the hand on the tiller and I am quite firm that the final decision is mine and the final vision is mine. I take full responsibility for that and if it fucks up then I am the one who has to wear it but I try and set up a creative, enjoyable and collaborative atmosphere with everyone still knowing that I am running it.

ISSUES FOR WOMEN

Having to put up with behaviour and attitudes that men don't have to. There is a whole layer of stuff that I've got to deal with all the time that my male colleagues don't.

It is very hard for women starting to direct. You're on your own. You do make an awful lot of mistakes – you're so tense and you want to make the most brilliant decisions all the time. Your delegation skills are not particularly high and you can be a pain in the arse to work with from the crew's point of view. So combine that with a woman going into a traditional male sphere, being in charge, well when anything goes wrong the level of sympathy for your mistakes is very low compared to a male director in the same position. Everyone knows how to direct better than the director, and if you are making mistakes, if you lose it, if you are indecisive and having a hard day, it affects everybody. So people get pissed off because it means that they are going to have to work late.

The trouble with being a female director, and it still holds true but much less today, is that you never know whether you are having problems because of your personality or because whoever you are talking to, and it's usually a male, can't cope with a woman authority figure. And I never know. It's also part of my personality, and I think it is a female thing as well, that I want to be liked by everybody, which is not possible but I certainly strove to achieve that. So I was being nice and wanting to be liked by everyone and that was the other big pressure. I do have a fairly strong personality, I get absolute tunnel visioned and run in and push people around and reorganise everything and piss people off.

Always having to grapple with the fact that things may not be happening for me because of my gender. I have heard some men complain that some of the government film bodies are all managed by women now, they are saying there is this female market. I say, 'Well sit back and bloody well know what it feels like – if you think you're having a rough time with them that's what women have to put up with most of the time'.

Having to fight harder than a man. There are shows that I may not get work on because I'm a woman, and having to deal with that all the time. Not knowing if I'm not getting a go on a show because I'm a woman, or whether it's because they don't like my directing, or whether it's because they don't like my personality, That's not an issue that I think most men even have to think about. I'm much less concerned about that now, but for those first five or six years it was tremendously difficult. I'm at the point now where I think, 'Well if they have problems with me being a female, that's their problem'. I don't give a shit, because I feel confident enough in my role as a director to know whether the way I'm coming across and what I'm doing is causing problems.

The isolation of working on a crew, particularly in commercial TV, where it's very blokey, it's a boys' club. It's got a lot better as I've got to know them. But even when I was doing continuity it's all the blokes and there's just one woman. So that isolation is really difficult. And most men I talk to don't understand it because they've never been in that situation. I'm sure only the men who have gone into traditional women's spheres of employment, like nursing, would understand that gender isolation.

The compromises I've had to make are not tearing someone's head off when they've made incredibly sexist comments but trying to find a tactful way to point out that I don't appreciate it, that that sort of thing is not okay. I'd prefer to tear their head off, but it's not productive. It's not productive in terms of me working with them, and I don't think it's productive in terms of getting them to understand the issues of sexism, because all they do is go into a defensive stance.

Sexist language

I don't get so angry about sexism any more because I know most of these guys well enough now, or their type, and know they're genuinely good human beings. They just hang out with a lot of blokes, they're not intellectuals, they're not politically inclined, they like going to the footy and the cricket and having a beer and stuff. So I just make jokes about it, so that they know I'm aware of the issues and that I'm not angry and hostile about it. I call them up on it before they can actually do anything about it. I often say, when I change my mind about a shot, 'Bloody women directors they just change their mind all the time – I would never have them on the crew, should get them right off the studio floor as far as I'm concerned'. And all the guys start laughing because I'm just getting in before them. I don't do it maliciously but I do make very broad jokes, and make jokes about all the women on the crew being premenstrual at the same time and the guys all laugh. That takes the edge off it but still points up their behaviour.

A classic term on a film crew is to call someone a 'big girl's blouse', they'll say 'Oh you big girl's blouse' to one of their mates. It's an affectionate putdown if someone's effeminate or is being a bit wussy. I'll turn around and say 'what's wrong with a big girl's blouse, I wear big girl's blouses all the time' and it points out what they're saying. It's a bit of a putdown without being too heavy about it.

I guess I'm feeling confident enough about myself as a woman now, and also my role as a director, to be able to joke. I started developing that technique quite a few years ago and it works really well. But half of the guys don't know when they're being sexist and they want to have a whinge about women because they shit them sometimes, and they do use derogatory terms to each other that are specifically female. If they have got an aggro woman coming down on them it just shoves them much further into a corner. Now that might be me also playing the classic stereotypical thing that women can't be aggressive, but I'm trying to deal with sexism in a positive way, so you can still get on with these guys and treat them as equals and as decent human beings and still point out that they're being sexist.

Problems with content

I've changed lines in dialogue which are fulfilling sexual or racial stereotypes on quite a number of occasions, and the producer's always agreed. The soaps do maintain racial and sexual stereotypes, but that's the dilemma with the soaps, people are very comfortable with those stereotypes. The messages are, the girls are always pretty, and usually Anglo-Saxon – I've been sneaking some non Anglo-Saxon extras in *Neighbours* in the last couple of months. But they are quite thoughtful on those programs about the sorts of things that they push. No-one smokes and drinks on those shows anymore, if you drive when you drink you're an idiot, it's not okay to treat women badly, indiscriminate sex is not something to be desired, particularly if you're a teenager, if you're going to sleep around you must use condoms, you must be responsible for yourself and your partner.

Feeling vulnerable

Probably all the time. I feel vulnerable when I am putting myself forward to a commercial producer for a show that I have not done before. I feel really vulnerable with the documentaries I am making because I am putting myself and my opinions and my artistic judgment out there in the middle for everyone to comment on and talk about. I am also always fighting that sense of feeling terribly naive.

Coping when things go wrong

I never consider that I can give up so I just keep putting one foot in front of the other. I figure, well, it is going wrong and it is a bloody nightmare but it will fix itself up one way or the other somewhere down the track. I just pick certain friends who help pick me up. I would say friends are important.

Managing your anger

I had trouble with anger, I don't yell and scream at people and I think that is to do with female conditioning. I am not comfortable with being angry. I am quite comfortable with acknowledging that I am really angry and I want to kill somebody when I am on my own. I can yell and scream around the house but I find it much harder expressing anger to someone face-to-face and at work.

When I am angry at work it is usually when someone has not done something which they should have done and it fucks me up, and then I usually say 'Look, I am really pissed off, I needed this and I will just have to work it out' so they know that I am annoyed. But usually in a working situation I try and set up an environment where the anger doesn't come up.

Coping with criticism

I find criticism really difficult. I have two responses to it: I either take it on board far too much in a totally neurotic way – if someone says 'Gee that wasn't very good' I think 'Oh I am a total failure, I am a hopeless director. Why did I ever think I could be a director, you idiot Helen' and start really beating myself up – or I get incredibly defensive and attack the person. So I am constantly struggling with managing criticism and taking it on board.

I often interpret advice and help as criticism and that is my tunnel vision because I have my ideas and I know the way it's gonna go and I actually don't care what anyone else thinks, so I feel they are just trying to stop me doing what I want. It's a constant struggle to be able to listen to it in the spirit in which it is intended.

Crying

I don't often want to cry but sometimes I do and it is usually when I am screening something to a producer for the first time and it does not go well or I don't get the feedback and I am tired and I feel I can't stand this tension. That does not happen very often but the producer's screening in commercial television is hell. When I'm working I don't usually think about whether I am doing a good job or not, and then when you actually sit down with the producer you suddenly think, 'Shit I think I did a bad job and I did not even know it'.

HELPING WOMEN

I try to help other women partly by being a positive role model, and partly by dealing with sexism without being aggro.

I talk to younger women. I'm a fairly accessible person, so if they want to come and talk to me and say, what do you think I should do, or how do you think I should do it, I'm really happy to give advice and encouragement, and say I think you should do this, and hang in there.

ADVICE

Do a film course. The path of being a director if you don't do a film course is much harder for a woman because the traditional way is to work your way through the camera department or through the AD's department and there is still a lot of barriers for women to fly through those easily.

There are more women who are directors now. No-one gets a

surprise when a woman walks on the floor, but there are still people around with reservations about training a woman up to be a director so I think it's easier if you can do a film course and walk into it from there. Also, doing a film course gives you three years to play around with your ideas. If you're doing commercial TV you haven't got any time to develop concepts. I'd like to go back to film school now and spend three years doing it. It would be fantastic.

Where you go from there depends very much on how you want to live your life. If you've got a burning desire to say something and if you don't mind being poor, you don't want to travel and you don't want to buy a house and you've been to a film school, particularly the AFTRS or Swinburne, then stick with the 'I'm a filmmaker' line, and you'll probably get somewhere. You're already taken seriously by the government film bodies when you come out of those film schools. I didn't have that burning obsession to say something at the cost of everything else in my life.

I also think working on a crew for a couple of years is invaluable, take any job that's going. You develop a sympathy for the role of every person in the crew, and you understand the parameters of what they're trying to do. You really need that as a director, so that when you're making requests you're not asking for something that's outrageous and impossible, or when you do ask for something that's outrageous and impossible, you can empathise with how much trouble and effort it's going to take to actually do it.

You can usually tell the directors who have worked on crews, because they have an understanding and a sympathy with what everyone else on the crew is doing. So I think you tend to get better work out of people when they feel supported and understood by the director. They're willing to go that extra mile for you.

Probably the main lesson I have learnt is to actually sit down and shut up. When I was younger I would just bowl in and say you should do this, this and this. I was really insensitive to structures that were already set up. It was very egocentric, so I have learnt to take a back seat a lot more and just watch and listen and try and fit in with the structure that is already there rather than impose my own.

Anything really worthwhile takes a long hard slog, and I am struggling with that now. One of my biggest assets is the tremendous amount of energy that I have and determination to crash through brick walls. It is effective sometimes but not all the time. So patience, collaboration and commitment to a long-term goal I think is really important in filmmaking.

RESEARCH

RESEARCH

RESEARCH

RESEARCH

RESEARCH

RESEARCH

RESEARCH

RESEARCH

RESEARCH

RESEARCH

Over the last twenty years the main arguments for having more women in all jobs, and the research that has underpinned those arguments, have been based in equity and social justice, which have given rise to anti-discrimination legislation and equal employment opportunity policies. More recently, however, other arguments have emerged:

▸ The economic argument – failure to use the brain power of one-half of the workforce can only result in less talent at the top (Townsend, 1995).

▸ The coping-with-change argument – women might be 'better prepared, culturally and psychologically' for the new economic conditions which have emerged through the rise of the information-processing and telecommunications industries. These industries require speed, intelligence and transferable personal and communications skills and women have traditionally had to explore new avenues, learn new skills, take risks, change jobs, work independently and drop in and out of the labour market more frequently than their male colleagues (Plant, 1997).

▸ The women-have-different-work-practices argument – women work differently from men and bring different perspectives which make for more diverse and richer decision-making. Research shows that women administrators are better than men at giving information, strengthening interpersonal relations, being receptive to ideas, encouraging effort and subordinate development, and at assuming supportive roles; women use an interactive leadership style rather than the more traditional command-and-control style (Kelly, 1991).

All this adds up to the conclusion which many industries are now supporting – that there should be a mix of perspectives in the workplace at all levels (Kelly, 1991).

THE FILM AND TELEVISION INDUSTRY

There have been two areas of relevant research in the film and television industry – the employment of women in different jobs within the industry, and the representation of women by the media.

The equity argument, supported by the research, has driven the initiatives to employ more women in film and television. The shortage of women in the key creative roles of scriptwriter, producer and director, and in television management, has also been seen as a factor in trying to get more balanced representations of women and women's points of view in films, television programs and advertising.

There has been a very valuable series of studies on women working in film and television since 1974 (UNESCO, 1976; Ryan et al, 1983; Pip et al, 1987; Cox & Laura, 1992). These show an increase from three percent of those employed in all 'upper level' positions on feature films in 1974 to 28 percent in 1990-91. (Upper level can generally be defined as a head of department, or someone who is authorised to make decisions without reference to a more senior person.) However, in the same year – 1990-91 – only five percent of upper level technical positions were held by women, and eighteen percent at the lower level. There had been no women working as sound recordists on feature films until the 1990-91 survey, when there was twelve percent.

These surveys showed that women tended to be better trained than men. In the 1990-91 survey of 680 women in film, television and video, 24 percent said that lack of support, no career prospects and working in small companies were the main barriers to progression; while 23 percent of women said that general sexism was the main barrier preventing their progress in the industry. This was confirmed in a survey of senior women in television conducted in 1996, when three-quarters of the 52 women interviewed said that subconscious and unintentional discrimination by men, the bureaucracy or the system, and the weakness or non-existence of female networks were factors which contributed to the lack of women in senior management roles. In the same survey, half thought that women's lack of confidence, the lack of female mentors and conscious or intentional discrimination by men were also factors (AFC, 1996).

The research into media portrayals of women has found that women are greatly under-represented (BAM SSB, 1994). But there has been very little research into the connection between the numbers and occupations of women working in the media and the representations of women in and by the media. This is because there have been too few women working in decision-making positions to make a relevant study. Therefore it has been taken for granted that if there were more women in management, in key creative decision-making positions of producer, writer, director, and a more balanced workforce, a more balanced portrayal of women would follow.

In the 1970s the women's film unit at the AFC and the Australian Women's Broadcasting Co-operative at ABC Radio were set up to give women production experience and to produce films and programs which had women's points of view (Rigg & Coppeland, 1985; Thornley, 1987).[1]

In the US there is a growing number of women in television senior management and women producers have been successful in producing shows encompassing women's perspectives. Marcy Carsey (*Roseanne*), Linda Bloodworth-Thomason (*Designing Women, Hearts Afire*), Diane English (*Murphy Brown, Love and War*) and Beth Sullivan (*Dr Quinn, Medicine Woman*)[2] have created independently minded heroines adept at handling men who refuse to take them seriously. The producers were described by Silverman, executive director of the Los Angeles-based Women in Film organisation: 'They are activist. They have a voice – and they use it'. However, Bloodworth-Thomason said 'Only a handful of women have clout, everyone else is way down the totem pole... I am tired of women raped, tormented and terrified. I wish women could rise up across the US and Canada and say, "Hell no, we are not going to watch this any more"' (Gregor, 1993).

Laura Ziskin, President of Fox 2000 Pictures USA and producer of *To Die For* and *Pretty Woman*, said that she was hired as the first woman senior executive at Fox because the management recognised that a large proportion of their audience was women but there were no women making the final decisions about what was made. She also said that she has heard a number of pitches from women which the men just don't understand.[3]

In Australia there are still relatively few women in positions where they can dictate exactly what they want to produce, write and direct, or the composition of their crew. However, some are producing films with strong female characters and perspectives.[4] In television there are too few women in program decision-making positions to be able to measure any connection. Women, who make up the majority of CEOs in the film funding bodies, are adamant that their decisions are based on merit and do not favour films with 'female sensibilities' (Crayford, 1997). Projects are usually assessed by peer review and it can still happen that women's projects are assessed by all-male panels.

> ▶▶ **Take risks, but be consistently outstanding.**
>
> **Be tough, but don't be macho.**
>
> **Be ambitious, but don't expect equal treatment.**
>
> **Take responsibility, but follow others' advice.**
>
> **(Morrison et al, 1992)**

If research into the effect of having women in key creative positions is scarce then research into the effect of having women in jobs that use equipment is non-existent.

It would need observational research to see whether women cinematographers, sound recordists and editors make different decisions to men about how they shoot, record and put stories together. The only observational research I am aware of is in the content area. In Denmark Else Jensen (1982) observed women journalists in a newsroom for two weeks and found that women journalist did make different decisions to the male journalists.

There is anecdotal evidence from digital artists, graphic designers, news camera operators and editors that women select different images, and there is also anecdotal evidence that the working environment can be different and more relaxed on a predominantly female crew. But does this produce a different film?

Would there be more interesting or a greater variety of films and programs if there were more women employed, not only in the key creative roles but in the crew roles? The answer is impossible to predict. One could argue that if women directors had the support of a more gender-balanced crew they might be more prepared to work in television or on big budget feature films and thus produce programs which have different perspectives; but that also means changes in the perspective of the decision-makers at the top.

OTHER RESEARCH

Because there is a paucity of research on the working conditions of women in film and television I have looked at other research which helps to identify the issues that women have raised. This research shows that although the industries may be different the issues are very much the same.

There has been a great deal of Australian and international research into women in 'non-traditional' jobs over the last 25 years which has identified similar problems. The most researched area is women in management but there have also been Australian studies into the building and construction industries, sciences, engineering, the defence forces and the electronics industry. In all these studies the problems and the techniques used to discriminate against women were the same (Burton, 1996; Pyke, 1993; Labour Research Centre, 1991).

The single most important hurdle for women is the persistent stereotype that associates a job with being male.

When women enter a workplace which has been a male area they set up an antagonism among the men at a number of levels. In the military it was particularly noted that women threaten some men's sense of their own masculinity so that the presence of women constitutes a threat to their 'manhood' and an invasion of their male space. Some men believe that their job has been degraded. 'I will lose some of my masculinity if women do my job'. This was called 'the fear of contagious effeminacy' when it was first identified. Men cope with this by either aggressive or passive-aggressive behaviour. This is evident in a number of stories about film and television crews and crew rooms, and particularly news camera operators.

SEXUAL HARASSMENT

The most aggressive behaviour constitutes sexual harassment. All Australian states and the Commonwealth have legislation making sexual harassment unlawful. In New South Wales the Equal Opportunity Tribunal accepted that sexual harassment could amount to sexual discrimination by saying that 'a person is sexually harassed if she or he is subject to unwelcome sexual conduct by a person who stands in a position of power in relation to him or her' (Equal Opportunities Commission, 1984).

Film

Film production is a stressful creative process with many variables, constant emergencies and deadlines. As Sue Kerr says (p62), 'filmmaking is a whole lot of palaver to capture performance in its absolute crystal best'. It is a prima donna industry and often egos are fragile and tempers are short. There are all-night shoots, weeks away from home and the adrenalin rush of working together against great odds and the euphoria of succeeding. Personalities and prejudices get exposed and emotional barriers are broken in a way that does not happen in a nine-to-five office job. These emotional highs and lows can be misconstrued and misused if those in power positions take advantage, even if it is relaxing off-duty.

Formal procedures for sexual harassment do not exist on film crews because they only come together for the production. The freelance nature of the film industry means that women have to renegotiate their working relationships in the predominantly male environment for each new film. Every new job for a woman can become another rite of passage and, depending on her experience, her own personality and the masculine fragility of the crew members, she may become the butt of sexist behaviour or comments meant to test her.

Most women tend to grin and bear sexist behaviour, in the hope that it will go away, rather than risk getting a reputation as someone who 'can't take a joke' when in fact the 'joke' may be behaviour which is totally unacceptable in the workplace. If it becomes bad they may go to the assistant director or the producer. The industry is so small and the length of a shoot is relatively short so that most women are not prepared to make a fuss because they feel that there would be little sympathy and it would hamper their opportunities for future work.

Some women confront difficult behaviour with quick repartee. Helen Gaynor (p323) and Gretchen Thornburn (pp45-47) both give examples of how they have been able to make jokes about sexist language and attitudes and turn it around. Others, like Jan Kenny (p20) and Annabelle Sheehan (pp86-8) deal with the situation later. Both tactics take a considerable amount of courage, particularly if you are young and inexperienced.

However, as more women get into positions of producers, directors and department heads they are able to employ the men who are sensitive to some of these issues and, as Sally Pryor (p171) and Dany Cooper (p156) have said, they just will not employ men again if they behave badly.

Television

In television women have to work in crew positions with the same men on the staff. The Griffith case in NSW,[5] the Ormond case in Victoria,[6] and the publicity surrounding the subsequent books, *The First Stone* by Helen Garner and *Bodyjamming* edited by Jenna Mead, have drawn attention to the issue of sexual harassment in the workplace. It was reported during interviews with staff of television stations that these cases had a profound effect on managements when they understood that a sexual harassment case could cost them money.

All television networks now have procedures to deal with sexual harassment internally in order to prevent it being taken outside to a tribunal, but the extent to which they have publicised the procedures varies. Many of the women I interviewed did not know that there might be a sexual harassment contact person, most said that they would go to their immediate boss, who was a man. Several women gave examples of sexual harassment that had occurred to them and explained how it had been dealt with. On the whole they were satisfied although there were a couple of instances where they had been told by their bosses not to pursue it because the men would lose their jobs.

There was general agreement that physical sexual harassment was no longer a major issue. One woman who is now in television management said, 'In the 1960s and '70s it was rife. A bloke would rub himself up against you by the filing cabinets, you didn't like it but you just had to put up with it. Today there are processes [to deal with it] and senior women who young women can go to'. In fact, very few women I spoke to in operations departments of stations where there was not a female human resources person employed could name a senior woman who they could go to.

How we Cope

Formal sex discrimination is now covered by discrimination laws, and there are financial penalties, which means that organisations are educating their workforces that certain practices are not acceptable. However, at either a conscious or unconscious level, informal discrimination is still played out in many subtle ways.

Women who work on their own with men find the passive aggressive behaviour particularly difficult. They have no support and they are constantly reminded that they are different. Pyke recommended to the building industry that workers and employers need the experience of women in those workplaces and that women should not be 'thrown to the wolves' without some kind of support mechanism. Therefore women should be employed in groups of three in order to establish a 'critical mass' to support women in male-dominated work cultures (Pyke, 1993). BTQ-7 Brisbane was sensitive to this when they employed two women technical trainees together.

Van Maanen (1976) suggests that there is a three-stage process that women go through in 'non-traditional' jobs. The experiences of many of the women interviewed for this book confirm the continuing validity of Van Maanen's hypothesis. The first stage is anticipatory socialisation, when the applicant takes on the values of the group to which she aspires. If she has not been socialised to accept the values of the occupation or organisation she will experience both conflict (due to the internal value clash) and frustration (because her values put her at variance with her male colleagues).

The second stage is reality shock. This is experiencing the reality of the organisation as opposed to the unrealistic rosy picture that she might have been given, or conjured up for herself, particularly if she was assured it was a non-sexist environment. She then finds it is not supportive and that there are informal networks which exclude women through overt ridicule and subtle intimidation and sexual jokes. The shock might come from self exclusion due to her confusion concerning inappropriate behaviour or from physical exclusion due to the removal of activities to private spaces such as the bar, the men's room, the golf course and private gatherings.

Women are also not well integrated into the mentor or coach system. The coach role is to develop a new identity for the learner by guiding her along a series of successful socialisation paths within the organisation. The peer group also eases a new recruit into the organisation but there is unlikely to be enough women for a significant peer group and women are unlikely to be integrated into groups composed mostly of their male colleagues. Therefore their token status creates barriers for them.

The last stage is metamorphosis. These are the solutions that a newcomer has adopted to address the problem. These have been identified as the 'mother', who represents the organisational extension of the traditional nurturing role; the 'seductress', who personifies the prize in the competition among men and does not focus on women's abilities or achievements; the 'pet', adopted by the male group as a cute little mascot, patronised and praised for exhibiting behaviours considered ordinary in a man; and, finally, the 'iron maiden', the tough non-emotional non-sexual strong woman who refuses to accept any of the other three clearly sex-linked roles but is, nonetheless, sexually defined by this very refusal and is often thought to be more militant and tougher than she really is.

These roles represent a forced choice offered by the dominant male group. This allows the male co-workers to deal with women in terms of these usual comfortable sexual and family roles of mother, sex partner, kid sister and maiden aunt. And of course by adopting them women assist men to cope with the conflict that their presence as women arouses in previously all-male territory (Betz & Fitzgerald, 1987).

DISCRIMINATION — PERSONAL

Although the procedures to eliminate formal discrimination may be in place, recent AFC studies identified discrimination at a conscious and unconscious level as still being an issue (Cox & Laura, 1992; AFC, 1996).

Leonie Still (1993) said that 'men's clubs' have dominated organisational culture since its inception because fewer women were in the workforce. Organisational structures, theory, language and processes were formed to suit male values. Those who are in control are not keen to share power with others who are different, so that men make rules that select and reward their successors. Men judge each other by their income status and paid work success and few are likely to prioritise family over their jobs. Therefore, women have to adjust and cope with management duties and loyalties based on total commitment measured in terms of time spent at the workplace because time, rather than efficiency, is often the only measure of management commitment.

Women managers operate from different values, assumptions and perspectives that reflect their female grounding but these are not widely represented or accepted in organisational life. Women, therefore, often feel alienated, different, out of place and that they are working in a hostile environment.

They are organisational migrants who try to accept and adopt the organisation's values, norms, culture and behaviour and, if successful, it means that they fit in. If women become managers then they are expected to discharge their home and family obligations while trying to fulfil the expectations associated with their male-dictated jobs. They often feel unaccepted despite their efforts towards enculturation.

Women managers have little impact on the organisational culture despite their growing numbers, because they avoid confronting the organisation with their unresolved issues (Still, 1993).

Kantor (1977) says that there are three types of pressure on women in senior positions: the job itself; being a female trailblazer; and being a minority. She says that token women at high levels are public creatures who attract attention with anything they do. They have to find a way to conform without being self estranged. They are stand-ins for all women and symbols of how women can succeed. They perform in a glasshouse, dreading the thought that they might fail. Gillian Armstrong has been very conscious of this pressure on her (pp206-17), and Carmel Travers identified it when commenting on her experiences at the Ten Network (p351). There is also the pressure of managing demands of life outside work, because career success can be a stigma for women who want relationships with men.

Breaking the Glass Ceiling (Morrison et al, 1992), another American study, suggested that women were put through a number of hoops when they entered management. They had to show toughness and independence at the same time; they had to contradict stereotypes that their male executives and co-workers had about women; they had to be seen to be different, 'better than women' as a group, but couldn't go too far to forfeit all traces of femininity because that would make them too alien to their superiors and colleagues. In essence, their mission was to do what wasn't expected of them while doing enough of what was expected of them as women to gain acceptance.

The real key to success was the women managers capacity to combine these two expectations consistently and to stay within a narrow band of acceptable behaviours. They had to accomplish feats in exactly the right way and that means combining seemingly contradictory behaviours:

Take risks, but be consistently outstanding.

Be tough, but don't be macho.

Be ambitious, but don't expect equal treatment.

Take responsibility, but follow others' advice.

— Morrison et al, 1992

Still (1993) says that those who don't adapt become mavericks and as soon as their numbers begin to rise, creating discord or discomfort in the organisation, there is a purge. In this way women are pressured to conform and it is therefore very hard for senior women to effect change if they themselves feel vulnerable. This is why equal opportunity officers have become important because they are change agents and become the token woman dissident. However they also have difficulty because they promote the interests of target groups who have traditionally had little power in the organisation and this leads to strong resistance and even opposition from the current powerbrokers.

As Still (1993) says, it takes strong action on behalf of senior management to begin a cultural shift.

Film

The 'management' on a film is the producer and the director and they can largely determine the environment of a film production by the people they employ.

Jackie McKimmie talks about the importance of personalities on a crew (pp224-32) and there are women such as Bronwyn Murphy who just do not like working on large crews (pp30-39). A film crew is like a family so you have to fit in and become a 'family member'; some women find that is easier on smaller productions.

Most women who have had the experience of working with women say that it is much more relaxing, there is no 'bullshit'. Sandra Levy employed a record number of women as heads of departments on *The Well* (1997) – writer, director, director of photography, editor and sound editor. At the forum 'Creative Partnerships – A Case Study of *The Well*' at the second Women in Film and Television (WIFT) conference in 1997 the women all said what a great experience it had been. Sandra made the general point that women are uncomfortable with direct conflict and are more reverential. Dany Cooper (editor) said that they were much more intimate and she talked about the trust and respect that they all had for each other so there were no grounds for direct conflict.

Television

Television managements are still very nervous about appointing women to senior positions. There was a short-lived period when the new Canadian owners of the Ten Network appointed a Canadian managing director, Peter Viner, and he totally restructured. He appointed three female executives who sat with four men to make up the senior management group. Carmel Travers, who was the first woman to become head of a news and current affairs department, described the experience of being in management as a 'blooding' and she said that for the first time in her career being a woman became an issue. 'A prominent columnist in Sydney described it as the pinking of the Ten Network and somehow we were supposed to feel flattered. I felt intensely irritated by it. Suddenly my femaleness became a public issue and it was the first thing that was said about me and it irritated the bejesus out of me. We were kind of thrust out there in too much limelight and once that has happened you can't actually switch the lights off. So you are under a microscope in a way you just hadn't anticipated.'

She said that that experience had made her aware of the very male culture and how women need support. 'When I got inside the organisation a great number of women there said "Thank God you're here, we've got some things we've got to talk to you about". A lot of them wanted to talk about the working conditions, the attitudes of men in the organisation. Some of them had been subjected to the most appalling harassment, some of them had had their careers severely truncated for one reason or another and I was able quite quickly to change that. Just my presence there was able to change a lot of those things' (Travers, 1997).

DISCRIMINATION — EMPLOYMENT

Informal inadvertent discrimination happens within organisational structures when one sex is given different treatment based on its gender rather than on work-related characteristics or performance. This is often informally sanctioned by organisations although it is not formal organisational policy. It happens when everyone is treated exactly the same but a gender standard applies which is not relevant to the job skills required and everyone is expected to meet it. It also happens when there is sex-typing of jobs, so that men and women will be systematically underrated for jobs stereotypically assigned to the other sex. Research shows that if there is only one position available and the candidates have equal qualifications, evaluators overwhelming select the stereotypical gender (Betz & Fitzgerald, 1987). As Margot Phillipson said, if a selection panel has an image of a man in the job then that becomes an unspoken criteria (pp256).

This cuts both ways, of course, so that men have difficulty getting into stereotypical female jobs, such as make-up, wardrobe and secretarial positions.

Other factors that influence so called 'gender neutral' procedures are tests that cannot clearly be shown to be job related, such as height and strength that exceed minimum qualifications, or hidden requirements such as physical attractiveness, which is called 'sex-typed goodness' – because she looks attractive she must be good.

Burton (1991) said that selection committees should be trained to ensure comprehensive job descriptions which identify required skills and performance using language which does not differentiate stereotypical men's and women's jobs. But she recognised that there is a paradox about selection criteria. The more attempts that are made to eliminate subjectivity from decision-making the more rigid become the criteria on which decisions are made, and that can exclude some applicants with relevant qualities or experiences which were not considered when the criteria were set up. She suggested that the way round this is to use selection criteria based on job outcomes and ask applicants to demonstrate the suitability of their qualifications and experiences to those outcomes.

Researchers have pointed out that in the restructuring and the move to multi-skilling the rigidity of traditional skill lines has broken down. This has provided an opportunity for redefining workplace skills and including those that have not been recognised, such as communication, interpersonal relationships, ability to do many things at one time, to provide emotional and physical caring, and organise and produce material without machines. These are often the home-learnt skills which neither men nor women have valued appropriately in the workplace (Cox & Leonard, 1994).

Film

There are no formal selection procedures for employment on film crews. People are employed by word-of-mouth and on the basis of who knows who. It is therefore very difficult to identify examples of sex discrimination where women have been denied jobs because they are women.

Thanks to the large number of women who have identified good properties in scripts and then been successful in producing them, the path has been made easier for other women to follow. Women producers are now being accepted as part of the industry although the high proportion of successful ones often distorts the overall picture. In 1992, 21 percent of sole executive producers were women, 15 percent of sole producers were women and 35 percent were women co-producing with men (Cox & Laura, 1992).

The producer and the director decide who they will employ as heads of departments. Some of those key choices can also be determined by the investors. Each department head selects the people she wants to work with. Decisions are made on the basis of experience, bankability or personality, which can hide sex discrimination. Women who object too strenuously to overt male behaviour are often seen as having a 'difficult personality' and therefore would not fit in.

There are anecdotes about men who have said that they will not employ women but when challenged they will retort that it was 'only a joke'. However the fact is that their crews or departments never do have women. There are stories like those of Mandy

Smith's, where investors have refused to have women directors, and key actors have refused to have women on the crew. So far no-one has been prepared to challenge it.

Within departments on a film crew there is a progression. In the cinematography department, for example, you may begin as a clapper loader and progress through to focus puller, camera operator and, ultimately, director of photography (DOP). Some women complain that a 'celluloid ceiling' is at focus puller level and it is very hard for women to progress to operator on feature films, no matter how many small films and documentaries they have made as an operator. One woman cinematographer had to go back to focus pulling for a year and a half after she had been both DOP and operator on her first feature film.

Television

Television stations present different issues because they recruit for full-time employment into career jobs. The ABC and SBS have, until recently, come under the Australian Public Service and therefore have had a formal selection process monitored by an equal employment opportunity officer. They have also had to conform to EEO requirements and report and implement set goals.

Until recently, hiring practices in commercial television were similar to the film industry and based on word-of-mouth and mates. One operations manager described the process: 'We pay top dollar for the best talent and if they don't make it in the ratings they're gone, and that attitude tends to permeate throughout the management to all the staff, so that we tend to treat people like pieces of meat to be bought and sold'.

The introduction of enterprise bargaining under the industrial relations legislation has introduced television stations to modern management techniques and the networks have all appointed human resource managers and developed selection procedures, identified skills and written formal job descriptions. If they employ more than one hundred people they have to submit an annual affirmative action report and show how they are working towards gender equity within their organisation. The organisations are graded for best practice on a scale of 1-5, with 4 and above indicating 'best practice'. Only the Nine Network has gained a grading of four or above by the Affirmative Action Agency.

The women's movement has been concerned about the impact of award restructuring on women in the workforce, believing that women would be in a weak bargaining position and further marginalised because they would lose the support they had achieved through union agreements. In fact, enterprise bargaining has been beneficial to women in television because it has introduced modern management practices which have incorporated sexual harassment procedures and brought women into human resource positions at a senior level with a brief to look after EEO and affirmative action matters. It has also made managements aware of the investment they have made in women and in some cases they have supported their careers and become more sensitive to issues that encourage women to stay on after pregnancy. Some managements are now talking about being 'family friendly' and negotiating part-time work. The Nine Network's agreement to six weeks' paid maternity leave is a major breakthrough for commercial television.

One of the first commercial stations to embody EEO principles was NWS-9 Adelaide which wanted to tender for state government work and therefore had to be accredited for having quality management practices (see Appendix 1). Now all networks say they advertise jobs internally and that women have a better chance of competing with men for the traditional male jobs.

Part of the restructuring process and enterprise bargaining has been a skills analysis which has involved a systematic process to identify the skills and competencies that are needed for each job. This provides the basis for job descriptions, which ensures fairer selection processes, and the foundation for performance appraisals. It has made managements look more closely at whether the traditional career paths are appropriate and this has made some jobs more accessible to women.

The career path to a director, for example, has traditionally been scene shifter, cable pulling, camera operator. Yet the director's assistant, who is invariably a woman, assists the director with all the pre-production, production and post production work. She sits beside the director in the control room.

However, with the introduction of skills analysis, the traditional progressions are breaking down and there is an emphasis on what the job requires and who is the person with the skills. Some director's assistants are becoming directors and at the Ten Network they are requiring directors to switch, so some women vision switchers have been trained to be directors. They are also providing each employee with a job description of what are the ideal characteristics and skills and experience needed for the job.

LACK OF CONFIDENCE

Over half the senior women in the AFC study (1996) said that lack of confidence is a factor in the low number of women in management. Many of the 50 women interviewed by Leonie Still (1990) believed their early socialisation prevented them from developing skills for management. They saw it as a process of conditioning that resulted in their learning to be agreeable and not to argue; learning not to be assertive or yell; needing to be liked and to not feel rejected; being fearful of confrontation; always apologising to others; and being fearful of breaking imposed moulds and expectations.

There have been a number of studies in schools on the way boys treat girls and vice versa. In 1991 a consultancy was undertaken for the Australian Educational Council (AEC) to study the situation of girls in Australian schools. One of the key findings was that in their day-to-day routine girls in co-educational classrooms and schoolyards suffer sex-based harassment from boys and sometimes from teachers (AEC, 1992). The girls reported that the boys hog the equipment or space; boys were disdainful, contemptuous, belittling; girls were ignored; boys flouted legitimate authority of female student office-holders or teachers; there was aggressive defence of some activities as 'boys only' or 'girls only'; nasty or hurtful teasing and name-calling; and comments on appearance or clothing. Girls also recounted unhappy experiences at the hands of teachers; sexual innuendo; sexist jokes; and some physical sexual harassment.

This environment has been called the sexual underworld of schooling. It is controlled by male sexuality with sexually abusive language, neglect and marginalisation of young women, and patronising behaviour towards female students that reinforces the traditional class and race-laden notions of femininity and masculinity (Wood & Lees, 1993). One male secondary teacher is quoted in the AEC report as saying that 'if parents knew what we know about the effects of boys' behaviour on girls there would be a political uproar. Everyone would insist on having their daughters in single sex classes'.

Film

Because the film industry is a freelance industry it means that women have to get out and sell themselves, and overcome their learnt behaviour to become assertive. Unfortunately not many training courses recognise this and give women the tools they need to operate in the male environment.

Television

Affirmative action programs are to correct the effects of past discrimination, to eliminate present discrimination or to prevent discrimination in the future. They do help those who find being assertive difficult. But very often there has been a backlash from men and women to these initiatives, and women have been made to feel that they have not got their job based on merit. This exacerbates their lack of confidence.

LACK OF MENTORS

Many studies of women in management identified having a mentor as the single most important factor helping women progress in their careers. A mentor knows how the organisation operates, advises on career paths through an organisation, provides opportunities for advancement and puts their protégés names forward at appropriate times for higher duties and training.

In the absence of mentors, performance appraisal is a tool that is helpful to women. It provides a formal process for managers to find out what their female and male employees' aspirations and goals are. The next step is to formally pair people up with appropriate mentors.

Film

A number of the women interviewed for this book identified men who had been important mentors. Russell Boyd, who employed Jan Kenny – the first Australian DOP to employ a woman on his crew, Bill Bennett who mentored Dany Cooper and provided time in his budget for her to learn Lightworks for *Last Man Hanged* (1992), Sid Butterworth who employed and guided Sue Kerr, and George Miller who provided working conditions for Annabelle Sheehan so that she could breastfeed while working on *Bangkok Hilton* (1989).

Because there are still so few senior women on large film crews female mentoring happens outside the production. WIFT has been organising a women mentor program for the freelance industry.

Television

Most mentoring is informal which means that there are not too many men who willingly take on female protégés in the male culture of television, because of the possible sexual connotations. Men by virtue of their 'boys' club' have an informal mentoring process which disadvantages women.

Women who have risen through the ranks have usually done so in the promotions and publicity departments, which in most television stations have come to be dominated by women. On the whole these women have been protected from the male culture by the growing number of women working in the field.

Often by virtue of their gender they have been made responsible for 'women's issues' at the station but are also very busy with their own senior positions and families. Being a mentor also makes them vulnerable in the organisation (see the research below on the need for women to distance themselves from their female colleagues).

WOMEN'S NETWORKS

In the AFC management study (1996) half the women reported the weakness or non-existence of female networks as a factor preventing them from getting into management. However a great deal of research shows that many women in non-traditional jobs, particularly management, are ambivalent about networking, particularly within an organisation.

Women in senior positions often distance themselves from other women and women's issues because masculine values prevail and the criteria for success are aligned with those values. Male peers rather than other women are a point of reference.

Women therefore accept the values of their male peers and unconsciously need to draw a line between the work they are doing and the work other women are doing, both in value terms and in identity terms (Burton et al, 1987). Research has found that many administrative and professional women will seek to distance themselves from secretarial workers in the expectation that they will be treated differently. Close relations with secretaries and other lower graded female workers, and actions on their behalf, might create confusion in how such women perceive themselves and are perceived by others (Game & Pringle, 1983).

This might be particularly the case if they have had to struggle to have their skills and experiences recognised.

Women have also sometimes been harsher than men in their judgments about other women's work. The price of being 'one of the boys' was a willingness to occasionally turn against 'the girls'.

Film

This distancing shows up in some women producers' nervousness in appointing women as heads of departments. A number of women in the freelance film industry complained that there are a small number of women who are worse than men in their sexist attitudes towards them. One suggested that there was a type of female producer who believed that because they had had it so tough themselves they didn't see why others shouldn't have to go through the same process.

Also, women producers, directors and writers have been loath to recognise that there is a woman's point of view because it can become a two-edged sword. They do not want to be put in a box labelled 'women' and prevented from working on 'men's' stories. This exacerbates the problem that there are few films with women protagonists. A WIFT survey conducted over 1993-94 showed that only five out of 32 feature films had a female protagonist. Women were co-leads in another five films but these were all stories about men. This was worse than a previous survey in 1991-92, which showed that one third of 37 feature films had been driven by female characters.[7]

Television

As a result of her experience at the Ten Network, Carmel Travers believes that it is really important for women to build up a critical mass of female support below, above, and around them, both inside and outside the organisation. 'Management boasts that they have women in senior executive roles but they have got to be prepared to pay a price and allow you to function as a woman and recognise that women may run things differently. They have to take on the social responsibilities of changing the imbalance.'

The ABC and SBS have formal women's support networks within their organisations. There are no formal networks in commercial television. Most of the women who work on equipment work in isolation and many do not want to mix with other women.

CAREER PATHS

Research has identified four types of male career patterns:

▸ The linear career, which is characterised by upward mobility predominantly within a given field. The majority of business executives appear to aspire to this materialistic, status-oriented and goal-directed path.

▸ The steady state career, characterised by one field for the duration of one's career, with little movement vertically or laterally.

▸ The spiral career, a newer concept whereby a person makes

major changes into a new field or occupation to build on current skills and develop new ones, although it still implies orderly and upward transitions.

▸ The transitory career, marked by many changes in jobs and occupational fields with more lateral than upward moves. The transitory career has been described as a consistent pattern of inconsistency. This does not fit traditional career concepts and it is viewed as a pattern of failure motivated by incompetence.

Women's career paths are different. They are more concerned with growth and identity and relationships with people, they are more influenced by role models and are more value-driven. None of the paths identified above encompass the sorts of career pressures faced by many women: temporary work, cessation, downward or lateral moves in order to accommodate the career move of a spouse, or a period of other responsibilities (Smith & Hutchinson, 1995). Women often experience strong career changes between 28 and 39, moving towards more autonomy between 40 and 50, which is the time when the establishment demands of men's careers tend to be diminishing.

Women who reach an equivalent status to men tend to do so through different, more specialised, routes. Men reach generalist positions more readily than women.

Men undertook most of their radical transitions fairly early in their careers whereas women maintained a higher rate of divergent mobility throughout their careers. Women moved faster between jobs with more radical switches, typically changing employers to achieve career progression. They maintained this pattern more continuously throughout their careers than did men, whose job moves became less radical as they aged (Still, 1990).

Film

Because it is a freelance industry women and men have to develop their own career paths by selecting appropriate jobs and being prepared to make a stand when they want to move on to the next level. Most of the women's stories in this book show how they have made definite decisions about their careers at various times.

Jan Kenny (pp11-25) was very definite about her change from focus puller to operator. Annabelle Sheehan (pp80-93) has crossed backwards and forwards between editing and teaching and made a stand to refuse to be a sound assistant.

Television

Eight of the 22 women managers interviewed had children and all but one had had them while they were employed at the station – but only two while they were in their senior positions, one of whom has since resigned. Only three have risen through the ranks of the same station (smaller city stations) and they must have taken time out to do other things when they were having children. All the others have job-hopped to get promoted and some have changed cities and gone overseas. Over a three-year period seven of these women have left the station and two of the vacated positions have been filled by women.

Most of them have had some problems with the male culture and to a greater or lesser extent have had to identify with it to succeed. However the appointment of senior women as human resource managers in all the networks, except for Seven, has helped with this problem.

NECESSARY SKILLS FOR A MALE MANAGEMENT CULTURE

The women managers in television have had to find a delicate balance between identifying with management, so as not to be marginalised, and representing what is seen as a minority interest.

Leonie Still (1990) has identified the attitudes and skills that women believe they need to acquire in order to operate effectively within the male managerial world:

- ‣ To accept the right to have human failings without rebuff or retribution.
- ‣ To accept that lack of expertise is not a condition to be hidden or spoken of as a failing.
- ‣ To reject differentials in salaries and opportunities.
- ‣ To overcome the fear factor; and to confront a person on an issue.
- ‣ To risk; to achieve; to do the unaccustomed.

- ▸ To assert one's views and achievements.
- ▸ To accept responsibility for one's own life and future and not blame others for one's failures or setbacks.
- ▸ To expect reward for effort.
- ▸ To learn that one's opinions are valid and to reject 'put downs'.
- ▸ To learn the games men play on each other and on women in the workplace.
- ▸ To become aware that men talk about how hard they work, while women actually do it and get it done quietly.
- ▸ To learn not to compromise one's desires and wishes to accommodate others.
- ▸ To learn to recognise the practices, behaviours and subtleties denoting discrimination.

A FINAL NOTE

In the Australian Film Commission's fifth edition of *Get the Picture* (1999), its regular report on the state of the Australian audiovisual industries, the following percentages of women were employed:[8]

Directors (film/stage/radio/TV)	29%
Directors of photography	11%
Camera operators	3%
Film/video editors	27%
Sound technicians	12%
Light technicians	11%
TV equipment operators	26%
Technical directors	11%

Based on 1996 figures, the report also noted that men were more likely than women to be in the higher income brackets in all the audiovisual industries. As an example, 23 percent of men and 13 percent of women in film and video production earned $52,000 or over. At the other end of the scale, 30 percent of women and 22 percent of men earned less than $20,800.

FOOTNOTES

1 More recently the same thinking has supported Indigenous units within ABC and SBS Television and the AFC. Frances Peters, a producer with the ABC Indigenous Program Unit, said that the unit gave Indigenous people political and creative control and had been extremely successful in producing high-quality programs on Indigenous issues for general audiences. But she stressed that it was a first step towards Indigenous people infiltrating the organisation to ensure that Indigenous perspectives were included in mainstream television (Jakubowicz et al, 1994).

2 This was the first dramatic series to be created and sole executive produced by a woman. For case study see Seger, 1996, 226-230.

3 At an International Women in Television breakfast organised by the Australian Film Commission, 5 November 1998, Sydney.

4 Producers Jan Chapman, Sandra Levy; writer Laura Jones; writer/directors Jane Campion, Jackie McKimmie, Shirley Barrett; director Gillian Armstrong.

5 In 1994 women who worked for Terry Griffith, the Minister of Police in NSW, charged him with sexual harassment and the NSW government settled the case for an undisclosed sum and he resigned. The case got a lot of publicity at the time.

6 The Master of Ormond College, Melbourne, lost his job due to charges of sexual harassment at a party, brought by two students.

7 Research conducted by Maggie Millar and Sue Maslin. Press release October 1994, 'What's Wrong with this Picture', issued by Women in Film and Television (Australia).

8 Compiled by the AFC from ABS, *Employment in Selected Culture/Leisure Occupations* (1996).

APPENDIX 1

>> **The process of working from the top down and ground up hopefully will ensure that permanent changes have been made.**

TELEVISION STRUCTURE

Throughout the 1990s there has been a gradual breaking down of the male culture in television. Each network has tackled it in a different way.

The commercial television sector is the largest employer. In the early years of television in Australia there were independently owned stations in the cities and large country towns that were loosely joined by network program buying agreements.

In the mid 1980s Australia's domestic satellite enabled programs to be distributed from Sydney to the rest of the country relatively cheaply. As well, changes to licensing and ownership restrictions enabled the commercial networks to expand into the country, providing country viewers with three commercial stations instead of one. As a result of these developments there were massive ownership changes in the late 1980s with a reorganisation of staff and a centralisation of production, mainly in Sydney. Today the Seven and Ten Networks own all the capital city stations in the mainland states and the Nine Network owns Sydney, Melbourne and Brisbane. The Perth and Adelaide stations in the Nine network are owned by independent companies.

The ABC was always a network, with production studios in each capital city, and initially in some regional cities, where local programs were produced. The head office and network management was always in Sydney and most of the network programs have been produced in Sydney or Melbourne. As a result of the growth of networking via the satellite and budget reductions forced by federal government funding cuts, the ABC has reduced its production in all its studios.

The SBS is based in Sydney, where it has a small production studio. It also has a small news facility in Melbourne. The network has been slow to cover the country because it broadcasts on the UHF band.

THE NINE NETWORK

The Nine Network, owned by the Packer family, is the oldest of the commercial networks. When licences were granted in 1955 the Packers were the only company to get both a Sydney and a Melbourne licence (TCN-9 Sydney and GTV-9 Melbourne). TCN-9 Sydney was the first television station on air, in September 1956.[1] Apart from three and a half years (1987 to 1990) when Alan Bond's company bought it, the Packers have controlled the Nine Network by virtue of their ownership of TCN-9 Sydney and GTV-9 Melbourne. These two stations cover 42% of the viewing audience, and provide a viable market for program production.

In the 1980s QTQ-9 Brisbane and STW-9 Perth were owned by Bond and joined Sydney and Melbourne when he bought TCN and GTV from Packer. However, Bond put all four stations up for sale in 1989: STW sold to a regional television operator and Packer bought GTV Melbourne, TCN Sydney and QTQ Brisbane. NWS-9 in Adelaide has always been owned independently of Sydney and Melbourne. From 1987 until 1998 it was owned by the Lamb family who then sold it to Southern Cross Broadcasting who also own a Canberra station and regional stations.

The three Nine Network stations and Northern Territory TV (also owned by Packer) employ 1725 people of whom 573 or 33% are women. There are 101 managers of whom 16 or 17% are women.[2]

The dominance of the Packer family on the Nine Network throughout most of its life meant that its management was the most stable (Bond did not make major management changes when he took over). The Nine Network was also the most successful of the networks in Sydney and Melbourne and since the mid '80s, when the satellite enabled the consolidation of network broadcasting across the country, all stations affiliated to the Nine Network have been leaders in the ratings.

There is an attitude within the Nine Network which is 'We are the top station, it works, so don't change it'. It was therefore not surprising to find that Nine is reportedly the most conservative of all the networks in its management practices. Women in many stations referred to the Nine management as the 'boys' club' and it has a reputation as a very macho culture. Its pre-eminence in news, football and its Saturday *World of Sport* program all support this macho image. However, things are changing. The Nine Network is the only broadcasting company which has been identified by the Affirmative Action Agency (AAA) as a 'best practice organisation'. The head office of the Nine Network has always been in Sydney and it is at TCN-9 Sydney where the changes are the most obvious.

The women who the station managements in the Nine Network nominated as the most senior in 1994-95 had quite different backgrounds from those at the other stations. Only one came from the television industry (head of publicity in Melbourne); four had come from other industries and worked in the human resources area. These four had either been brought in to sort out management problems, as was the case with Karen Marks at STW Perth and Sam Thomas at NWS Adelaide, or been appointed in other senior positions in the station and then taken on the role of human resources. Susie Waters at TCN had been the network's legal counsel before being appointed network director of human resources. Jennifer Murray at QTQ Brisbane was the chief executive's assistant. She had come from the public sector in the late 1980s. She saw the lack of procedures, career paths and training and gradually took on the human resources duties by default.

From a slow start in the mid 1990s the three stations owned by the Nine Network had caught up, introducing a number of practices which had already been accepted at NWS Adelaide and the Seven Network. It overtook them with the AAA best practice assessment in 1997.

When Bruce Gyngell was appointed chairman in the early '90s he recognised that, while women made up half the viewing audience, there were very few women in the network who management consulted. He engaged a consultant to look at management practices and a task force was set up to work with the consultants. Susie Waters, who was then the network's legal officer, was the only woman on the task force. She had joined the staff in 1993 as a company lawyer from Freehill Hollingdale and Page, a large Sydney law firm which had a 50-50 gender split, to a position where she was the only woman senior executive. She was interested in employment law and had taken an interest in equal employment and affirmative action issues.

One of the recommendations of the consultancy was to set up a human resources department and to conduct a staff survey to collect information about employees' perceptions both of their jobs and of management.

Subsequently, in 1995, the network carried out a confidential survey among all staff in the three stations (TCN, GTV, QTQ). They were anxious for a high return rate, so scheduled people into the studio to complete the survey during work time. There was a 78 percent response rate. The survey showed very high job satisfaction but identified other areas where staff wanted change.

In 1996 Susie Waters was made director of human resources and given the job of formulating strategies to meet the needs identified in the survey.

One of the problems at TCN-9, which did not help when initiating change, was that it was very decentralised. The programs were separate entities in separate cottages, responsible for their own staffing. This decentralised, competitive structure was obviously very successful in terms of ratings, so no-one wanted it changed. It was therefore difficult to dictate from the centre and break down the entrenched 'old boys' culture that existed in some of the program units.

However, TCN introduced management training in selection processes and performance appraisal. This meant that every manager had to sit down with each staff member once a year and talk about her or his individual performance. While this was very time consuming it ensured good communication within departments and provided a formal process for concerns to be discussed and opportunities for departmental heads to hear from the staff.

Quite fortuitously, around this time a number of senior women in the station returned to work after having children, including Susie Waters herself. This provided role models for women and I was told that managers became more accommodating about rearranging rosters, particularly if there were couples with children employed at the station. The women no longer felt that their need to take time off to look after sick children was of a lesser concern to managers than the men's golf days.

In four years there was an increase from one to three women on the executive third floor at TCN and more women were represented at the senior executive committee meetings.

So the Nine Network's culture slowly changed. The initiatives piloted in Sydney were gradually extended to Melbourne. Brisbane had already introduced a number of them. The three stations in the network now have six weeks' paid maternity leave, a first for commercial television and one that helped give them a 100 percent return rate for women on maternity leave, along with flexible working practices such as options for part-time work and work from home. (Paid maternity leave was introduced many years ago into the public service and therefore enjoyed by staff in the ABC and SBS.) The Nine Network decision gave the staff a major signal that women employees are important and the network wanted to retain them. The network also paid for a childcare advisory service but the management was not convinced that there was a need for the expense of childcare facilities.

The director of human resources estimated she spent twenty percent of her time on affirmative action which was the same amount as NWS-9, ten percent more than the Ten Network and seventeen percent more than the Seven Network.

The Nine Network did not provide details of its senior management structure in its 1997 Affirmative Action Report but independent investigations in 1996 suggest the following: two men in Tier 1, two women out of fifteen in Tier 2 and eleven out of 51 in Tier 3 – a total of thirteen out of 68.[3]

NWS-9 Adelaide

The most forward looking of the stations in the Nine Network, in terms of changing the male culture, was NWS Adelaide when it was owned by the Lamb family. Of all the thirteen capital city stations that I visited NWS was the most proactive in changing its male management practices and adopting EEO practices. However I understand the new owners do not have the same approach.

NWS has always been owned independently of the Nine Network. It is the oldest station in Adelaide and had a blokey reputation in the past. In 1997 it employed 227 staff of whom 84 or 37 percent were women.[4] (The new owners have cut the staff by nearly half.)

NWS then had five women on its fifteen-person executive committee: the head of programs and promotions (who was third in line to the general manager), and the heads of human resources, information technology and finance and sales.

In 1993 it was the first station in the network and in Adelaide to appoint its own human resources manager, a woman, Sam Thomas. At that time the Nine Network was still at the stage of appointing consultants to review their management practices. I understood that the NWS-9 management was not just paying lip service to employing more women but they had a policy to change male attitudes, although it was not happening as fast as some women would have liked.

This early proactive approach was due to the demise of local production. NWS wanted to tender to the South Australian government to produce training tapes, which meant that it had to be accredited for total quality management. It engaged management consultants who recommended a range of policies in order to get accreditation. These covered recruitment, training, career development opportunities, defining strategic objectives for five years ahead and the appointment of a human resources person.

Tyrrell Talbot, the then general manager, initiated the recommendations and admitted that properly conducted selection procedures and appraisals was a much fairer way of operating. He proudly showed me the staff board with everyone's photograph and job. 'It's a simple thing but it means that people working on shifts know who everyone is.'

Sam Thomas was new to television. She had worked with a major agency in the public sector and had managed change in other work cultures in Adelaide. She brought a totally different approach to management.

The cultural change process was established through teams with team leaders who had the responsibility of managing their work areas instead of all the direction coming from the top. Job descriptions were developed and team work partnerships evolved.

Other affirmative action initiatives were that women on maternity leave were provided with information, training and notification of vacancies. There were also exit interviews with all staff.

The number of women employed increased and male managers started to comment on how well the female employees had done and to encourage their participation at all levels. However, three years later there were still no women directors.

Sam realised that it had been hard for men to understand that women have a major role in organisations and a major contribution to make. 'Sometimes I had to take a back seat and try another approach. It would be fair to say that sometimes males have seen the promotion of women as a threat which is incorrect as, after all, we are all there to do a job'.

'Within one particular area there were women who were undertaking similar roles to the men but they were not treated equally. The women were apprehensive that if they spoke up there may be a backlash. I advised that this would not happen and as a team they devised a plan which had equal job roles and recognition and gender balance within them and it has now become fully operational'.

Sam admitted that changing the culture had been a long process 'but it is slowly happening and the process of working from the top down and ground up hopefully will ensure that permanent changes have been made'. She didn't reckon on the sale of the station at a price which meant massive job losses, including her own in 1998.

THE SEVEN NETWORK

The Seven Network was established by Christopher Skase in 1988. It consists of TVW Perth, SAS Adelaide, BTQ Brisbane, HSV Melbourne and ATN Sydney. Until the mid '80s ownership shake-up, ATN and BTQ had been owned by Fairfax, HSV and ADS by the Herald and Weekly Times in Melbourne and SAS and TVW by Holmes à Court. HSV Melbourne and ATN Sydney had traditionally been fiercely independent in their station management policies, having had different local owners for most of their existence. The take-over of the two stations, with the head office located in Sydney, altered that power balance.

In 1991 the Seven Board asked Chris Chapman, who was then managing director of ATN – he had initially come from a large law firm to Seven as the network's legal counsel – for advice on developing enterprise bargaining agreements. He attended some seminars and realised that 'In terms of our development, staff, goodwill and trust in management levels, understanding business literacy, understanding industrial relations, we were about one out of ten. The station had good old fashioned values, our integrity was quite high so that was not an issue. I said to the Board "Forget about enterprise agreements for two years, you have a network that is reactive, conservative, run of the mill, a chauvinistic, discriminatory environment where second is good enough. Unless you get rid of all that, you're not going to have an enterprise agreement that will have longevity". They accepted that, and we surveyed all our staff.'

Chapman's view was that 'Good, old fashioned male chauvinism has stopped women getting into senior positions and if you acknowledge that, and that there is no logic to it, and it is counter-productive, then you can begin to deal with it'.

In 1993, network management introduced a blueprint for a

continuous improvement program, which included performance appraisal, a network human resources manager to oversee the new policies, which included equal opportunity and affirmative action, a network training manager and a traineeship scheme. Chapman believed that training and affirmative action were very much related. 'You can't really talk about one without the other.' The network also set up uniform management practices across all its stations and affirmative action committees in each station.

Chris Chapman was the most proactive managing director that I met. He was committed to changing the management structure and culture. All the senior women at Seven who had dealings with him praised him for his attitude and for improving the status of women within the network.

'Chris was very tuned in to giving opportunities to women in the network. I think it was because he was that much younger, the old management was very traditional, their wives stayed at home and looked after the kids', said one long-time employee.

In 1995 there was a change of ownership and management at the network. Chris Chapman left the company in 1996. In 1998 there was another change of CEOs but under the same ownership.

The new management in 1996 came in with an agenda of budget cuts and redundancies. The continuous improvement program and the position of training manager were dropped. Management training continued in Sydney in conjunction with Macquarie University and there were four women participants out of a total of twelve. The performance appraisals were dropped because they were seen to be taking up too much time with very little result. The policy was changed to 'mainstream' the initiatives. Managers were expected to discuss the performance of their staff regularly instead of once a year, and it was assumed that the managers were sufficiently aware of equal opportunity issues to regularly apply them.

Scott Blakeman, the director of human resources, pointed out that there were a growing number of women in very senior positions in the network. They were all based in Sydney – Maureen Plavsic, the national sales director, Janeen Faithfull, head of network production ('a first for any network'), Judith Howard, company secretary, as well as Catherine Rothery, regulatory and business affairs. In 1995 there had been only three senior women and they were less senior than any of the women mentioned.

The network had introduced the Seven Network Assistance Program (SNAP), an independent counselling service for its staff in all states. It was free and time was granted in working hours for the initial interview. The staff could go for guidance and support for any problems that they did not want to take to the director of human resources or his female personnel manager, who were both sexual harassment officers.

Seven was the first network to own all the mainland capital city stations and institute a centralised network human resources responsibility. In spite of the initiatives in Sydney the other stations owned by the network had not been as progressive towards women. There were no women in senior management in Adelaide or Perth and some staff said that, for all the lip service paid to selection processes, there were still examples of mates being employed and that the affirmative action committees in each of the stations hardly met. They also regretted that the impressive induction program had ceased.

Two to three percent of the time of human resources staff was spent on affirmative action. The network's 1997 report to the Affirmative Action Agency said that as a goal it would increase women in management and encourage women in operations crews to apply for traditionally 'male' jobs. News camera, directing, production floor managing and technical positions were all nominated for these goals. When these sorts of positions became available, women would be encouraged to apply if they had not done so initially, despite having equal or more experience than their male colleagues. They estimated a 30% success rate, although it was difficult to measure.

At the time of the 1997 AAA report, there were four women out of 21 in Tier 1 management positions, eleven out of 76 in Tier 2, and thirteen out of 67 in Tier 3.[3] Since 1996 there had been a very large increase in management positions but the percentage of women in these roles had reduced from twenty percent to seventeen percent. The network employed 2609 people in its six stations in 1997, of whom 839, or 32 percent, were women.

THE TEN NETWORK

The stations in the Ten Network were established in 1964-65, much later than those in the other two commercial networks. NEW Perth only came on air in 1988. The network suffered the most from the major ownership changes that occurred in 1987-88. It was broken up and sold off with the Sydney, Melbourne and Brisbane stations ending up in receivership. CanWest, a Canadian company, rescued TEN Sydney, ATV Melbourne and TVQ Brisbane in 1993 and took over ADS Adelaide and NEW Perth in late 1995.

Ten has been the least successful of the networks and has always had the lowest ratings. This has meant that the stations did not pay well and expected staff to be multi-skilled. One effect of this is that all stations in the network were training grounds and gave women opportunities that they were unlikely to have had elsewhere. The common characteristic of each station was the youthfulness and enthusiasm of the female staff, who were all anxious for the network to succeed.

Ten has had a chequered career in relation to senior women. The new management in 1993 had not been shy in appointing women into senior positions. Female staff praised Peter Viner, the Canadian CEO, for having the courage to appoint three women to his management team: Carmel Travers, the first woman to head news and current affairs, Kristen Marlow, the first woman head of network programming and Valerie Hardy, who was head of drama.

This had been a source of pride and inspiration to all women in the network, particularly when Kristen Marlow, who was only just 30, was promoted. Many women saw them as role models and an example that women could succeed in the network. All three have now left, and that momentum seems to have disappeared, although there are some senior women.

In 1997 John McAlpine, who had been head of network sales, took over as CEO from Peter Viner. The three senior executives responsible for network policy were then all male. The most senior woman was Susan Oddie, general manager business affairs. She was one of the seven senior executives when she had a baby, providing a new experience for her management colleagues to adjust to.

The Ten Network in Sydney moved into a modern new building in 1997 and it has been struggling to prove itself. There were no women working in the camera or sound areas but a decision to make directors do their own vision switching meant that some of the female switchers were being trained to direct.

There was a recognition that job-sharing and part-time work could help child rearing but the leanness of the station made flexibility difficult. Also, childcare had not got much support when a survey on the options for the use of the next door building was conducted.

The other stations in the network varied in their culture and operation. ATV Melbourne lost its production studios in the ownership shake-ups and had a small staff working out of city offices. ADS Adelaide had suffered from the ownership shake-out in 1987. It was sold by HSV-7 Melbourne and had to swap its network programming to the Ten Network but was not then owned by it, which meant it stopped producing network programs. The management culture was very male. Although there were no women on its management team, the station employed a number of young women in the operations area who were very enthusiastic and loyal. It is now owned by the Ten Network, has a new CEO and comes under the network human resources initiatives in Sydney.

NEW Perth, being an '80s station, always had a good representation of senior women on its management and had the only woman program manager in a capital city commercial station (Glenys Gill, see pp259-61). (Kristen Marlow had a brief period as network program manager.)

The human resources department based in Sydney is responsible for all the stations. Policy and procedures manuals and performance appraisals now exist and managers in the six capital city stations have been trained in equity matters by the human resources department.

Ten percent of the human resources department budget was spent on affirmative action. In the five stations in the network there was one woman and five men in Tier 1 of the management structure, eight women out of twenty in Tier 2 and eight out of 30 in Tier 3. The network employed 1291 people in its six stations in 1997, of whom 568, or 44 percent, were women.[3]

THE AUSTRALIAN BROADCASTING CORPORATION

ABC Television is a government statutory authority managed from its head office in Sydney. Unlike commercial television it has always been a national network. It started in the 1950s, when large studios were built in each capital city and staff were employed under the Australian Public Service Act, which meant they had 'cradle to grave' employment. The ABC had a comprehensive training program for all production and technical staff, and people moved from the smaller city stations to Sydney and Melbourne to work on large programs and move into network management positions. The stations outside Sydney and Melbourne were known as the BAPH states (Brisbane Adelaide Perth and Hobart), and were often used for training.

The equal opportunity and affirmative action policies initiated by the federal government in the late 1970s meant that the ABC could no longer only employ women in stereotypical jobs such as those requiring typing speeds, as experienced by Gillian Armstrong and Mandy Smith. The women employed at the ABC demanded equal opportunities and the organisation started to recruit women from the typing pools and other typically female jobs for training in the operations area.

However, men held tenured positions, so that progress was slow. Even so, there were proportionately more women working in sound, camera and editing in the ABC stations than in the commercial stations. But the ABC produces fewer programs in each capital city than do the commercial stations. In Sydney and Melbourne the policy now is that network productions should be outsourced to production houses, which come in and use the studio facilities and bring their production crews with them.

It is ironic that at a time when many of the older men in middle management were retiring, and when affirmative employment policies were starting to change the male culture, there was major downsizing of the ABC. Both men and women have been laid off so that there are fewer job opportunities for anyone.

However, in the engineering area, in spite of the funding cuts, the ABC has been able to continue an affirmative action policy. In 1998, in the engineering and technical group, there were two traineeships for women in NSW and one each in Victoria and Queensland. There was also a scholarship scheme for engineering students which provides payment and three weeks' work experience. Scholarships have been awarded in Sydney and Melbourne, extended to Hobart and Perth and then to all states. A number of these scholarship recipients are now fully employed in the ABC.

There are still occasional opportunities in all the city stations for women to be employed on a contract basis for a particular production, and sometimes there is freelance work. Women have been accepted as editors and graphic artists for many years but there are still not many in sound or on cameras in the studio or in the field. However, in 1997 Chantal Abouchar, a news camera operator in Sydney, won the prestigious Walkley Award for her camerawork.

The ABC, as a Commonwealth employer, is bound by Commonwealth sex discrimination and equal employment opportunity legislation. Their Equal Employment Opportunity report does not provide separate figures for television staff, but states that in August 1998 there was a total of 4031 non-casual staff, of whom 1726 or 43 percent were women. There is an over-representation of women in production support (78%) and administrative positions (63%) while the lowest participation rates are in engineering/technical (6%) and production operations (15%). However there has been an improvement of 3 percent in the former and 1.3 percent in the latter since June 1993. There were 78 women senior executives representing 31 percent, 48 in production services (34%) and 79 in production operations (15%). (See Appendix 2 for the table, Women by Occupation, ABC.)

The most senior women in the ABC were the three who sat on the nine-person executive committee: the chief of staff, the head of human resources and the head of regional services.

When David Hill was managing director he tried to help women get management experience and break down perceptions that only men could be heads of departments by initiating a policy that women be given first opportunity to act in the position of manager if a manager was away. However this caused a lot of animosity and some women believe that despite the good intentions, it almost set them up to fail because it created so much bad blood and they were not in the job for long enough to prove themselves.

In Sydney there was a continual battle by women in management to correct the gender imbalance. When Sue Chapple was manager TV, NSW, in the mid '90s she had three women out of eight on her management team and introduced one-year traineeships for women in areas where there was low female employment. She also let it be known when recruitment occurred that she wanted a good proportion to be women to redress the imbalance in the various operational departments. This was difficult against a background of redundancies but she took the view that you have to keep the talent coming in for the future even if you reduce it. She was also keen to develop men to redress the balance in female dominated areas.

Sue changed the assessment process and insisted that senior women be on assessment panels, not just token women administrators, even if this meant flying women with the required knowledge of the job from interstate. She saw this as one way of stopping assessment criteria of 'the best person for the job' being used against women.

She said that it was hard to get the message through as a senior manager when you have male managers with traditional views about women's roles. 'You have to have perseverance and a lot of follow up and then make sure that you hear about it if it is not happening.' She thought that being a woman she probably did have good feedback because women found it easier to talk to her.

ABC Sydney and Melbourne both have childcare facilities

for their staff. This had been a great help for women coming back to work, and men with children had also come to realise its benefit. There was also a women's network in Sydney, Network 99, which met irregularly, usually with a guest speaker, and provided opportunities to discuss problems and provide support to some women.

The ABC has worked hard to dilute its white Anglo-Saxon male image. On the whole it had a better understanding of what affirmative action meant and less opposition from male managers than the commercial stations. A side effect was that the organisation has also addressed EEO and affirmative action issues relating to Indigenous Australians, non-English speaking groups and people with disabilities.

THE SPECIAL BROADCASTING SERVICE

SBS is the youngest network and came on the air in 1980. It is a statutory authority with its own act of parliament that requires it to be a 'good employer'. It has most of its television staff in Sydney but there are some in Melbourne and a few in Canberra. Its regular productions are all made in Sydney from small studios using a presenter format. Its administration is in Sydney.

Until 1994 SBS staff were employed under the provisions of the Australian Public Service Act. It then became independent, with its own enterprise agreement, and chooses to report to the Public Service Commissioner. The last five years have seen a great change in employer/employee relations and SBS is proud of having a family friendly enterprise agreement with flexible working conditions and provisions for people working at home.

There were 418 staff working in television in 1997-98 of whom 210 or just over 50 percent were women. There were 93 staff in the operations area of whom 38 (41 percent) were women. There were three women out of 23 (13 percent) in engineering and studio support, no women in sound, no women directors, and women number seven out of the thirteen (54 percent) editors and five out of sixteen (31 percent) in videotape.

The gender profile of management has also changed. Maureen

Crowe, head of resources, was the most senior woman. When she arrived in 1993 she was the only woman on the six-person management committee. She was later joined by two other women: the head of marketing and the policy manager. Maureen was responsible for all resources, financial, transmission, building and human. The enterprise agreement provided the opportunity to make the organisation much more sensitive to equal opportunity issues, and with over seventy language groups there were additional cultural issues relating to gender, particularly within specific cultural groups.

SBS has always been a small operation and its television staff profile is closer to a small capital city commercial station. It relies on freelance crews and production houses to supplement its core staff for occasional productions or additional work.

Maureen Crowe believed that new digital equipment could provide 'a golden time for women technical people. Everyone will have to learn new techniques and women could grasp the initiative'.

SBS had an EEO officer, Sophia Catharios, a feisty woman who has been with the organisation since its beginnings. She was well known at SBS as a wise woman and I was told the story, several times, of how she had gone to Melbourne and when the blokes refused to remove the girlie pictures in the crew room she ripped them down herself and was called an 'interfering bitch'.

SBS negotiated a joint venture childcare centre with Willoughby Council in Sydney to provide 35 places, of which 23 would initially be taken up by SBS staff. There was also a women's network at the station.

1 Commencement dates for all the major metropolitan commercial stations are:
  Sydney TCN-9 16 September 1956, ATN-7, 2 December 1956, TEN-10 5 April 1965;
  Melbourne HSV-7 4 November 1956, GTV-9 19 January 1957, ATV-10 1 August 1964;
  Brisbane QTQ-9 16 August 1959, BTQ-7 1 November 1959, TVQ-10, 1 July 1965;
  Adelaide NSW-9 5 September 1959, ADS-7 24 October 1959, SAS-10 26 July 1965;
  Perth TVW-7 16 October 1959, STW-9 12 June 1965, NEW-10 20 May 1988.

2 Affirmative Action Agency report, 1997.

3 See Table 2: Women in Senior Management in Appendix 2 (p383) for definitions of the management levels included in these Tiers.

4 1997 report to the Affirmative Action Agency.

APPENDIX 2

TABLE 1: WOMEN BY OCCUPATION, COMMERCIAL TELEVISION

Occupational Group	Channel 9*			Channel 7			Channel 10			NWS-9			STW-9			Industry#		
	Total	Women	%	Total	Women	%	Total	Women	%	Total	Women	%	Total	Women	%	Total	Women	%
Managers	101	17	17	70	11	16	51	14	27	2	0	0	19	2	11	1094	299	27
Professionals	347	125	36	953	266	29	238	92	39	14	6	43	30	12	40	3026	1019	34
Para-professionals	726	152	21	923	172	19	519	128	25	38	15	39	99	20	20	3600	807	22
Trade	172	30	17	168	47	28	57	27	47	115	17	15	13	4	31	1105	183	17
Clerk	235	195	83	328	287	88	251	203	81	47	43	91	26	21	81	2952	2360	80
Sales and Services	79	52	66	92	34	37	175	104	59	10	3	30	7	2	29	4686	2587	55
Plant Operations	34	2	6	4	–	0	–	–	–	–	–	–	–	–	–	302	138	46
Labour	31	–	0	91	22	24	–	–	–	1	–	0	5	–	0	326	96	29
Total	1725	573	33	2609	839	32	1291	568	44	227	84	37	199	61	31	17091	7489	44

Source: Affirmative Action Agency reports for 1997.

Those figures compiled by AAA for Picture Radio and Television Services.

* Channel 9 – Brisbane, Sydney, Melbourne and Darwin. NWS Adelaide and STW Perth are independent stations.

TABLE 2: WOMEN IN SENIOR MANAGEMENT, COMMERCIAL TELEVISION

	Channel 9*			Channel 7			Channel 10		
	Total	Women	%	Total	Women	%	Total	Women	%
Tier 1	2	-	0	21	4	19	6	1	17
Tier 2	15	2	13	76	11	14	20	8	40
Tier 3	51	11	22	67	13	19	30	8	27
Total	68	13	19	164	28	17	56	17	30

Source: Affirmative Active Agency reports 1997.

* Not stated in 1997 report (these are 1996 figures).

NWS and STW figures not available.

The Affirmative Action Agency definitions are:

- Tier 1 directs and is responsible for the organisation and its development; primarily responsible for long term strategic planning and policy formation; ultimate control of resources; typical titles include CEO, chief general manager, executive director, etc;

- Tier 2 is directly below and assists Tier 1 management; may head a state office or other major division or group; typical titles include divisional manager, state manager;

- Tier 3 is responsible to Tier 2 management; responsible for a functional sub-division or sub-branch, eg accounting, computing, training; formulates policies and plans for their area of control and manages a budget and staffing resources; is the interface between Tier 2 management and supervisors, section leaders and operations staff but is not primarily a supervisor.

TABLE 3: WOMEN BY OCCUPATION, ABC

Occupational Group	All Staff No.	Women Staff June 1993		August 1998*	
		No.	%	No.	%
Senior Executives	250	83	28.6	78	31.2
Administrative Officers	1009	793	61.5	636	63.0
Journalists/Reporters	722	305	42.1	346	47.9
Musicians	–	174	38.3	–	–
Engineering/Technical	244	10	2.8	14	5.7
Prod. Support (TV)	201	193	74.5	157	78.1
Producers/Directors (TV)	133	54	34.6	52	39.1
Production Services (TV)	141	53	23.6	48	34.0
Transmission (TV)	20	4	21.1	4	20.0
Production Ops (TV)	544	83	13.2	79	14.5
Broadcaster (R & RA)	767	317	35.2	312	40.7
Total	4031	2069	39.0	1726	42.8

Source: ABC Equal Employment Opportunity Annual Report, 1997-1998.

* excluding subsidiaries

The total number of women staff members at 31 August 1998 is 1726, representing 42.8% of total non-casual staff. This represents about the same percentage as the previous year, 42.9%, with a steady increase since June 1993 from 39.0%. The number of women who departed the ABC under redundancy arrangements totalled 201, which is 47% of all redundancies.

APPENDIX 3

MY STORY

My family moved to England when I was twelve and was lucky enough to go to a progressive co-educational school in London where I fell in love with drama. I trained at RADA (the Royal Academy of Dramatic Art) and was on the stage in repertory theatre for a number of years. I also did small film and TV parts. I had wanted to direct but it was the early 1950s and women just didn't direct on the stage in those days.

However, Betty Box and Wendy Toye were directing films and women were beginning to direct in television. I was told that if I wanted to work behind the camera I should learn shorthand and typing so I could do continuity or be a producer's assistant. So I did, and got a job as a secretarial gopher in a small production house which made corporates, commercials and B grade features.

In my spare time I borrowed their 16mm Kodak special and also did some assisting in the editing room. I bought my own 16mm Bolex, did a weekend course on filmmaking and went off and filmed the Women's Caravan of Peace, which was organised by Dora Russell. We spent three months travelling through western and eastern Europe in 1958 when the iron curtain was well and truly down.

In 1959 I got my first job in television as a writer of commercials with Tyne Tees Television in the north of England, before the station went on air. I had written a few corporate scripts for the production company and a book about my life as an actor in repertory. I moved to other regional stations as a researcher for current affairs programs and occasionally was allowed to direct small film segments. Finally, in 1961, I got a job as a director/producer with ATV, one of the major independent television companies in Birmingham, where I was responsible for a half-hour slot once a fortnight to produce social documentary programs.

I then became interested in educational television and went to the US and worked with WGBH, an educational TV station in Boston, until returning to England to get married. For three years I freelanced and taught television production. My husband was also working in television. He had been a teacher so we set up our own company to teach teachers to use television, because closed circuit television was beginning to be introduced into teachers' colleges.

In 1967 our first daughter was born. Peter got a job as a producer with the television service at Sydney University and so I came back to Sydney. Because there was no childcare available in those days, and partners as carers were unheard of, I spent eight years child-rearing until my two daughters were old enough to go to school.

During that time I did a degree by correspondence with London University and was on a lot of committees to fight for a film industry, more Australian content on television and better children's programs. Through these activities I got to know people in the industry while I was child-rearing. In 1973 I was appointed to the first council of the AFTRS.

In 1975 I was employed to set up the AFTRS research unit and was there for eight years. I was then appointed as a full-time member to the Australian Broadcasting Authority, where I spent five years and, in 1990, became the first professor of film and media at Griffith University. I used my study leave in 1994 to start interviewing women for this book.

THE ISSUES

Every one of the interviews I did raised issues for me about my own career. The unresolved one is – did I really want to be a documentary cinematographer but was put off by the lack of role models and the very male environment? Who knows? All the cinematographers I knew were men twenty years older than I was and I didn't want to assist any of them. Would it have been different if there had been women cinematographers?

I am older than all the women I interviewed and, like Sara

Bennett, I came late in life to understand gender issues. Although I had been brought up in a feminist household and my mother and Dymphna Cusack (who shared a house with us for two years while they wrote *Come in Spinner*) were role models – they were a continuation of the first wave of feminists who had fought for the vote. But they were of the generation that accepted that once a girl married and had children ideally she stayed at home until they went to school and then she could try to find a job that had suitable hours. My mother made it clear she would not provide childcare for grandchildren and, so, when I returned to Australia with one child and was offered a job as a director in the education department at the ABC, I turned it down. A new country, a new job, and no child-minding facilities just seemed too hard.

I accepted that, being a woman, I had to make my own opportunities; no-one was going to look after me. I knew that I was most unlikely to be promoted within an organisation and therefore I had to change jobs to get opportunities to become a director. I tried to be at the forefront of new initiatives to get those opportunities. I spent a year making scrapbooks of cuttings from local newspapers in two cities in England where I knew they were going to start television stations so that I would be better qualified than others to apply for a job as a current affairs producer.

I sought to follow the path of television director because it was an expanding industry and there were some women role models who had come up through the film industry as production secretaries and then producer's assistants. I could also see that there were other acceptable women's jobs and I acted, wrote and did research. There were no women theatre directors and although I won the director's prize at RADA no-one suggested it would lead to a directing career for me.

Because I started as an actor where there is no sex discrimination in your daily working life and I had a supportive mother and no brothers or a father around I never had anyone to say I couldn't do things. Like Carolyn Reid and Camilla Rudd, I was the tomboy who always found out how things worked and fixed them. Like many of the young women I interviewed in television stations, I was blithely ignorant about sex discrimination at a personal level. I just accepted that there were certain jobs I could not do because of my gender, in the way that I had accepted, once I became a professional actor, that I could no longer play the good boys' parts, as I had at school.

I had thought that women being denied certain jobs was an obstacle to overcome or get round rather than something to be changed. I never minded being overlooked because I was a woman; in fact I got a perverse sense of power from it. If conversations went on as if I wasn't there I delighted in thinking how stupid the men were for making the assumption that I was nobody, and my ears flapped and I picked up very useful information. I have only learnt to get angry recently but have never acquired the skills to use that anger.

When I was young I used to be flattered to be regarded as 'one of the boys' because, as a tomboy, I identified with that role. I cannot remember any examples of specific sexist language in the television stations but I was always conscious that I was the outsider. I was the one who had to make the compromises, I was the one who had to sit and listen, I was the one who had to stroke the egos. I was not able to lose my temper and shout when I was angry; I had to try and hide my tears. Like most women I became my harshest critic because there was no-one to tell me I was doing a good job or give constructive criticism without making it a power game. Like all women, I had to tread that delicate balance of being matey but not sexy in order to get the male crews to put themselves out when things went wrong. I identify with Leonie Still's research of absorbing the culture, and recognise her descriptions of assimilation (see p356).

When I started to direct I can remember consciously thinking I could either play the dumb flirting female to get the boys to help me, or try to establish one-on-one relationships with each head of department so that I could learn about their jobs and they could respect what I was trying to do. My personality dictated that there was really no choice, but at times I was envious of a woman director in London who batted her eyelids and got great results. In Betz & Fitzgerald's terms I am sure I was typecast as the maiden aunt (see p348). Before I was married my sex life became the subject of gossip at one television station because I was hauled into the boss's office and asked to confirm or deny the rumour that I was married and had a husband behind the iron curtain! When I laughed about this to others I discovered they had all heard the rumour.

I only ever had to work with two really difficult men. One was a floor manager, who I dreaded because he was so uncooperative he had to be told to do anything that was not within the strict line of duty, and then did it with bad grace. The other was a gaffer. The two-person television film crew was very helpful without the gaffer but when he joined them they became very tiresome. I did not recognise this as sexist behaviour – I put it down to personality problems – but I am now sure that it was the former and I would like to have confronted it.

I found the film crew situation much more difficult because it is more personal and when you're on the road with a small crew the behaviour is not constrained by the formal hierarchical structure of studio television and the schedule. (Some of the women I interviewed made the same distinction between the formality of the feature film which is easier than the informality of a documentary shoot.) I just tried to avoid interior locations when I knew that gaffer was rostered on.

It was only when I had children, which coincided with my returning to Australia, that I started to lack confidence in myself. I was totally humiliated at an interview I did for a job as a lecturer in television production at Gore Hill Technical College in the early 1970s. The all-male selection panel from the electronic engineering department started asking me about ohms and volts. I said that in my ten years experience in television studios in England and the US I had never had to understand electronics. I knew from a floorplan test they had given to all interviewees that I was the only one who had any real experience but they so humiliated me that all I wanted to do was crawl under a rock and disappear.

In spite of these experiences I was guilty of distancing myself from other women I worked with. I was one of the 'I've done it, why can't you' brigade, which I now understand, having read the women in management research, is not uncommon. It was not until my first year at the AFTRS, which coincided with International Women's Year, that I was sensitised to feminism.

Jerzy Toeplitz, the first director of the AFTRS and vice president of CILECT, the international organisation of film schools, was coordinating a report on the status of women in film and television in six countries, including Australia, and I had to take over the initiatives he had started. I learnt an enormous amount very fast and for the first time started to question why women were not able to do certain jobs just because of our gender and why men had privileges that we did not.

I became a convert. I helped establish the women's courses at the AFTRS in the 1970s. I became vigilant about the gender balance of selection committees and staff and students. However, what I now realise is that you have got to work from the bottom up in an organisation in order to effect change. The history of EEO at NWS-9 as opposed to ATN-7 shows us that (see Appendix 1).

Like so many of the women I interviewed for this book, I believe that we have got to change the culture towards women. It is the same sort of problem that we have in changing the culture towards Indigenous Australians. Women, like Indigenous Australians, are visibly different from white males, we cannot hide our differences and assimilate and neither do most of us want to. We believe that we have something of value to offer the world we all live in and we should be allowed to share it equally.

Young women today are much more aware of their rights to equal opportunity and self worth than I ever was when I started out but this presents them with a difficult dilemma. Should they 'fit in' to the male culture and accept being second class citizens until they have the experience and standing to challenge it, as I unwittingly did; or, with their greater sense of self worth, should they challenge sexism when they come across it and risk being given a really hard time by the men who still get angry when their behaviour is questioned?

I hope this book will help give women the strength to challenge and give men some understanding of the male culture that they condone by not challenging it themselves.

REFERENCES

Aitkin, David J, Moorman, Jay, Lin, Carolyn A, 1993, 'Ready for Prime Time: Network Series Devoted to Working Women in the 1980s', *Sex Roles: A Journal of Research*, Vol 25, Nos 11/12, Plenum Publishing Corporation, New York, NY.

Alexander, S, 1979, *Stop Organising – Be Creative*, Australian Film and Television School, Sydney.

Australian Educational Council, 1992, *Listening to Girls: A Report of the Consultancy Undertaken for the Australian Educational Council Committee to Review the National Policy for the Education of Girls in Australian Schools*, Curriculum Corporation for the Australian Education Council, Carlton, VIC.

Australian Film Commission, 1999, *Get the Picture*, Sydney.

Australian Film Commission, 1996, *Women in Television: Career Advancement*, Sydney.

BAM SSB, 1994, *Advertising Through Women's Eyes*, AGB McNair/BAM SSB, Sydney.

Betz, Nancy and Fitzgerald, Louise, 1987, *The Career Psychology of Women*, Academic Press, San Diego.

Bail, Kathy, ed, 1996, *DIY Feminism*, Allen & Unwin, Sydney.

Birke, Lynda, et al, ed, 1980, *Alice Through the Microscope: The Power of Science Over Women's Lives*, The Brighton Women and Science Group, Virago, London.

Burton, Clare, Raven, Hag and Thompson, Gay, 1987, *Women's Worth: Pay Equity and Job Evaluation in Australia*, AGPS, Canberra.

Burton, Clare, 1991, *The Promise and the Price*, Allen & Unwin, Sydney.

Burton, Clare, 1996, *Women in the Australian Defence Force: The Cultural, Social and Institutional Barriers Impeding the Merit Based Progress of Women*, Defence Centre, Canberra.

Cox, Eva and Laura, Sharon, 1992, *What Do I Wear for a Hurricane: Women in Australian Film, Television*, Video and Radio Industries, AFC, Sydney.

Cox, Eva and Leonard, Helen, 1994, *Recognising Women's Skills: Readings in Non-Formal Learning*, Deakin University, VIC.

Crayford, Peter, 1997, 'Leading Ladies: The Film Industry Reverses the Gender Roles', *Australian Financial Review*, 8-9 November.

Equal Opportunities Commission, 1984, 92-023 at 75, 496, cited in Morgan, Jenny, 1997, 'Sexual Harassment: Where Did it Go in 1995?' in Meade, Jenna, *Bodyjamming*, Random House, Sydney.

Game, A and Pringle, R, 1983, *Gender at Work*, Allen and Unwin, Sydney.

Garner, Helen, 1995, *The First Stone: Some Questions about Sex and Power*, Picador, Sydney.

Gregor, Anne, 1993, 'Designing Women: Women in Television', *Maclean's*, 29 March, Vol 106, No 13, Maclean Hunter, Canada.

Grieve, Anna, 1987, 'Big Mother/Little Sister: The Women's Film Fund' in Blonski, et al, *Don't Shoot Darling: Women's Independent Filmmaking*, Greenhouse Publications, Richmond, VIC.

Jakubowicz, A, Goodall, H, Martin, J, Mitchell, T, Randall, Lois, Seneviratne, K, 1994, *Racism, Ethnicity and the Media*, Allen & Unwin, Sydney.

Jensen, Else, 1982, paper presented at 13th International Association of Mass Communication in Paris referred to in 'Communication in the Service of Women', 1985, *End of Decade of Women Media Report*, UNESCO.

Kantor, Rosebeth Moss, 1977, *Men and Women of the Corporation*, Basic Books, New York.

Labour Research Centre, 1991, *Against the Current: Career Paths for Women in the Electronics Industry*, AGPS, Canberra.

Kelly, RM, 1991, *The Gendered Economy: Work, Careers and Success*, Sage Publications, Newbury Park, London, New Delhi.

Meade, Jenna, 1997, *Bodyjamming*, Random House, Sydney.

Morrison, Ann, White, Randall, Van Velsor, Ellen and The Centre for Creative Leadership, 1992, *Breaking the Glass Ceiling*, Addison-Wesley Reading, Mass.

National Working Party on the Portrayal of Women in the Media, 1993, *Women and Media*, Department of the Prime Minister and Cabinet, Office of the Status of Women, Canberra.

Pip, C, Marsh, M, Cox, E, 1987, *Women in Australian Film, Video and Television Production*, AFC, Sydney.

Plant, Sadie, 1997, *Zeroes + Ones: Digital Women + the New Technoculture*, Fourth Estate, London.

Pyke, Jo, 1993, *Women in Building: The Missing 51%*, Department of Employment Education and Training, Canberra.

Rigg, Julie and Copeland, Julie, 1985, *Coming Out! Women's Lives*, Nelson Publishers, Melbourne.

Ryan, P, Eliot, M and Appleton, G, 1983, *Women in Australian Film Production, Women's Film Fund*, Australian Film and Television School, Sydney.

Sally Hartnett and Associates, 1988, *The Portrayal of Women in Advertisements*, Office of the Status of Women, Canberra.

Saulwick Weller and Associates, 1987, *Sex Role Portrayal of Women in Advertisements*, Office of the Status of Women, Canberra.

Seger, Linder, 1996, *When Women Call the Shots: The Developing Power and Influence of Women in Television and Film*, Henry Holt, New York.

Smith, Catherine R and Hutchinson, Jacquie, 1995, *Gender: A Strategic Management Issue*, Business and Professional Publishing, Sydney.

Speed, S, 1987, 'Voices from the Silent Era' in Blonski, et al, *Don't Shoot Darling: Women's Independent Filmmaking*, Greenhouse Publications, Richmond, VIC.

Spender, Dale, 1980, *Man Made Language*, Routledge and Kegan Paul, London.

Stapleton, C, 1987, *Industry Training Fund for Women: Summary of the Review of On-the-Job Training Scheme for Women and Recommendation for an Industry Fund for Women*, Australian Film and Television School, Sydney.

Still, Leonie, 1990, *Enterprising Women: Australian Women Managers and Entrepreneurs*, Allen & Unwin, Sydney.

Still, Leonie, 1993, *Where to From Here? The Managerial Woman in Transition*, Business and Professional Publishing, Sydney.

Thornley, Jeni, 1987, 'Past, Present and Future: The Women's Film Fund', in Blonski, et al, *Don't Shoot Darling: Women's Independent Filmmaking*, Greenhouse Publications, Richmond, VIC.

Townsend, Kathleen, 1995, 'Women in the APS: More Than Just Numbers', Paper given at joint conference, Public Service Commission and Department of Finance, 11 December, Canberra.

Travers, Carmel, 1997, *New Girls on the Block*, WIFT Conference, Tools of the Trade, October, Sydney.

UNESCO, 1976, *Women in the Media: The Professional Participation of Women in the Audio Visual Media – Film, Radio and Television*, Film and Television School, Sydney.

Van Maanen, J, 1976, 'Breaking in: Socialisation to Work', in Dubin, T, ed, *Handbook of Work Organisation and Society*, Rand McNally, Chicago.

Wood, J and Lees, S, 1993, in Arnot, Madeleine and Weiler, Kathleen, eds, *Feminism and Social Justice in Education: International Perspectives*, The Falmer Press, London.

Wyndam, D, 1986, *On the Job Training Scheme for Women: Evaluation*, Australian Film and Television School, Sydney.

Zoe, Sofia, 1993, *Whose Second Self? Gender and (Ir)rationality in Computer Culture*, Deakin University Press, Geelong.